DICTIONARIES OF
FOREIGN LANGUAGES

DICTIONARIES OF FOREIGN LANGUAGES

A Bibliographical Guide to the General
and Technical Dictionaries of the Chief
Foreign Languages, with Historical and
Explanatory Notes and References

BY

ROBERT L. COLLISON

Fellow of the Library Association;
Reference Librarian, City of Westminster

THE HAFNER PUBLISHING COMPANY

NEW YORK

1955

Printed in Great Britain at the Villafield Press, Bishopbriggs, Glasgow

To Dr. Lawrence Clark Powell and his
Staff at the Library of the University
of California at Los Angeles, who made
my year with them so memorable.

CONTENTS

TABLES

ACKNOWLEDGMENTS

This work was originally based on the holdings of the Library of the University of California at Los Angeles. To the knowledge gained from the splendid collection of dictionaries and philological periodicals possessed by that Library, I have since added further information from many libraries in the London area. I am greatly indebted to Mr. J. H. P. Pafford, Goldsmiths' Librarian of the University of London, and to Mr. J. D. Pearson, Librarian of the School of Oriental and African Studies of that University, for permission to make use of collections which are particularly rich in lexicographical material. And I gratefully acknowledge the generous help given me by Miss Joan Ferrier, Librarian of the Church Missionary Society; Dr. W. Guy Atkins of the School of Oriental and African Studies; and Mr. Anthony Curwen of Westminster Central Reference Library.

R. L. C.

Hampstead, 1955.

FOREWORD

Professor Pierce Butler, whose wise words often brought unexpected dignity to library work, once said that " the universe of books is chaos ", and then he defined bibliography as " the geography of the book world ". Mr. Collison, a chartered explorer, provides us here with a new *Baedeker* for an important sector of the chaotic book world.

Some people consider dictionaries the most civilized form of light reading; others give the palm to bibliographies. Here the two are happily made one. This book then should have a large and faithful audience. What could be a tedious but useful listing is illuminated by an intriguing historical and critical commentary that will probably set many readers to further searches into lexicographical history. One would like to know more about the romantic life of Richard Perceval, the Elizabethan compiler of a Spanish and English dictionary, and about Adoniram Judson, the well y-clept American who published " the first part of his *Burmese and English Dictionary* at Moulmein on his own hand-press ". And how many lexicographers were also librarians? I found five in these pages.

But this is the sort of graceful and efficient work we have come to expect from the Westminster Reference Librarian. With him the making of reference books is a " profession of maturity and responsibility ", praise he would give to the dictionary-maker. Like the missionary dictionary-makers of whom he reports, Mr. Collison came from London a few years ago to the " remote outstation " of Los Angeles, and this volume is one more chapter in his productive Anglo-American library career.

" Dictionaries are truly international," Mr. Collison reminds us; this compilation has an international character of another kind. The compiler, an Englishman, working in an American library, used a " splendid collection " that had been enriched by the private libraries of several European, notably Scandinavian, philologists. At least one of them, Verner Dahlerup, comes into these pages.

As one of the UCLA staff members to whom the book is so generously dedicated, I am delighted to be associated with it in this small way. It provides a happy means of recording that the Collison year was memorable for all concerned and fruitful for librarianship.

With all his tenacity Mr. Collison knowingly has not exhausted the field. The Asian section is rich and that on Africa ranges extensively through fields little known to the parochial American, from Acholi through Ewe and Ga to Zulu, by way of Igbo and Twi. We are reminded he must return, in another edition, and do as well by American Indian and Polynesian dictionaries. The field is as wide and the names as fruity. Like lexicography, bibliography is a " never-ending task ". But Mr. Collison's diligence and competence likewise seem never-ending.

ROBERT VOSPER
Director of Libraries
University of Kansas

FOREWORD

It is a pleasure to write a foreword to Mr. Collison's *Dictionaries of Foreign Languages*. Such a work has long been a desideratum, as all librarians whose readers use foreign dictionaries will agree. It will be invaluable to the librarian and to the private individual, to the amateur and the professional translator. Much fuller information on dictionaries is available here than is to be found in the wider field covered by Malclès and Mudge. On the technical side too it will supplement Holmstrom. The author gives us, too, concise accounts of the rise of dictionary-making in many countries, a guide to the confusing language situation in Norway and an illuminating description of the position to-day of many of the lesser European languages, but alas! he has (probably wisely) found little time to browse among dictionaries for those entertaining definitions such as Cotgrave's " Fleureter: only to touch a thing in going by it (metaphorically from the little Bees nimble skipping from flower to flower as she feeds)" or that definition of the wicket-keeper in one of the early editions of a now famous and valued American dictionary as " the player who protects the wicket from the ball ".

Mr. Collison throws his net very wide and there will be few readers who do not find the information they require. The specialist however may regret the omission of some works and studies which seem important to him but which obviously could find no place in a general reference work of this kind. The wise librarian will interleave and annotate his own copy for the better guidance of himself and his specialist reader. For myself the following entries I propose to add in my interleaved copy provide me with much specialist information, not properly relevant in Mr. Collison's work:

For early dictionaries and language studies in French:—	Bibliographies in Brunot's *Histoire de la langue française*. 1905– .
For Italian dialect studies:—	Prati, I vocabolari delle parlate italiane. 1931.
For early Italian dictionaries and grammars:—	Fontanini, Biblioteca dell'eloquenza italiana. 1803.
For early Spanish dictionaries and grammars:—	Conde de la Viñaza, Biblioteca histórica de la filología castellana. 1893.

and there will be a growing list of specialist studies culled from linguistic periodicals.

May I wish Mr. Collison's work every success and hope that his publishers will find it possible periodically to issue supplements and addenda.

D. M. SUTHERLAND
Librarian
Taylor Institution,
Oxford

INTRODUCTION

The first step in making a literature in any hitherto unwritten language is to standardise the form in which it is to be written, so that what one man has thought another may be able to read. Even to-day there are some languages—most of them African—which still await this basic process. And in Africa the grammars and the dictionaries have very often preceded the newspapers, the books, the letters and the inscriptions, so that variations in spelling and usage have thus been eliminated from the start. But in the older civilisations the evolution of language has been different. Dictionaries have come fairly late, and when at last they have been constructed their compilers have been faced with all the difficulties of equating pronunciation with spelling, literary meaning with current idiom. In the older languages, in fact, the recording of a nation's tongue in the form of a dictionary marks a definite and important stage in the development of the people. It not only recognises the fact that the language has emerged from the other languages with which it is akin into a distinct identity of its own: it also announces that its speakers are at last aware of the necessity for ensuring that it is used accurately and properly. Dictionary-making is therefore a profession of maturity and responsibility. With these considerations in mind it is possible to understand why the dictionaries of the languages of France and Italy should have preceded those of some of their eastern neighbours by many years. But it is not as easy to explain why some of the best work on the lexicography of a nation should have been done by people alien to its soil.

The visitor who sits down at the piano and plays more ably than anyone living in the house is immediately recognised both for his talent and for adaptability in performing well on an instrument with which he is not familiar. So it is with linguistics: a Jespersen can quickly outstrip the British on the subject of English grammar; a Vasmer can supersede a Preobrazhensky in the field of Russian etymology; Gamillscheg and Wartburg both know more about the French language than any man west of the Rhine. What could be more personal than a language?—and yet a Conrad can write better English than all but a few of our greatest writers. It is nevertheless comforting to know that lexicography admits no national barriers, for—were it otherwise—

many African and native American languages would have been lost for ever as their speakers died out or became assimilated in other nations.

Almost equally a cause for wonder is the fact that so many lexicographers have been amateurs: Littré and the brothers Grimm—all three outstanding figures in the history of language—were dictionary-makers more by way of interest than of design, and it was first necessary for them to train themselves by a long and hard discipline. Even though the science of linguistics becomes daily more technical and daily requires a higher degree of training and concentration, the amateurs continue their very necessary work, often in spite of themselves. Foremost among these must be the missionaries and the social workers among primitive peoples who, without any special leaning toward language study, find that their work depends for its success on their intimate understanding of the people around them. So it is that the remote outstations of the Christian missions continue to produce the first grammars, the first dictionaries and reading-books and Bibles in little-known languages and dialects. These may be, and very often are, both amateur and linguistically unsound: they remain valuable contributions on which the research workers of the future will gratefully base their more learned studies.

For the user, the dictionary represents an immediate broadening of outlook. Apart from the encyclopaedias, the dictionaries are almost the only form of book which avoids the narrow confines of one subject or of a group of related topics. Owing to the accidental placing of entirely unrelated information in close proximity through the artifice of alphabetical order, the reader, in spite of himself, is brought into contact with subjects and ideas of which he might otherwise have known nothing. It is the least curious of persons who can refer to a dictionary and not permit his glance to be caught by an unusual word or spelling which will lead him to browse among other equally strange words and topics. In many cases the knowledge thus gained may be of little practical value to the reader either then or even later on, but there is nevertheless the chance that a mind may be stimulated into exploring a fresh field of thought, or that a flagging interest may be newly revived. The value of the dictionary-maker to his own country and to the world at large cannot be measured: the influence of such a man is ever-increasing and permanently beneficial.

The reader only slowly becomes aware of the immense variety of dictionaries: from the idea of a dictionary of a language which explains its terms in the same language, he finds no difficulty in proceeding to the concept of the bilingual dictionary which will translate English words into German, or Italian into Russian or Amharic. Even polyglot dictionaries will appear a logical development, though their arrangement may confuse him. But he is still at the threshold of this vast field of reference. Beyond it lies the territory of the expert, in which each dictionary is assessed according to whether it gives the derivation of each word, its history, an adequate outline of its changes in meaning and pronunciation, sufficient quotations from standard authors to illustrate this information, and an indication of any differences of spelling at various times throughout the centuries. And then there is the world of specialist dictionaries, in which there are not only dictionaries which are restricted to the language of one region, one town, or one class of people, but also dictionaries which may concentrate on a particular trade or profession, or which may concern themselves with a hobby or a period in time. And again, beyond all this, there are the dictionaries which may be devoted to historical lexicography, to etymology or pronunciation, to correct usage, or even to abstruse subjects such as figurative usage, similes, prefixes and suffixes, synonyms and antonyms, abbreviations, or individual books and authors. The diligence with which a myriad men have tried to harness the stubborn languages which interested them is only surpassed by the obscurity of their efforts. Few lexicographers achieve fame, and those who do owe much of it to those who do not.

Lexicography is a never-ending task: language is constantly changing and adding to itself, and the new word is more elusive than its predecessors. It is a task which is not made easier by the well-meaning efforts of modern governments who try to help their subjects by codifying grammatical rules, spelling, alphabets, and scripts, thereby rendering all existing dictionaries out-of-date and yet making them even more important, since they record a language in its previous form in which the majority of its printed matter has been written. Within living memory such countries as Sweden, Turkey, the Netherlands, the USSR, Denmark and numerous others have made substantial official changes in their languages—Norway has already had three spelling reforms in this century—and the process continues as more and more nations become convinced of the necessity of bringing their languages into line with current requirements of literature and commerce. Even so, it may be some time before those peoples who have one language for everyday use and a more inflexible and ceremonial version for their literatures can arrive at an acceptable mean.

No one dictionary of a language is sufficient: each has its advantages and defects, and the more dictionaries there are, the richer the people. It is noticeable how well some of the smaller language areas, such as the Armenian and Bulgarian, have been served by the lexicographers.

This may be for the same reason that many a small parish may have a more adequate written historical account than the average large city— it is easier to do justice to a Hitchin than to a Nottingham, or to a Bergen County than to a Kansas City. What is needed however is a clear indication of the interdependence of one dictionary upon another: no dictionary is completely without debt to its predecessors, and most compilations are nowadays based on the best preceding models.

Interdependence is, of course, the keynote of philology: without it, little could be done. Philologists rarely specialise in one language to the exclusion of all others: most of them have a lively interest in many other tongues, and their names may appear on the title-pages of books in several different languages. For instance, the talented Major R. C. Abraham wrote a grammar and a dictionary of Tiv, a book on the principles of Idoma, and a grammar of spoken Hausa, in addition to his work on Amharic. In the same way there is a mutual inter-dependence between nations, dating from the time when the institution of the Accademia della Crusca could stimulate the creation of the Académie Française for the same basic purposes.

But to determine the degree of debt which one dictionary owes to another, it is essential to establish not only the dates of first publication, but also the dates of actual compilation. Neither is immediately obvious in every case, for there are still some dictionaries in revision and in use which were compiled over one hundred years ago—an extreme example is that of the most influential of all Portuguese dictionaries, António de Moraes e Silva's *Grande dicionário da lingua portuguesa*, whose tenth and latest edition is now in course of publication, but which was first published as the *Diccionario da lingua portugueza* as early as 1789. Then, in the same language, there is Francisco Julio Caldas Aulete's *Dicionario contemporâneo* whose first edition was not published until 1881, even though Caldas Aulete died more than eighty years earlier. And in many languages there are other dictionaries which, on the other hand, have had no effectual revisions or additions within the past thirty years or more. Then there are the languages which have no dictionary really worthy of the name. There is room, in truth, for a world-wide investigation into the present lexicographical position with regard to the main languages, so that attention may be turned to those which at present are being neglected owing to the haphazard nature of dictionary-making.

There is a strange fascination in the lives of many of the dictionary-makers: Johnson marking the significant passages for his six assistants to work on; Cleasby, the wealthy but delicate Englishman, with his vast quantities of careful entries on Old Norse; Kohnen writing his dictionary of the Shilluk language in German shorthand during his internment in Egypt during the first World War; the persecuted Alexandre de Rhodes managing to provide the world of the seventeenth century with its first real dictionary of the languages of Indo-China. Their characters vary immeasurably, but there are certain basic ingredients: an immense curiosity, and an unflagging perseverance in the face of adversity, opposition and indifference.   In spite of the many thousands of dictionaries in the world to-day, we can never have too many more, for the man who is searching for a particular word or phrase will remain unsatisfied as long as he does not find it, whether there be one or fifty dictionaries.

    *   *   *   *   *   *   *   *   *   *   *

It is therefore with the idea of helping all those who use dictionaries—translators, writers, librarians, scholars, and plain readers—that the following brief guide has been compiled.   For each language the chief general dictionaries have been given, together with some notes—wherever possible—on their history, contents and use; to these have been added at times information on more specialised dictionaries, and in the larger chapters these have been arranged in the following order:

(*a*) General Dictionaries
(*b*) Etymological Dictionaries
(*c*) Specialist Dictionaries: synonyms and antonyms, etc.
(*d*) Dictionaries relating to Special Periods
(*e*) Slang and Dialect
(*f*) Bi-Lingual Dictionaries: for the most part English, but with some important foreign-language dictionaries from time to time.

And, finally, an Appendix of polyglot and technical dictionaries has been added, the latter being arranged alphabetically by (1) language, and (2) subject.

In the main part of this book details have been kept to a minimum, but titles are generally given in full, since these often throw valuable light on viewpoint, approach, treatment, and special features.   In the same way, both publisher and place of publication have been given, since it may be important to know that a particular Russian dictionary was published in Riga, or a German lexicon in Paris, and the name of the publisher may often give the reader some idea of the standing of the work.   Latest editions are quoted wherever possible, but dates of first publication are frequently stated to help with the overall assessment and to indicate the limits of possible influences and dependence.   The number of volumes or pages are shown, since some slight idea of the

2

size of a dictionary may be gained from the fact that it has 235 or 1235 pages, even though this will not tell whether it has two or three columns per page, or what size of type has been used.

Most of the dictionaries listed in this book are good; occasionally a poor or a really bad dictionary has been included, but only for the sake of illustrating some historical or other valid point, and always with sufficient warning of its real nature.

It is well to keep in mind that dictionaries are truly international: the lexicon which is issued to-day in Prague or Benares, may be on sale the same year in New York or Buenos Aires with the title-page of a local publisher, and sometimes with a different title. It should be assumed that few of the titles listed are unavailable, however obscure their provenance, and that recourse to a good bookseller will bring the book quickly to hand.

Manca un profilo generale
della lessicografia, e solo
parzialmente vi suppliscono
le storie della filologia e
della linguistica.
Enciclopedia Italiana, xx: 968.

FRENCH DICTIONARIES

Although the Académie Française was founded as early as 1635 and commenced work on its great dictionary almost immediately, its efforts were preceded by those of César-Pierre Richelet (1631–98) who compiled his remarkable *Dictionnaire français* and had it printed in two volumes clandestinely at Geneva in the years 1679–80. The edition was small and, owing to Richelet's incautious boasting, fifteen hundred copies which had been smuggled into France were seized and burnt. The publisher died of chagrin, and the bookseller who had betrayed Richelet's confidence was assassinated shortly afterwards. Richelet was the first compiler of a dictionary to express extensively his personal likes and dislikes, and many of his definitions are satirical or even, say some critics, scabrous. An interesting article on the subject has been written by M. Spire Pitou under the title " Richelet, forerunner of Samuel Johnson and de Lormes " on pages 474 to 476 of the November 1949 number of *Modern language notes*. Other editions of Richelet's dictionary appeared, notably:

> Richelet, César-Pierre. Nouveau dictionnaire françois contenant généralement tous les mots anciens et modernes, et plusieurs remarques sur la langue françoise; ses expressions propres, figurées et burlesques, la pronunciation des mots les plus difficiles, avec leur ortographe, le genre des noms, la conjugaison, des verbes, leur régime, celui des adjectifs et des prépositions; et les termes les plus connus des arts et des sciences. Le tout tiré de l'usage des bons auteurs . . . Nouvelle édition, revue, corrigée et augmentée considérablement des termes latins, de tous les mots, et phrases proverbiales, qui manquoient dans les précédentes, et d'un grand nombre d'exemples: avec un abregé de la vie des auteurs dont ces exemples sont tirés . . . Amsterdam, Jean Elzevir, 1709. 2 volumes.

The verbose title has been repeated almost in full since it clearly indicates that the early dictionary-makers had a good understanding of their task and had set themselves high standards.

Chapelain, the poet, was the first to conceive the idea of an authoritative dictionary. He was one of the original members of that little café-haunting group of friends who unwillingly agreed to Cardinal Richelieu's request to form themselves into an academy on the Italian model. Richelieu, no doubt inspired by the example of the Accademia della Crusca which had already produced its dictionary in Venice, was instrumental in having one of the most important articles inserted in the constitution of the newly-founded Académie Française. It was number 26, and it read: " Il sera composé un Dictionnaire, un Grammaire, une Rhétorique et une Poétique." The Statutes and Rules were signed by the Cardinal in 1635, and Vaugelas assumed the editorship of the dictionary, but the first edition did not appear until 1694: it was in two folio volumes, and the contents were arranged by families of words. On receiving a copy of this great work, Louis XIV said: " Je lirai à mes heures de loisir et je tâcherai d'en profiter."

It was only with the second edition, issued in 1718, that alphabetical order was first adopted for the Dictionary. By 1813, five editions had appeared, and of the fifth M. Chesnier du Chesne relates in " Une édition du Dictionnaire pendant la Révolution " (*Les Annales politiques et littéraires*, volume 114: pages 186 to 190. 25 August, 1939) that it was prepared by the Academy, but finished by men who were not Academicians, at a time when—owing to the Revolution—the Academy had ceased to exist. Nevertheless, it was recognised and adopted by the Academy when that body was reconstituted.

The latest edition of the Dictionary is:

Académie Française, *Paris*. Dictionnaire de l'Académie française. 8th edition. Paris, Hachette, 1932–35. 2 volumes.

Although the Dictionary is recognised universally as the standard reference work on the French language, it has always come under heavy fire from the scholars—especially in its own country—for it has always been a conservative publication to which new words are only very cautiously admitted and, even so, at a date long after they have become current both in conversation and in literature. Typical of the kind of criticism levelled at the Dictionary is M. A. Barthélemy's "Dictionnaire de l'Académie française " (*Mercure de France*, volume 234: pages 251 to 252. 15 February, 1932) which is severely critical of the first volume. And, as M. Chesnier du Chesne points out in his " Le Dictionnaire est fini " (*Les Annales politiques et littéraires*, volume 106, pages 287 to 289. 25 September, 1935), France still lacks its equivalent of the Oxford English dictionary, the Académie having commenced the preparation of an historical dictionary in 1850, but only to abandon it after publishing the first four volumes.

Independent lexicographers were no doubt encouraged by the

infrequent publication of new editions of the Dictionary which has only achieved eight editions in more than two hundred years. One of the most popular efforts was that of Pierre Claude Victoire Boiste who compiled his *Dictionnaire universel de la langue française* in the late eighteenth century; it had reached its thirteenth edition by 1851. But it was in the nineteenth century that the great scholars of the language made their appearance. Emile Littré, who was born in 1801, started as a student of medicine and was only prevented from completing his studies owing to family misfortunes. He devoted himself instead to the history of medicine and to philology, learning many languages to equip himself thoroughly for his studies. His was an encyclopaedic mind, and he became a voluminous writer on many subjects, but his most important work was his:

> Dictionnaire de la langue française contenant . . . la nomenclature . . . la grammaire . . . la signification des mots . . . la partie historique . . . l'étymologie . . . Paris, Hachette, 1873–78. 4 volumes, and Supplement.

which includes many examples drawn from the literature of the past three centuries and an account of the use of each word prior to 1600, together with its etymology. To the Supplement is added an etymological dictionary of all the words of oriental origin, by Marcel Devic. An abridged edition edited by A. Beaujean was first issued in 1914 (latest edition, Paris, Editions Universitaires, 1950. 1294 pages), and the original dictionary was reprinted in 1950. In spite of the fact that it is now out of date for much of its material, it remains a rich source for all students of the history and grammar of the French language. Even after the publication of his dictionary, Littré's candidature for membership of the Académie Française was rejected by that body which only accepted him eight years later.

Louis-Nicolas Bescherelle, a Parisian, was appointed Librarian of the Louvre in 1828 at the age of 26. He was a grammarian who, basing his work on the dictionaries of the Académie and of Boiste, published his *Dictionnaire national* in the middle of the century; it was many times reprinted. He also published a dictionary of verbs, containing the conjugation of some seven thousand regular and irregular words.

One of the most important works of the century was the achievement of a publisher. Pierre Larousse, with the aid of a host of specialists, issued:

> Larousse, Pierre. Grand dictionnaire universel du XIXe siècle, français, historique, géographique, mythologique, bibliographique,

littéraire, artistique, scientifique, etc. Paris, Larousse & Boyer, 1866–90. 15 volumes, and Supplement in 2 volumes issued 1877–90.

This, which is encyclopaedic not only in scope but in treatment as well, includes an immense range of vocabulary. A number of related volumes in many editions followed, of which the chief are:

Dictionnaire complet illustré, comprenant: 1° langue française . . . 2° des développements encyclopédiques . . . 3° la géographie, l'histoire et la mythologie, 4° les locutions étrangères: latines, anglaises, etc., 5° une liste complète des académiciens, des sénateurs et des députés actuels . . . 95th edition. Paris, Larousse, 1898. 1464 pages. illustrated.

Larousse du XXe siècle . . . publié sous la direction de Paul Augé . . . Paris, Larousse, 1928–33. 6 volumes. illustrated.

Nouveau Larousse universel: dictionnaire encyclopédique . . . publié sous la direction de Paul Augé. Paris, Larousse, 1948–49. 2 volumes. illustrated.

Nouveau petit Larousse illustré: dictionnaire encyclopédique publié sous la direction de Claude Augé. Paris, Larousse, 1924. 1760 pages. (since reprinted many times, with corrections and additions).

A work which obtained the Jean Reynaud prize was:

Hatzfeld, Adolphe *and* Darmesteter, Arsène. Dictionnaire général de la langue française du commencement du XVIIe siècle jusqu'à nos jours. Paris, Delagrave, 1895–1900. 2 volumes.

of which a sixth edition was issued in 1920. This covered pronunciation, etymology, examples of first employment and subsequent changes in spelling and meanings, arranged historically, together with a three-hundred page treatise on the formation of the language, in volume two.

The more important of the many dictionaries published in recent years include:

Dictionnaire Quillet de la langue française: dictionnaire méthodique et pratique rédigé sous la direction de Raoul Mortier. Paris, Quillet, 1946. 3 volumes.

Rozoy, A. *and others*. Dictionnaire français illustré. Paris, Simon, 1947. 757 pages. (Known also as *Simon's Nouveau dictionnaire illustré*. Previous editions were also published by the University of London Press. Definitions are elementary).

Sève, André *and* Perrot, Jean. Ortho: dictionnaire orthographique. Chambéry, Editions Scolaires, 1950. 640 pages. (Known as *Ortho vert*, to distinguish it from the less detailed *Ortho jaune*: 1er degré of 1947, and *Ortho rouge*: 2e degré, the second edition of which was issued in 1948).

Etymological Dictionaries

The first etymological dictionary of the French language was written by Gilles Ménage in 1650 under the title *Dictionnaire étymologique, ou origines de la langue françoise*, and was an immediate success, being reprinted with additions many times in the next fifty years. But it was Friedrich Christian Diez who first showed scholars how an etymological dictionary should be compiled. The publication of his *Etymologisches Wörterbuch der romanischen Sprachen* at Bonn in 1853 no doubt inspired Auguste Scheler in his preparation of a popular etymological dictionary of the French language. Scheler, a Belgian scholar born in Switzerland, became Librarian to King Leopold in 1854 and German tutor to his children. His work:

Scheler, Auguste. Dictionnaire d'étymologie française d'après les resultats de la science moderne . . . new edition. Brussels, C. Muquardt, 1873. (3rd edition published 1888).

was not as important—even though he had himself contributed to the later editions of Diez—as that of Hatzfeld and Darmesteter mentioned above, which contains considerable etymological material. It was in any case superseded by:

Clédat, Léon. Dictionnaire étymologique de la langue française. 8th edition. Paris, Hachette, 1923. xviii, 686 pages. (includes a list of common nouns derived from proper names).

Körting, Gustav. Etymologisches Wörterbuch der französischen Sprache. Paderborn, F. Schöningh, 1908. 414 pages.

Even though Clédat's dictionary was crowned by the Académie Française, it has now—together with that of Körting—lost its importance owing to the brilliant work of two foreign scholars:

Wartburg, Walther von. Französisches etymologisches Wörterbuch: eine Darstellung des galloromanischen Sprachschatzes. Bonn, Klopp, 1928– volume 1- (reprinted: Tübingen, Mohr, 1948 onwards, and now being published at Basle by Helbing & Lichtenhahn. some early parts (fascicles 7 onwards) were

published by the author at the press of Sauerländer & Cie,
Aarau, in 1927).

—— Beiheft. Ortsnamenregister, Literaturverzeichnis, Übersichts-
karte. 2nd edition. Tübingen, Mohr, 1950. xiv, 135 pages.

which includes all the dialectical variants, arranged under the original
Vulgar Latin words, and gives the historical development of the meanings
of the words and the influences they have experienced. Wartburg
himself explains his method in an interesting article " Autour d'un
article du *Französisches etymologisches Wörterbuch*: comment naît un
article de mon dictionnaire " (*Modern philology*, volume 38: pages 251
to 266. February, 1941). The other scholar, a professor at the
University of Berlin, compiled a much smaller work:

Gamillscheg, Ernst. Etymologisches Wörterbuch der französischen
Sprache . . . mit einem Wort- und Sachverzeichnis von Heinrich
Kuen. Heidelberg, Winter, 1928. xxvi, 1136 pages. (published
in parts, 1926–28).

which excludes patois, but includes learned words and utilises phonetics
to the fullest extent in discussing doubtful etymologies.

The pursuit of etymology never ceases, however, and although
Wartburg's dictionary is not yet completed, two new works have
appeared:

Bloch, Oscar *and* Wartburg, Walther von. Dictionnaire étymologique
de la langue française. 2nd edition. Paris, Presses Universitaires de France, 1950. xli, 651 pages. (first issued in 1932
in two volumes).

This dictionary devotes itself to modern French, and places derivatives
under the main words, giving earliest dates of appearance and historical
information. On Bloch's method there is a short article by R. Georgin
" Aux sources de la langue à propos du livre *Dictionnaire étymologique
de la langue française* d'O. Bloch " (*Journal des débats*, volume 39, pages
717 to 718. 6 May, 1932). The other work is:

Dauzat, Albert. Dictionnaire étymologique de la langue française.
5th edition. Paris, Larousse, 1950. xxxvii, 804 pages.

which includes lexicological and chronological supplements, and is of
a more popular character than the last three dictionaries mentioned.

Specialist Dictionaries

There is a handful of specialist dictionaries which may assist writers and translators. On the subject of synonyms and antonyms, one of the earliest works was Jean Pons Victor Lacoutz de Levizac's *Dictionnaire universel des synonymes de la langue française: nouvelle édition corrigée et augmentée par P. N. de Rabaudy* (London, Cox, 1826. xxiii, 427 pages. First published in 1807). More modern dictionaries on this subject include:

Bailly, René. Dictionnaire des synonymes de la langue française. Paris, Larousse, 1946. 626 pages.

Lafaye, Benjamin. Dictionnaire des synonymes de la langue française. 8th edition. Paris, Hachette, 1903.

Maquet, Charles. Dictionnaire analogique: répertoire moderne des mots par les idées, des idées par les mots, d'après les principes de P. Boissière. Redigé sur un plan nouveau. Paris, Larousse, 1949. 591 pages.

Robert, Paul. Dictionnaire alphabétique et analogique de la langue française: les mots et les associations d'idées. Paris, Presses Universitaires de France, 1951– volume 1– .

The last has been crowned by the Académie Française, and is published for the Société du Nouveau Littré. It is to be completed in 25 fascicles by 1955. As its compiler explains: " un mot n'est pas défini complètement par son étymologie, son classement grammatical et la signification de ses divers emplois. Il ne prend sa pleine valeur que *par* rapport aux autres mots qu'il évoque logiquement: non seulement ses synonymes, homonymes et antonymes, mais encore les termes auxquels se rattachent sa famille, sa place dans la phrase et les liens multiples de l'association d'idées . . . En effet, pour trouver un mot dans un dictionnaire alphabétique, il faut, d'abord, que ce mot soit déjà connu, ensuite, qu'il affleure à l'esprit. Impossible de découvrir si l'on ignore son existence ou s'il reste enfoui au fond de la mémoire défaillante. C'est au dictionnaire analogique à le tirer du néant ou de l'oubli, au bénéfice de chacun, étudiant ou savant." This dictionary makes extensive use of examples drawn from the works of recent and contemporary writers.

Special Periods

More attention has probably been paid to the state of the language at definite periods in French history than that of the language of any other country except perhaps Britain. The research into Old French has been particularly thorough:

> Godefroy, Frédéric Eugène. Dictionnaire de l'ancienne langue française et de tous ses dialectes, du IXe au XVe siècle, composé d'après le dépouillement de tous les plus importants documents, manuscrits ou imprimés, qui se trouvent dans les grandes bibliothèques de la France et de l'Europe, et dans les principales archives départementales, municipales, hospitalières ou privées . . . Publié sous les auspices du Ministère de l'Instruction Publique. Paris, Vieweg, 1881–1902.   10 volumes.

The last two volumes of this work are supplementary, and include words which still survive in the language of to-day.   A shorter version, omitting the examples and a number of the words, was published under the title of *Lexique de l'ancien français* (Paris, Welter, 1901) which achieved one-volume size by these means.   Godefroy's dictionary remains the standard work, but its position may one day be challenged by:

> Tobler, Adolf.   Tobler-Lommatzsch Altfranzösisches Wörterbuch: Adolf Toblers nachgelassene Materialien bearbeitet und mit Unterstützung der Preussischen Akademie der Wissenschaften, herausgegeben von Erhard Lommatzsch . . . Berlin, Weidmann, 1925–   volume 1– .

which gives emphasis to the literary language, but includes all words extinct and surviving, indicating useful parallels in other Romance languages, and giving the history and examples of use of each word, with references to any special studies published elsewhere.   Tobler began work on this immense dictionary as early as the middle of the nineteenth century, but it did not begin to appear until fifteen years after his death.   Publication was interrupted by the war, but has since been resumed under the imprint of Franz Steiner of Wiesbaden, and has now reached the letter E.   There are also three other works to which attention must be drawn:

> Grandsaignes d'Hauterive, Robert.   Dictionnaire d'ancien français, moyen âge et renaissance.   Paris, Larousse, 1947.   592 pages.
>
> Roques, Mario.   Recueil général des lexiques français du moyen âge (XIIe–XVe siècle).   I. Lexiques alphabétiques, tome Ier. Paris, Champion, 1936.   xxxiii, 523 pages.   (Bibliothèque de l'Ecole des Hautes Etudes, Sc. hist. et philol., fasc. 246).
>
> Vandaele, Hilaire.   Petit dictionnaire de l'ancien français.   Paris, Garnier, 1940.   536 pages.

Grandsaignes d'Hauterive indicates his sources and gives etymologies but these have been questioned by the critics (e.g. *Bulletin critique du livre français*, volume III, page 522. July, 1948). Roques' dictionary is to be arranged in five parts: I. alphabetical lexicons, II. methodical, III. separate glossaries, IV. textual glossaries, V. Anglo-Norman and Provençal lexicons. The present volume gives the text of five Latin-French lexicons of the last quarter of the thirteenth century.

For the sixteenth century there is, in addition to what is contributed incidentally by the works just mentioned, a new dictionary:

> Huguet, Edmond Eugène Auguste. Dictionnaire de la langue française du seizième siècle. Paris, Champion, 1925– volume 1–

which was also interrupted during the war but which is now continuing again. This dictionary is especially rich in material, and has been praised for its careful workmanship and for its documentation. It includes not only those words which have disappeared from use, but also those whose form or meaning has altered, and even those remarkable only for date of first appearance. Slang is included, and verbal forms are grouped and illustrated by apt examples. The complete work is planned to consist of seven or eight volumes of some eight hundred pages each.

The seventeenth century has received much more attention:

> Cayrou, Gaston. Le français classique: lexique de la langue du dix-septième siècle expliquant d'après les dictionnaires du temps et les remarques des grammariens, le sens et l'usage des mots aujourd'hui vieillis ou différemment employés. 6th edition. Paris, Didier, 1948. xxviii, 884 pages. (first published 1923).

> Génin, François. Lexique comparé de la langue de Molière et des écrivains du XVIIe siècle, suivi d'une lettre à M. A. F. Didot, sur quelques points de philologie française . . . Paris, Firmin Didot, 1846. lxxxvi, 465 pages.

> Huguet, Edmond Eugène Auguste. Petit glossaire des classiques français du dix-septième siècle, contenant les mots et locutions qui ont vieilli ou dont le sens s'est modifié . . . Paris, Hachette, 1907. v, 409 pages.

> Livet, Charles-Louis. Lexique de la langue de Molière comparée à celle des écrivains de son temps, avec des commentaires de philologie historique et grammaticale . . . Paris, Imprimerie Nationale, 1895–97. 3 volumes.

Huguet's work is intended primarily for students, while Cayrou addresses himself to a more informed public and, utilising both the sources of contemporary dictionaries and the writings of contemporary authors, provides copious examples of grammatical and literary usage in the seventeenth century. Livet's lexicon, which was crowned by the Académie Française, is the most substantial in form and content of these four works.

Slang and Dialect

While it is not the intention of this guide to list more than the very important dialect dictionaries in each language, those interested in French dialects will find more comprehensive lists in Walther von Wartburg's *Bibliographie des dictionnaires patois* (Paris, Droz, 1934. Société de Publications Romanes et Françaises, tome 8), and in George S. C. Adams's *Census of French and Provençal dialect dictionaries in American libraries* (Lancaster, Pa., Lancaster Press, 1937. Linguistic Society of America, special publication).

Among the many dictionaries of slang, the following are worthy of mention:

Bauche, Henri. Le langage populaire: grammaire, syntaxe et dictionnaire du français tel qu'on le parle dans le peuple de Paris, avec tous les termes d'argot usuel. Paris, Payot, 1929. 256 pages. (first published in 1920).

France, Hector. Dictionnaire de la langue verte: archaismes, néologismes, locutions étrangères, patois. Paris, Librairie du Progrès, 1907. 495 pages.

La Rue, Jean. Dictionnaire d'argot et des principales locutions populaires, précédé d'une histoire d'argot par Clément Casciani. new edition. Paris, Flammarion, 1948.

French Dialect Dictionaries

Bal, W. Lexique du parler de Jamioulx. 1949. (Mémoires de la Commission de Toponymie et Dialectologie, Sect. Wall., V).

Beaufort, D. Lexique liégeois (Li bon walon d'oûy). Dinant, Bourdeaux-Capelle, 1933.

Bloch, Oscar. Lexique français-patois des Vosges méridionales. Paris, Champion, 1917. ii, 186 pages.

Castellana, Georges. Dictionnaire niçois-françois. Nice, the author, 1952. ii, 276 pages.

Chataing, Jean. Vocabulaire français-patois de la vallée supérieure de l'Ance. Clermont-Ferrand, 1934. (Mémoires de l'Académie des Sciences, Belles-Lettres et Arts de Clermont-Ferrand, sér. 2, tom. 34). 111 pages.

Coppens, Joseph. Dictionnaire aclot, wallon-français, parler populaire de Nivelles. Notes étymologiques de Henri Ferrière, dessins de Paul Collet. Nivelles, Fédération Wallonne, 1951. 420 pages.

Dauzat, Albert. Glossaire étymologique du patois de Vinzelles. Montpellier, Société des Langues Romanes, 1915. 289 pages. (Publications spéciales, tom. 25).

Descroix, J. Glossaire du patois de Lantignié-en-Beaujolais (Rhone). Paris, Droz, 1946. (Société de Publications Romanes et Françaises, XXIV). 119 pages.

Dottin, Georges. Glossaire des parlers du Bas-Maine (département de la Mayenne). Paris, Welter, 1899. 682 pages.

Duraffour, Antonin. Lexique patois-français du parler de Vaux-en-Bugey (Ain), 1919-40. Grenoble, 1941.

Ernault, Emile. Vocabulaire breton-français. Saint-Brieuc, Prud'-homme, 1927. x, 685 pages. (Bibliothèque de l'Académie Bretonne, I).

Eynaudi, Jules and Cappatti, Louis. Dictionnaire de la langue niçoise. Nice, 1931-35.

Gauchat, L. and others. Glossaire des patois de la Suisse romande; par L. Gauchat, J. Jeanjaquet et E. Tappolet. Neuchâtel & Paris, Attinger, 1924- volume 1-

Glossaire du parler français au Canada; préparé par la Société du Parler Français au Canada. Quebec, Action Sociale, 1930. xix, 709 pages.

Gonon, Marguérite. Lexique du parler de Poncins, Loire. Paris, Klincksieck, 1947. xii, 340 pages. (Publication d'Association des Chartes du Forez, Montbrison).

Haust, Jean. Dictionnaire liégeois, illustré de figures par Remouchamps et Salme. Liège, Vaillant-Cormanne, 1929-33. 766 pages. (Le Dialecte Wallon de Liège, II).

Haust, Jean. Dictionnaire français-liégeois, publié sous la direction d'Elisée Legros. Liège, Vaillant-Cormanne, 1948. xxvi, 512 pages. (Le Dialecte Wallon de Liège, III).

Musset, Georges. Glossaire des patois et des parlers de l'Aunis et de la Saintonge; avec la collaboration de Marcel Pellisson et Charles Vigen. La Rochelle, Masson et Renaud, 1929- volume 1-

Pirsoul, Léon. Dictionnaire wallon-français: dialecte de Namur. 2nd edition. Namur, Imprimerie Commerciale et Industrielle, 1934. 331 pages.

Prajoux, J. Dictionnaire du langage roannais: mots d'argot, termes familiers, locutions populaires, expressions locales. Roanne, Journal de Roanne, 1936. vii, 255 pages.

Quiévreux, Louis. Dictionnaire du dialecte bruxellois. Brussels, Dessart, 1951. 201 pages.

Sjoegren, A. Lexique français-guernesais. Paris, Droz (SPRF), 1939.

Vallée, François *and others*. Grand dictionnaire français-breton: par François Vallée, E. Ernault et R. Leroux. Rennes, Imprimerie Commerciale de Bretagne, 1931–34. xli, 817 pages.

Vasseur, Gaston. Lexique serrurier du Vimeu. Lille, Giard, 1950. 79 pages. (Société de Publications Romanes et Françaises, Publication 29).

Verdier, Roger. Dictionnaire phonétique, étymologique et comparé du patois du Haut-Maine. Le Mans, Graffin, 1952– volume 1–

Villié, Emile de. Glossaire du patois de Villié-Morgon en Beaujolais. Geneva, Droz, 1950. 147 pages. (Société de Publications Romanes et Françaises. Publication 31).

Zéliqzon, Léon. Dictionnaire des patois romans de la Moselle. Paris & Strasbourg, Istra, 1922–25. 720 pages. (Publication de la Faculté des Lettres de l'Université de Strasbourg). (Supplements 1929–).

Bi-Lingual Dictionaries

The interest in the French language in England—and the fact that Caxton had himself spent so many years on the Continent at a French-speaking court—led to the publication of one of the earliest books printed in England:

[Vocabulary in French and English. London, Caxton? 1480?]

The details are given in square brackets for there was no title-page to this book, and the information concerning printer and date of publication is by no means certain. The volume opens with the words: " Cy commence la table De cest prouffytable doctrine . . ." and closes " Here endeth this doctrine at Westmestre by London In fourmes emprinted In whiche one everich May shortly lerne Frenssh and englissh." In the sixteenth century another work—this time a translation—was issued:

Sainliens, Claude de. The treasurie of the French tong: teaching the waye to varie all sortes of verbes . . . Gathered together and set forth by Cl. Hollyband . . . London, Bynneman, 1580.

and not long afterwards the Secretary to William Cecil, Lord Burghley, dedicated his dictionary to his master:

Cotgrave, Randle. A dictionary of the French and English tongues. London, A. Islip, 1611. 976 pages.

Cotgrave presented a copy of his work to Prince Henry, eldest son of James I, who gave him ten pounds in acknowledgment. Another edition, with an English-French section by Robert Sherwood, was issued in 1632. Recently interest has been revived in Randle Cotgrave and in his pioneer work in dictionary-making: a reprint of his dictionary, with an introduction by William S. Woods, has been issued (University of South Carolina Press, 1950), and " extra volume no. 25 of the Johns Hopkins Studies in Romance Literatures and Languages " comprises Vera E. Smalley's *The sources of 'A Dictionarie of the French and English Tongues' by Randle Cotgrave (London*, 1611): *a study in Romance lexicography* (Baltimore, Md., Johns Hopkins Press, 1948. 252 pages).

A friend of Ben Johnson and Kenelm Digby, and himself a minor writer, improved on Cotgrave's effort:

> Howell, James. A French and English dictionary, composed by Mr. Randle Cotgrave: with another in English and French [by Robert Sherwood.] Whereunto are added sundry animadversions, with supplements of many hundreds of words never before printed; with accurate castigations throughout the whole work, and distinctions of the obsolete words from those that are now in use. Together with a large grammar and a dialogue consisting of all Gallicisms . . . 2nd edition. London, William Hunt, 1660. 2 volumes.

of which the first edition had been published in 1650, and a later edition "with other refinements according to Cardinal Richelieu's late Academy" was to be issued in 1673. Howell also contributed to a *Lexicon tetraglotton, or an English-French-Spanish-Italian dictionary*, 1659–60. Two other early efforts were Guy Miege's *The great French dictionary* (London, Thomas Basset, 1687–88. 2 volumes), which was an enlarged edition of the work which this former under-secretary to the Earl of Carlisle had first issued in 1677; and Abel Boyer's *Le dictionnaire royal françois-anglois et anglois-françois* (London, C. Bathurst, 1773. 2 volumes), which was first published in the Hague in 1702.

For modern use the principal dictionary is:

> Mansion, Jean Edmond. Harrap's standard French and English dictionary. London, Harrap: New York, Heath, 1934–39. 2 volumes.
>
> —— Supplement. new edition. Compiled by R. P. L. Ledésert. London, Harrap; New York, Heath, 1954.

The American work substitutes the name of the New York for that of the London publisher in the title. In addition to the main work, there are two smaller editions available: the *Shorter French-English, English-French dictionary* (1940); and the *Concise French-English, English-French dictionary* (1949) which omits the more abstruse words and some of the examples in the former.

Of the smaller modern dictionaries, the three most in general use are:

Bellows, John.   French dictionary: French-English, English-French. 4th edition, revised by H. H. Lucas.   London, Longmans, 1951. 766 pages.

Cassell's French-English, English-French dictionary.   With an appendix of proper names, weights and measures, etc.; by Ernest A. Baker.   Revised by J. L. Manchon.   London, Cassell, 1951.   xxiv, 727; 557 pages.

Chevalley, Abel *and* Chevalley, Marguerite.   The concise Oxford French dictionary.   Oxford, Clarendon Press, 1947.   1190 pages. (first published 1934).

Bellows's dictionary is especially interesting, for it adopts the idea of the divided page*, a horizontal line drawn across the middle of each page enabling the English-French and French-English vocabularies to be printed parallel to each other, with the advantage of being able to compare words of similar spelling in the two languages. Proper names are included in the Chevalleys' dictionary.

For the use of translators and students of the French language, there are several important and useful works which pay particular attention to idiom:

Anderson, James Gauchez.   Le mot juste: a dictionary of English and French homonyms.   Revised . . . by Lewis C. Harmer. New York, Dutton, 1938.   ix, 205 pages. (first published 1932).

Boillot, Félix François.   Le vrai ami du traducteur anglais-français et français-anglais.   Paris, Presses Universitaires de France, 1930.   266 pages.

Clarke, George Herbert *and* Charpentier, Alfred.   Manuel lexique des difficultés linguistiques du français: prononciation, vocabulaire, grammaire, synonymie.   London, Harrap, 1029.   315 pages.

Crowhurst, P. O.   Cassell's dictionary of French synonyms.   London, Cassell, 1933.   vii, 207 pages.

Derocquigny, Jules.   Autres mots anglais perfides . . . pour faire suite au livre intitulé *Les faux amis: ou, Les trahisons du vocabulaire*

---

* Webster's *New international dictionary of the English language* also uses the divided page, but in this case merely for the purpose of relegating obsolete and rare words to a subordinate position.

anglais, de MM. Koessler et Derocquigny.   Paris, Vuibert, 1931. xii, 107 pages.

Kettridge, Julius Ornan.   French for English idioms and figurative phrases, with many quotations from French authors.   London, Harrap, 1940. vi, 278 pages.

Koessler, Maxime *and* Derocquigny, Jules.   Les faux amis: ou, Les trahisons du vocabulaire anglais (conseils aux traducteurs). 4th edition.   Paris, Vuibert, 1949.

Pradez, Elisabeth.   Dictionnaire des gallicismes les plus usités, expliqués brièvement, illustrés par des exemples et accompagnés de leurs équivalents anglais et allemands.   Lausanne, Payot, 1949. vi, 367 pages.   (first published in 1914).

Boillot supplements Koessler and Derocquigny, and distinguishes between ambiguous words and their meanings.   Clarke and Charpentier include examples of current usage, synonyms, and adjectival forms of many French towns and regions, etc., most of the meanings being given in French.   Crowhurst lists more than a thousand groups of synonyms, with brief definitions and a full index.   Koessler and Derocquigny give many examples—incidentally, Chevally's *Concise Oxford French dictionary* marks " faux amis " with an asterisk.

On the subject of slang, there are three bilingual dictionaries of note :

Barrère, Albert Marie Victor.   Argot and slang: a new French and English dictionary of the cant words, quaint expressions, slang terms and flash phrases used in the high and low life of old and new Paris.   London, Bell, 1911. lx, 483 pages.   (first published 1889).

Kastner, L. E. *and* Marks, J.   A glossary of colloquial and popular French. revised edition.   London, Dent, 1930. vii, 376 pages. (first published 1929).

Leroy, Olivier.   A dictionary of French slang.   London, Harrap, 1935. 237 pages.

Kastner and Marks include examples, and some derivations and historical notes.   Leroy includes colloquial and child speech, and corrupted forms.

There is one French-German dictionary to which special attention must be drawn owing to its high standards of scholarship and accuracy:

Sachs, Karl *and* Villatte, Césaire.   Enzyklopädisches französisch-deutsches und deutsch-französisches Wörterbuch.   Methode Toussaint-Langenscheidt. 4e Bearb. Berlin, Langenscheidt, 1952. 2 volumes.   (*i.e.* 1. Französisch-deutsch, von Karl Moser.   33e Aufl. mit Nachtrag.   2. Deutsch-französisch, von Adolf Biel, u.s.w.   29e Aufl.)

Another dictionary which is especially designed for students of Old French is:

Urwin, Kenneth.   A short Old French dictionary for students. London, Chaterson, 1946.   x, 108 pages.

In addition to the dictionaries of the French language recorded in the Library of Congress bibliography and its Supplement (*see* General Bibliography, page 191), attention is drawn to the following list of further items: " Une bibliographie supplémentaire des dictionnaires du français moderne," by Raphael Lévy (*PMLA*, June 1947, pages 556 to 571).

GERMAN, DUTCH AND AFRIKAANS DICTIONARIES

The absence of any German equivalent to the French and Italian academies, and the comparatively late unification of Germany under a single ruler contributed to the delay in the development of German lexicography. The division of Germany during so many centuries into many different states, each with its own version of the German language which was almost a separate language rather than a dialect, gave rise to a situation where there were many substantial works on the languages of individual regions from quite early on, but that attempts at overall surveys—as in the case of Adelung's preoccupation with the Saxon dialect—were unlikely to be entirely free from prejudice.   One of the first attempts at a more general dictionary was:

> Neues vollkomenes und nach alphabetischer Ordnung wohleingerichtetes Wörterbuch. Worinnen die Wörter nach Art, wie sie buchstabiret werden müssen in Sylben abgetheilet, derer gleichlautender Unterscheid gewiesen, und Ihr Ursprung meistens gezeiget wird, welches bey der heut zu Tage nöthigen Rechtschreibekunst nützlich zu gebrauchen, und der Jugend zu liebe verfertiget worden. Chemnitz, C. Stösseln, 1722. 286 pages.

This comparatively short dictionary was in two parts, with continuous paging. It was quickly followed by:

> Wachter, Johann Georg. Glossarium germanicum continens origines et antiquitates linguae germanicae hodiernae. Specimen ex ampliore farragine decerptum. Leipzig, Schuster, 1727. 33; 342 pages.

which must be one of the earliest dictionaries to include bibliographical footnotes. Wachter, who, among other posts, held that of Librarian to the City of Leipzig, followed this with a larger work:

> Wachter, Johann Georg. Glossarium germanicum, continens origines et antiquitates totius linguae Germanicae, et omnium paene vocabulorum, vigentium et desitorum. Opus bipartium et quinque indicibus instructum. Leipzig, 1737–

which has since proved a mine of information for the brothers Grimm and for later lexicographers.

Throughout the history of German lexicography there is a noticeable tendency to cleanse the language of alien words and phrases. Was not Daniel Sanders himself called to Berlin as late as 1876 to help the Ministry of Education in its work of eliminating all foreign terms and expressions from the German language? The move towards a good language received a great stimulus from the works of the dramatist and literary critic, Johann Christoph Gottsched. Gottsched, who was responsible for a very useful catalogue of German plays and operas, helped to purify the language by his linguistic writings, such as his *Grundlegung einer deutscher Sprachkunst*, 1748, which went into five editions in the next fifteen years, and his *Beobachtungen über den Gebrauch und Missbrauch vieler deutscher Wörter und Redensarten*, 1758. His influence could perhaps have been more lasting had he not adopted an autocratic attitude in setting himself up as an arbiter of literary taste. Nevertheless, it could plainly be seen in:

> Popowitsch, Johann Siegmund Valentin. Versuch einer Vereinigung der Mundarten von Teutschland als eine Einleitung zu einem vollständigen teutschen Wörterbuche, mit Bestimmungen der Wörter und beträchtlichen Beitragen zur Naturgeschichte: aus den hinterlassenen Schriften . . . Vienna, Kurzböck, 1780. 649; 60 pages.

Heinrich Braun, a leading educational theorist of his day and Director-General of Schools in Bavaria, once held a university professorship in the—for that time—unusual subject of the German language. As a result of this, he compiled:

> Braun, Heinrich. Deutsches orthographisch-grammatisches Wörterbuch, mit einem Verzeichnisse ausländischer Wörter und Redensarten, welche im gemeinen Leben am öftesten vorkommen, und lieber deutsch gegeben werden sollen. Auf kurfürstlichen höchsten Befehl zum Gebrauche der deutschen Schulen herausgegeben: nun nach H. J. Ch. Adelungs grossem Wörterbuche, und andern guten Sprachlehrern um die hälfte vermehrt, durchaus verbessert und mit einigen kritisch- und etymologischen Anmerkungen versehen von Vincent von Pallhausen. Munich, Joseph Lentner, 1793. xviii, 326; 41 pages.

Almost contemporary with Heinrich Braun was the famous philanthropist, philosopher and educationalist, Joachim Campe, who was noted for sleeping only five hours each night. His writings and translations were voluminous and deservedly popular. In addition to a dictionary of foreign words in the German language, he compiled:

Campe, Joachim Heinrich. Wörterbuch der deutschen Sprache. Veranstaltet und herausgegeben von J. H. Campe. Brunswick, Schulbuchhandlung, 1807–11. 5 volumes.

This was an advance on previous work in this field, but the great dictionary of the German language was yet to come. The remarkable brothers Grimm, whose knowledge and tastes were so catholic, wrote their fairy tales as a hobby or at least as an escape from their more serious work. The main part of their lives was devoted to the compilation of a vast dictionary which only now is approaching completion, one hundred years after the publication of the first volume:

Grimm, Jacob *and* Grimm, Wilhelm. Deutsches Wörterbuch. Im Auftrage des deutschen Reiches und Preussens mit Unterstützung des Reich-Ministeriums des Innern, des preussischen Ministeriums für Wissenschaft, herausgegeben von der Preussischen Akademie der Wissenschaften. Leipzig, S. Hirzel, 1854– volume 1–

The brothers Grimm set out to cover the whole of the printed German language from the Middle Ages to the present time, giving derivations, subsequent history and changes in meaning and use both nationally and in different regions, with examples drawn from contemporary works. At the time of Jacob Grimm's death only two volumes of the work had been published, and it was due to the energetic organisation of the famous publisher Salomon Hirzel that work on the enormous dictionary was continued by the foremost scholars of the day. Incidentally, Wilhelm Grimm was once Assistant Librarian at Göttingen.

From the first, the great dictionary was subject to much criticism, notably by Daniel Sanders and Christian Wurm. As a result of his detailed scrutiny of the first volumes, Sanders published:

Sanders, Daniel. Wörterbuch der deutschen Sprache. Mit Belegung von Luther bis auf die Gegenwart. Leipzig, O. Wigand, 1860–65. 2 volumes in 3.

and this was followed by two later works:

Handwörterbuch der deutschen Sprache. 8., neubearb. und verm. Aufl. von J. Ernst Wülfling. Leipzig & Vienna, Bibliographisches Institut, 1912. 887 pages. (first published 1859–65).

Ergänzungs-Wörterbuch der deutschen Sprache. Eine Vervollständigung und Erweiterung aller bisher erschienenen deutschsprachlichen Wörterbücher (einschliesslich des Grimm'schen). Mit Belegung von Luther bis auf die neueste Gegenwart. Berlin, Abenheim (G. Joël), 1885. 691 pages.

Wurm reacted as quickly with his *Zur Beurtheilung des Deutschen Wörterbuches von Jakob und Wilhelm Grimm, zugleich ein Beitrag zur deutschen Lexikographie* (Munich, G. Franz, 1852. 34 pages), which he followed up with his own dictionary:

Wurm, Christian Friedrich Ludwig. Wörterbuch der deutschen Sprache, von der Druckerfindung bis zum heutigen Tage . . . Freiburg im Breisgau, Herder, 1858–   volume 1–

which was to stand against the Grimm dictionary. But only the 960 pages of the first six fascicles (carrying the work to AUSHAUER) were ever published, and the rest of this enormous compilation remains in manuscript in the Hof- und Staatsbibliothek at Munich.

Friedrich Weigand, a great friend of Jacob Grimm and, after the latter's death, the greatest of German lexicographers, not only collaborated in the preparation of many of the later volumes of his friend's dictionary, but himself published:

Weigand, Friedrich Ludwig Karl. Deutsches Wörterbuch. 5. Aufl. . . . Nach des Verfassers Tode vollständig neu bearb. von Karl von Bahder . . . Hermann Hirt . . . Karl Kant. Herausgegeben von Hermann Hirt . . . Giessen, A. Töpelmann, 1909–10. 2 volumes.

Other dictionaries issued towards the end of the nineteenth century include:

Heyne, Moriz. Deutsches Wörterbuch. 2. Aufl. (nach der neuesten amtlichen Rechtschreibung). Leipzig, Hirzel, 1905–06. 3 volumes. (first published 1895).

Hoffmann, Peter Friedrich Ludwig. Wörterbuch der deutschen Sprache in ihrer heutigen Ausbildung; mit besonderer Berücksichtigung der Schwierigkeiten in der Bedeutung, Beugung, Fügung und Schreibart der Wörter und mit vielen erläuternden Beispielen aus dem praktischen Leben. 10. Aufl., bearbeitet von Martin Block, mit Beiträgen von Gustav Mohr und Walter Weber. Leipzig, F. Brandstetter, 1936. xvi, 700 pages.

Paul, Hermann. Deutsches Wörterbuch. 4. Aufl., bearb. von Karl Euling. Halle, Niemeyer, 1933-35. vii, 688 pages. (first published in 1897).

Sarrazin, Otto. Wörterbuch für eine deutsche Einheitsschreibung. 2. verm. Aufl. nach den Beschlüssen des Königl. preussischen Staatsministeriums von 11. juni 1903, bearb. Berlin, W. Ernst, 1903. 120 pages. (first published January, 1903).

Viëtor, Wilhelm. Deutsches Aussprachewörterbuch . . . 3. durchgesehene Aufl. besorgt von Ernst A. Meyer. Leipzig, Reisland, 1921. xxii, 469 pages. (first published in 8 parts, 1908-12).

Vogel, August. Ausführliches grammatisch-orthographisches Nachschlagebuch der deutschen Sprache . . . mit Einschluss der gebräuchlicheren Fremdwörter nebst deren Aussprache, Angabe der Silbertrennungen und der Interpunktionsregeln; . . . 7. verb. Aufl. 71.-85. tausend, mit einem Verzeichnis geschichtlicher und geographischer Eigennamen. Berlin-Schöneberg, Langenscheidt, 1909. xl, 568 pages.

Weber, Ferdinand Adolf. Handwörterbuch der deutschen Sprache, nebst den gebräuchlichsten Fremdwörtern, Angabe der Betonung und Aussprache und einem Verzeichnisse der unregelmässigen Zeitwörter. 25. Aufl. völlig umgearb. und den Regeln der neuesten Rechtsschreibung angepasst, von Siegfried Moltke und Alfred C. Schmidt. Leipzig, Tauchnitz, 1908. xxxii, 896 pages.

William Viëtor indicated the pronunciation of every word according to the system of the International Phonetic Association.

Between the first and second World Wars, several more dictionaries appeared, notably:

Trübners Deutsches Wörterbuch im Auftrag der Arbeitsgemeinschaft für deutsche Wortforschung herausgegeben von Alfred Götze. Berlin, de Gruyter, 1939-   volume 1-

Weidemann, Gerhard. Das neue Wörterbuch der deutschen Sprache. Ausführliches, orthographisches, grammatisches stilistisches Handbuch in alphabetischer Anordnung, mit vielen Beispielen und leichtfasslicher Grammatik. Ein praktischer Führer durch die Hauptschwierigkeiten im deutschen und ein Ratgeber in Fällen schwankender Ausdrucksweise. Zum täglichen Gebrauch . . . Halle-Saale, Buchhandlung des Waisenhauses, 1931. xviii, 662 pages.

The former, whose progress has been somewhat impeded by the divided administration of Germany during the post-war era, is to be completed in seven volumes, of which well over half have already appeared.

The publishing firm of Brockhaus in Leipzig, founded by Friedrich Arnold Brockhaus, first made its name in the nineteenth century with the publication of its *Conversations-Lexikon*, the first edition of which was for some time banned by the Cabinet in Berlin. The house of Brockhaus can to some extent be compared with that of Larousse in Paris. Both firms are famous for the series of encyclopaedias which they have issued, and for the many reference works which they have commissioned and published. In addition, Brockhaus have issued:

> Sprach-Brockhaus: der deutsches Bildwörterbuch für Jedermann. 6th edition. Wiesbaden, Brockhaus, 1951. 799 pages. (first published in 1935).

which is an illustrated abridgment of the two-volume Brockhaus encyclopaedia. There is also a special dictionary of illustrations:

> Basler, Otto. Der grosse Duden: Bildwörterbuch der deutschen Sprache, bearbeitet von der Fachschriftleitung des Bibliographisches Instituts . . . Mit 342 Tafeln in Strichätzung und 6 Farbentafeln. Leipzig, Bibliographisches Institut: London, Harrap, 1935. x, 795 pages.

This, like the Duden series in other languages, helps to describe and to identify words by means of clear and simple illustrations. Readers are also reminded of the lexicographical resources of the great German encyclopaedias—especially Brockhaus* and Meyer—which give additional assistance in the identification and definition of words, and of the very considerable help given by the many illustrations in these works which are of particular aid for many of the more specialised and technical words.

Etymological Dictionaries

One of the best of the etymological dictionaries of the German language is:

> Kluge, Friedrich *and* Götze, Alfred. Etymologisches Wörterbuch der deutschen Sprache. 15th edition. Berlin, de Gruyter, 1951. xvi, 933 pages. (first published in 1881).

---

* of which a post-war edition is now appearing

A pioneer in this field, Kluge did not allow the blindness which struck him in 1902 and affected the last twenty-five years of his life to prevent his improving and amending his dictionary. In this he was aided by many eminent scholars, and later editions have been amended by Alfred Götze and Wolfgang Krause. Included is a *Sachverzeichnis*, in which the vocabulary is arranged under significant headings, and there is also a list of *Lehnübersetzung*. An English edition of the fourth German edition was published in 1891. There is also:

> Pinloche, Auguste. Etymologisches Wörterbuch der deutschen Sprache; enthaltend: ein Bildwörterbuch mit erklärenden Legenden zu 5700 Abbildungen; ein Verzeichnis der Eigennamen und eine grammatische Übersicht . . . unter Mitwirkung von Theodor Matthias. Paris, Larousse; Leipzig, Brandstetter, 1922. xiii, 1203 pages.

which contains illustrations, maps and musical examples.

Specialist Dictionaries

Johann August Eberhard, an eighteenth century philosopher and theologian, who spent most of his life vainly seeking recognition from the theologians who could not bring themselves to pardon his early apology for Socrates, compiled the first main work on German synonyms: *Allgemeine Synonymik der sinnverwandten Wörter der hochdeutschen Sprache* (1795– . 6 volumes), which he followed with his *Versuch einer allgemeinen teutschen Synonymik in einem kritisch-philosophischen Wörterbuche* (Halle, 1795-98). The second edition of the latter was augmented by Maass, and the third by Gruber (Halle, 1826–30). The abridged edition first appeared anonymously at Halle in 1802, and in its eighth edition (Berlin 1837) received the title under which it now appears:

> Eberhard, Johann August. Synonymisches Handwörterbuch der deutschen Sprache. 17. Aufl., durchgängig umgearb., verm. und verb. von Otto Lyon. Mit Übersetzung der Wörter in die englische, französische, italienische und russische Sprache. Leipzig, Grieben, 1910. 1201 pages.

Friedrich Weigand, who has already been mentioned, wrote a *Handbuch der sinnverwandten Wörter der deutschen Sprache*, 1836, which finally developed into a work which superseded the efforts of Eberhard, Maass and Gruber:

> Weigand, Friedrich Ludwig Karl. Wörterbuch der deutschen

Synonymen. 2nd edition. Mainz, Kupferberg, 1852. (first published in 3 volumes in Mainz, 1840–43).

Daniel Sanders also compiled a *Wörterbuch der deutschen Synonymen* (Hamburg, 1871. 2nd edition, 1882), and there are also two more recent works:

> Dornseiff, Franz. Der deutsche Wortschatz nach Sachgruppen geordnet. 3rd edition. Berlin, de Gruyter, 1943. 722 pages.

> Hoffmann, Peter Friedrich Ludwig. Volkstümliches Wörterbuch der deutschen Synonyme: Erklärung der in der deutschen Sprache gebräuchlichsten sinnverwandten Wörter. 10. durchgesehene Aufl. von Wilhelm Oppermann. Leipzig, Brandstetter, 1936. iv, 254 pages.

a new edition of the former being in active preparation.

Probably the earliest list of foreign words in the German language was *Ein teutscher Dictionarius . . . publiciert: durch Simon Roten. Gedruckt zu Augspurg bey Michaël Manger*, 1571, which was reprinted in recent years:

> Roth, Simon. Simon Roths Fremdwörterbuch, herausgegeben von Emil Öhmann. (*Mémoires de la Société Néo-Philologique de Helsingfors*, 1936: pages 225 to 370).

Campe compiled a dictionary of foreign words (Brunswick, 1801. 2nd edition, 1813), and Sanders another (2 volumes, 1871. 2nd edition, 1891). More modern dictionaries of foreign words include:

> Keysers Fremdwörterlexikon. Herausgegeben von Rich. von Kienle. Heidelberg, Keyser, 1950. 473 pages.

> Liebknecht, Wilhelm. Volksfremdwörterbuch. 21st edition. Berlin, Dietz, 1948. xvi, 562 pages.

> Schulz, Hans. Deutsches Fremdwörterbuch, fortgeführt von Otto Basler. Strassburg, Trübner; Berlin, de Gruyter, 1913–42. 2 volumes. (Wörterbücher der deutschen Academie, II).

> Tesch, Albert. Fremdwort und Verdeutschung: ein Wörterbuch für den täglichen Gebrauch . . . Leipzig & Vienna, Bibliographisches Institut, 1915. 244 pages.

Special Periods

One of the greatest of sources for the older words in the German language, and one of the finest of the early dictionaries is:

Adelung, Johann Christoph.   Versuch eines vollständigen grammatisch-kritischen Wörterbuches der hochdeutschen Mundart, mit beständiger Vergleichung der übrigen Mundarten, besonders aber der Oberdeutschen . . . Leipzig, Breitkopf, 1774–86.   5 volumes.

Adelung, who was Librarian to the Elector of Saxony until his death in 1806, wrote a history of " Menschliche Narrheit ".   His aim as a lexicographer was to purify the language and lay down sound laws concerning what writers should and should not use.   He has been compared to Samuel Johnson in his contribution to the lexicography of his country, and the details he gave of each word—pronunciation, orthography, inflexions, construction and use—were of lasting value to later scholars.   The second (1793–1801) and subsequent editions of his dictionary have the title: *Grammatisch-kritisches Wörterbuch der hochdeutschen Mundart*.   The second half of volume five, which was to have contained additions and corrections, was never published.

Of the dictionaries devoted to special periods in the history of the German language, the following are notable:

Kehrein, Joseph.   Alterneuhochdeutsches Wörterbuch: ein Beitrag zur deutschen Lexikographie . . . Würzburg, Stahel'schen Buch- und Kunsthandlung, 1865.

which includes sources from church songs and hymns, and psalms from the earliest-printed German prayerbooks and hymnals.

Lexer, Matthias von.   Mittelhochdeutsches Taschenwörterbuch. 26th edition. Stuttgart, Hirzel, 1951.   viii, 343 pages.   (a reprint of the 25th edition of 1949.   first published in 1881).

Steinmayr, Elias von.   Althochdeutsches Wörterbuch.   Leipzig, 1952–   volume 1–

Lexer, who collaborated in the preparation of several of the later volumes of the Grimm dictionary towards the end of the last century, compiled as a supplement to the pioneer work of Beneke, Müller and Zarncke:

Lexer, Matthias von.   Mittelhochdeutsches Handwörterbuch. Leipzig, Hirzel, 1872–78.   3 volumes.

Steinmayr's *Wörterbuch*, which is being published under the auspices of the Saxon Academy of Sciences at Leipzig, has been compiled by Theodor Frings and Elisabeth Karg-Gasterstädt, and will be completed in five or six volumes.   In addition to providing a throughgoing examination of the entire vocabulary of Old High German according to form, syntactical function and meaning, it will have a Latin-Old High German index, and will replace Eberhard Graff's *Althochdeutscher Sprachschatz*, 1834–46.

German Dialect Dictionaries

Autenrieth, Georg Gottlieb Philipp. Pfälzisches Idiotikon: ein Versuch. Zweibrücken, F. Lehmann, 1899. 197 pages.

Berghaus, Heinrich Karl Wilhelm. Der Sprachschatz der Sassen: ein Wörterbuch der plattdeutschen Sprache in den hauptsächlichsten ihrer Mundarten. Brandenburg, A. Müller, 1880–84. 3 volumes in 2 (A-Paddeln only. no more published).

Crecelius, Wilhelm. Oberhessisches Wörterbuch: auf Grund der Vorarbeiten Weigands, Diefenbachs und Hainebachs sowie eigner Materialien bearbeitet. Darmstadt, Selbstverlag des Vereins für das Grossherzogtum Hessen, 1897–99. 2 volumes.

Fischer, Hermann von. Schwäbisches Wörterbuch: auf Grund der von Adalbert von Keller begonnenen Sammlungen und mit Unterstützung des Württembergischen Staates. Tübingen, H. Laupp, 1904–36. 6 volumes in 7.

Frischbier, Jermann. Preussisches Wörterbuch: Ost- und westpreussische Provinzialismen. Berlin, Enslin, 1882–83. 2 volumes.

Heinzerling, Jakob *and* Reuter, Hermann. Siegerländer Wörterbuch. Siegen, Vorländer, 1932–38. xxiv, 354 pages.

Holthausen, F. Altfriesisches Wörterbuch. Heidelberg, Winter, 1925. xviii, 152 pages. (Germanische Bibliothek, I., iv, 5).

Hönig, Fritz. Wörterbuch der Kölner Mundart. Cologne, J. P. Bach, 1905. viii, 312 pages.

Hügel, Franz Seraph. Der Wiener Dialekt: Lexikon der Wiener Volkssprache. (Idiotikon Viennense). Vienna, Hartleben, 1873. 224 pages.

Jungandreas, Wolfgang. Niedersächsisches Wörterbuch. Auf Grund der Vorarbeiten von Hans Janssen und unter Mitwirkung eines Arbeitskreises niedersächsischer Mundartforscher, herausgegeben von der Abteilung für niedersächsische Mundartenforschung des Seminars für deutsche Philologie der Universität Göttingen. Neumünster, Wachholtz, 1953.

Leithaenser, J. Wörterbuch der Barmer Mundart. Wuppertal, Martini & Grüttefien, 1929–36.

Luxemburger Wörterbuch; im Auftrage der Grossherzoglich Luxemburgischen Regierung herausgegeben von der Wörterbuchkommission,

auf Grund der Sammlungen, die seit 1925 von der Luxemburgischen
Sprachgesellschaft und seit 1933 von der Sprachwissenschaftlichen
Sektion des Grossherzoglichen Instituts veranstaltet worden sind.
Luxemburg, 1954–

Martin, Ernst Eduard *and* Lienhart, H.   Wörterbuch der elsässischen
Mundarten.   Im Auftrage der Landesverwaltung von Elsass-
Lothringen . . . Strasburg, K. J. Trübner, 1899–1907. 2 volumes.

Mensing, O.   Schleswig-Holsteinsches Wörterbuch.   Neumünster, K.
Lachholtz, 1935. 5 volumes.

Mojmir, H.   Wörterbuch der deutschen Mundart von Wilamowice.
Cracow, Gebethner, 1931.   xxiii, 355 pages.   (Polska Akademja
umiejętnósci. Prace komisji językowej, 18, 1).

Müller-Fraureuth, Carl.   Wörterbuch der obersächsischen und erzge-
birgischen Mundarten. Dresden, W. Baensch, 1911–14. 2 volumes.

Schmeller, Johann Andreas.   Bayerisches Wörterbuch.   2. mit des
Verfassers Nachträgen verm. Ausg.   Munich, R. Oldenbourg,
1872–77. 2 volumes.

Schmid, Johann Christoph von.   Schwäbisches Wörterbuch mit etymologischen und historischen Anmerkungen. 2nd edition. Stuttgart,
E. Schweizerbart, 1844. xvi, 630 pages.

Schöpf, Johann Baptist.   Tirolisches Idiotikon.   Innsbruck, Wagner,
1866. xvi, 835 pages.

Schmoeckel, Hermann *and* Blesken, Andreas.   Wörterbuch der Soester
Börde: ein Beitrag zur westfälischen Mundartenforschung.   Soest,
Westfälische Verlagsbuchhandlung, 1952. 15 pages, 342 columns.
(Soester Wissenschaftliche Beiträge, Bd. 5).

Schuster, Mauriz.   Alt-Wienerisch: ein Worterbuch veraltender und
veralteter Wiener Ausdrücke und Redensarten der letzten sieben
Jahrzehnte.   Vienna, Österreichischer Bundesverlag, 1951.   232
pages.

Schütze, Johann Friedrich.   Holsteinisches Idiotikon: ein Beitrag zur
Volkssittengeschichte: oder, Sammlung Plattdeutscher. Hamburg,
H. L. Villaume, 1800–06. 4 volumes in 1.

Schweizerisches Idiotikon: Wörterbuch der schweitzerdeutschen Sprache.
Gesammelt auf Veranstaltung der Antiquarischen Gesellschaft in
Zürich unter Beihülfe aus aller Kreisen des Schweizervolkes. Herausgegeben mit Unterstützung des Bundes und der Kantone. Bearbeitet
von Friedrich Staub und Ludwig Tobler.   Frauenfeld, J. Huber,
1881–   volume 1–

—— Verzeichnis der literarischen Quellen mit den dafür gebrauchten
Abkürzungen. Sammt einem ergänzten Verzeichniss der abgekürzten
Ortsbezeichnungen. Frauenfeld, Huber, 1903. 6 pages.

Siebs, T. *and* Jungandreas, Wolfgang.   Schlesisches Wörterbuch.
  Breslau, Korn, 1935–   volume 1–
Wossidlo, R. *and* Teuchert, H.   Mecklenburgisches Wörterbuch.
  Neumünster, Wachholtz, 1937–   volume 1–
Ziesemer, Walther.   Preussisches Wörterbuch: Sprache und Volktum
  Nordostdeutschlands.   Im Auftrag und mit Unterstützung der
  preussischen Akademie der Wissenschaften, der Deutschen For-
  schungsgemeinschaft und der Provinz Ostpreussen.   Königsberg,
  Gräfe & Unzer, 1935–   volume 1–

Bi-Lingual Dictionaries

There are many bilingual dictionaries of the German language:
of those issued during the nineteenth century, the more important
include:

Flügel, Johann Gottfried.   Allgemeines englisch-deutsches und
  deutsch-englisches Wörterbuch.   3. verb. und verm.   Abdruck
  der 4. gänzlich umgearb. Aufl. von J. G. Flügels *Vollständigem
  Wörterbuch* . . . Brunswick, Westermann, 1908–12.   2 volumes
  in 3. (first published in 1847–52).

Grieb, Christoph Friedrich.   Englisch-deutsches und deutsch-
  englisches Wörterbuch, mit besondere Rücksicht auf Aussprache
  und Etymologie neubearb. und verm. von Arnold Schröer.
  11. Aufl.   Berlin-Schöneberg, Mentor-Verlag, 1911.   2 volumes.

Hilpert, Joseph Leonhard.   Englisch-deutsches und deutsch-
  englisches Wörterbuch.   Neue, im Preis ermässigte Ausg. . . .
  Karlsruhe, G. Braun, 1857.   4 volumes in 2.

James, William.   Dictionary of the German and English languages
  . . . 43rd edition, entirely rewritten and greatly enlarged and
  now augmented by all the latest expressions connected with
  aviatics, motoring, travelling, sport, etc.   German-English,
  English-German, New York, Macmillan, 1916.   x, 532; 592
  pages.

Klatt, Edmund.   Langenscheidts Taschenwörterbuch der englischen
  und deutschen Sprache.   19th edition.   Berlin-Schöneberg,
  Langenscheidt, 1949.   2 volumes in 1.

Koehler, Friedrich.   Handwörterbuch der englischen und deutschen
  Sprache.   Gänzlich umgearb. und verm. von Hermann Lambeck.
  30th edition.   Leipzig, Reclam, 1892.   2 volumes in 1.

Lindemann, Hermann. Taschenwörterbuch der englischen und deutschen Sprache, mit Angabe der Aussprache nach dem phonetischen System der Methode Toussaint-Langenscheidt . . . zusammengestellt von Hermann Lindemann. 8th edition. Berlin-Schöneberg, Langenscheidt, 1912. 2 volumes in 1.

Schmidt, Immanuel. Flügel-Schmidt-Tanger, a dictionary of the English and German languages for home and school . . . With special reference to Felix Flügel's *Universal English-German and German-English dictionary*, edited by Immanuel Schmidt and G. Tanger. 8th edition. Berlin-Schöneberg, Langenscheidt, 1910. 2 volumes.

The dictionary on which Schmidt was based was itself a complete revision of Flügel's *Vollständiges . . . Wörterbuch*. Flügel, incidentally, had lived for some time in the United States at the beginning of the nineteenth century, before returning to his own country to become a university lecturer in English at Leipzig.

The outstanding example of modern bilingual German dictionaries is:

Muret, Eduard *and* Sanders, Daniel. Enzyklopädisches englisch-deutsches und deutsch-englisches Wörterbuch. Parallelwerk zu Sachs-Villattes *Französisch-deutschem und deutsch-französischem Wörterbuche*. Mit Angabe der Aussprache nach dem phonetischen System der Methode Toussaint-Langenscheidt. Grosse Ausg. Berlin-Schöneberg, Langenscheidt, 1908. 2 volumes in 4.

A small school edition, in two volumes, was issued by the same publisher in 1910, and a *Nachtrag*—in two parts—in 1931. A new edition of the main work is now in preparation. Details of the important Sachs-Villatte dictionary have already been given in the chapter on French Dictionaries (page 16).

Other useful, and more modern dictionaries include:

Barker, Marie Louise *and* Homeyer, Helene. Pocket Oxford German-English dictionary. Oxford University Press, 1946. xvi, 432 pages.

Carr, Charles Telford. Pocket Oxford English-German dictionary. Oxford University Press, 1950. 222 pages.

These two volumes were issued in one in 1951. They omit archaic forms.

Bellows, Max. Dictionary of German and English, English and German. 2nd edition. New York, Holt, 1936. xxxii, 772 pages. (reprinted 1946).

4

which is remarkable for its use of the divided page (see page 14 of the chapter on French dictionaries).

> Bithell, Jethro.   German-English and English-German dictionary. 4th edition. London, Pitman, 1949. 1034 pages.

> Breul, Karl Hermann. Cassell's new German and English dictionary with a phonetic key to pronunciation . . . Revised and enlarged by J. Heron Lepper and Rudolph Kottenhahn. London, Cassell, 1939. 813; 687 pages.

The latter is also known as *Heath's new German dictionary* (Boston, Heath, 1939).

> Köhler, Friedrich *and others*. Reclams Wörterbuch der englischen und der deutschen Sprache. Völlig neubearb. Aufl. Mit Aussprachebezeichnung nach d. Regeln d. Association phonétique internationale. Nuremberg, Sebaldus-Verlag, 1948–   volume 1–

> Pfeffer, Jay Alan. Dictionary of everyday usage, German-English, English-German. Handbuch der amerikanischen und deutschen Umgangsprache. New edition. New York, Holt, 1947. xxx, 873 pages.

Pfeffer's dictionary was originally published by the Intensive Language Program of the American Council of Learned Societies.

> Schoffler, Herbert. English-German pocket dictionary: completely revised and much enlarged by E. Weis. London, Allen & Unwin, 1951. xi, 611 pages.

which was originally published as the *Taschenwörterbuch der englischen und deutschen Sprache. v.I.* (Stuttgart, Klett, 1949).

> Schröer, Arnold. Neuenglisches Aussprachwörterbuch mit besonderer Berücksichtigung der wichtigsten Eigennamen. Heidelberg, C. Winter, 1913. 522 pages.

> Wildhagen, Karl. English-German, German-English dictionary: a comprehensive and strictly scientific representation of the vocabulary of the modern and present-day languages, with special regard to syntax, style and idiomatic usage. 3rd revised and enlarged edition. Wiesbaden, Brandstetter; London, Allen & Unwin, 1952–54. 2 volumes in 3.

The latter, which is written by a former Professor of English Philology at the University of Kiel, gives special emphasis to present-day language at the expense of the older and rarer words.

Pattermann, Wilhelm *and* Reitterer, Theodor. Deutsch-englisches Wörter- und Phrasenbuch, mit Berücksichtigung des amerikanischen Englisch. Vienna, Alexa-Verlag, 1949–52. (reissued in 1 volume, 1953).

where again the emphasis is on current usage and on the differentiation of shades of meaning. Two other important dictionaries of special aspects of the German language have appeared recently:

Farrell, R. B. A dictionary of German synonyms. Cambridge University Press, 1953. viii, 428 pages.

Spalding, Keith. An historical dictionary of German figurative usage. Oxford, Blackwell, 1952– volume 1–

Farrell's dictionary is based on those English words whose translation into German is made difficult by the abundance of German equivalents: each shade of meaning in the German words is examined in detail, and plentiful examples of the use of the words in different connections are given. Spalding is to be completed in twenty-four parts. It records figurative expressions, proverbs, quotations, and other established phrases appearing in German literature since about 1750; annotations illustrating the uses or changes of meaning are often drawn from sources which precede this date. English translations for each entry are equivalent, not literal. A complete list of sources is planned for the conclusion of the work.

Recent terms are included in the following dictionaries of contemporary usage:

Brinitzer, Carl. Cassell's War and post-war German dictionary. London, Cassell, 1945. 254 pages.

Kremer, Edmund Philipp. German-American handbook: a collection of current idioms, colloquialisms, familiar quotations, localisms, dialectical and slang expressions and words not generally found in German-English dictionaries. Philadelphia, Lippincott, 1939. 390 pages.

Paechter, Heinz *and others*. Nazi-Deutsch: a glossary of contemporary German usage, with appendices on government, military and economic institutions. New York, Frederick Ungar, 1944. 128 pages.

The last-mentioned includes explanations of new terms coined by the Nazis, and of old terms used by them in senses different from the original meanings.

Dutch Dictionaries

The standard dictionary of the Dutch language which is still in course of publication is:

> Woordenboek der nederlandsche taal. The Hague, Nijhoff, 1882– volume 1–

while recent dictionaries and new editions of older works include:

> Brouwers, Ludovicus. Het juiste woord: beteekenis-woordenboek der nederlandsche taal. 2nd edition. Turnhout, Brepols, 1942. 1466 pages. (synonyms).

> Dale, Johan Hendrik van. Nieuw groot woordenboek der neder-landse taal. Bewerkt door C. Kruyskamp en F. de Tollenaere. 7th edition. The Hague, Nijhoff, 1948-50. xxxv, 2379 pages. (more concise editions are also published in frequent editions under the same imprint.)

> Koenen, M. J. and Endepols, J. Verklarend handwoordenboek der nederlandse taal (tevens vreemdewoordentolk). 23rd edition. Groningen, Wolters, 1951. viii, 1248 pages.

> Verschueren, J. Modern woordenboek. 5th edition. Turnhout, Brepols, 1949-50. 2 volumes.

> Vries, Matthias de and Winkel, Lambert Allard te. Woordenlijst voor de spelling der nederlandsche taal, met aanwijzing van de geslachten der naamwoorden en de vervoeging der werkwoorden. 7th edition. The Hague, Nijhoff, 1914. xliv, 500 pages.

There are also two etymological dictionaries:

> Franck, Johannes. Franck's etymologisch woordenboek der neder-landsche taal. 2. druk door N. van Wijk. Met registers der nieuwhoogduitsche woorden, enz. The Hague, Nijhoff, 1912. xvi, 897 pages.

> —— Supplement, door C. B. van Haeringen. The Hague, Nijhoff, 1936. xvii, 235 pages.

> Vercoullie, Jozef. Beknopt etymologisch woordenboek der neder-landsche taal. 2nd edition. Ghent, Vuylsteke, 1898. xx, 464 pages.

and two dictionaries of the older language:

> Verdam, Jacob. Middelnederlandsch handwoordenboek, enver-randerde derde herdruk, en van het woord Sterne af opineuw

bewerk door C. H. Ebbingen Wubben.   The Hague, Nijhoff, 1946. vi, 811 pages.

Verwijs, Eelco *and* Verdam, Jacob. Middelnederlandsch woordenboek. The Hague, Nijhoff, 1885–   volume 1–

Of the bilingual dictionaries, the more important are:

Bruggencate, Karel ten.   Engels woordenboek.   new edition. Groningen, Wolters, 1948–51. 2 volumes.

Calisch, Isaac Marcus.   New complete dictionary of the English and Dutch languages. 2nd edition, revised by N. S. Calisch. Tiel, Campagne, 1890–92. 2 volumes.

Jansonius, Herman.   Groot nederlands-engels woordenboek voor studie en practijk. Leiden, Nederlandsche Uitgeversmaatschappij, 1950. 2 volumes.

—— Supplements. (issued 4 times a year).

Neck, M. G. van *and* Theunis-van-Neck, M.   Nederlandsch-engelsche klank- en zinverwandte woorden. Leiden, Brill, 1946. 296 pages. (synonyms and antonyms).

Prick van Wely, Franciscus Petrus Hubertus.   Cassell's English-Dutch, Dutch-English dictionary. London, Cassell, 1951. xv, 1376 pages.

Renier, Fernand G. Dutch-English and English-Dutch dictionary. London, Routledge, 1949. xviii, 571 pages.

Swaen, Adriaan Ernst Hugo.   Engelsch woordenboek.   Zutphen, Thieme, 1933– volume 1–

Afrikaans Dictionaries

Boshoff, Stephanus Petrus Erasmus.   Etimologiese woordeboek van Afrikaans. Cape Town, Nasionale Pers., Beperk, 1936. 121 pages.

Bosman, Daniël Brink *and* Merwe, Izak W. van der. Tweetalige woordeboek. Cape Town, Nasionale Pers., Beperk, 1946–49. 2 volumes.

Kritzinger, Matthys S. *and others*   Woordeboek afrikaans-engels, engels-afrikaans en die afrikaanse spelreëls van die Akademie vir Taal, Lettere en Kuns. new edition. Pretoria, van Schaik, 1928. 1290 pages.

Le Roux, Thomas Hugo *and* Pienaar, Pierre de Villiers. Uitspraak-woordeboek van afrikaans. 2nd edition. Pretoria, van Schaik, 1950.

Potgieter, Dirk Jacobus *and* Potgieter, Johannes Marthinus. Juta's dictionary Afrikaans-English and English-Afrikaans (in accordance with the latest spelling of the Akademie). 2nd edition. Cape Town, Juta, 1932. 676 pages. (reprinted 1947).

Woordeboek van die afrikaanse taal. Redaksie: P. C. Schoonees. . . . Pretoria, Staatsdrukker, 1950–   volume 1–   (known as *Die afrikaanse woordeboek*).

ITALIAN DICTIONARIES

Academies flourished in most of the great Italian cities many years before the founding of the Académie Française and their half-mocking titles emphasised the dilletante nature of the intellectual pursuits of the majority of these groups. The academy which was responsible for Italy's first real dictionary was established comparatively late and its origin was almost as haphazard as its French counterpart. Previous attempts at dictionary-making had been limited mostly to the construction of vocabularies of the works of single authors such as Dante, Petrarch, and Ariosto, but Francesco Alunno compiled an early dictionary of the language as a whole in his *Della fabrica del mondo* (Venice, G. P. Porta, 1584) and the all-embracing interests of Leonardo da Vinci inspired him to attempt the same task.

The Accademia della Crusca had been founded in 1582, but it did not commence its work on the dictionary until 1591. The first edition:

Vocabolario degli accademici della Crusca. Venice, 1612.

was published in a single volume but, as H. H. Vaughan writes: " The vocabulary of the Italian language is enormous, being surpassed only perhaps by that of English; in fact, it is even possible that there are more words in use to-day by Italian than by English authors. Any attempt therefore to make a dictionary of the two languages in less than 1000 octavo pages is doomed to fail." (*Italica*, volume I: pages 31 to 34. November, 1924). But the Accademia did its work well, drawing on the writings of the standard authors for examples, and setting a good standard for the national dictionaries of the other European countries. The second edition was published in the same city in 1623, but was little more than a corrected reprint. Expansion came with the third edition which was issued in three volumes in Florence in 1691, and with the fourth which was also printed there in six volumes in the years 1729 to 1738. But after that the Accademia fell on evil days and was at one time compelled to amalgamate with other moribund academies. It eventually managed to regain its independence in the nineteenth century, and set itself to compile the fifth edition, the first volume of which was published in 1863, in Florence. But the Accademia lacked energy, and by 1923 the dictionary had reached only the letter O and the eleventh volume.   It was at this point that the dictionary was abandoned, but in 1935 a new start was made, and after six years the first volume of a completely new edition was issued under the title:

> Accademia d'Italia, *Rome*. Vocabolario della lingua italiana ... Milan, Società anonima per la pubblicazione del Vocabolario della lingua italiana, 1941–   volume 1–

and now that peace has been established, this great work will no doubt be completed.

Independent attempts in the nineteenth century compensated in part for the tardy work of the Accademia. One great work corresponds to some extent to the Oxford English dictionary:

> Boccardo, Gerolamo. Nuova enciclopedia italiana: ovvero, Dizionario generale . . . 6th edition. Turin, Unione Tipografico—Editrice Torinese, 1875–88. 25 volumes in 26. Supplement, 5 volumes in 6, published 1889–99.

which, like the Larousse encyclopaedia in France, was important for its definitions until almost the present day.   Another and earlier work was also held in great esteem:

> Vocabolario universale della lingua italiana: edizione eseguita su quella del Tramater di Napoli, con giunte e correzioni . . . Mantua, Negretti, 1845–56.   8 volumes.

which was first issued in 1829, and was reprinted in 1878.   And there was a smaller dictionary, first published in 1855:

> Fanfani, Pietro. Vocabolario della lingua italiana.   Florence, Le Monnier, 1922.

which had three editions in the nineteenth century and was valued for its concise definitions.   But the most important of all nineteenth century dictionaries was:

> Tommaseo, Nicolò. Dizionario della lingua italiana, nuovamente compilato dai . . . Nicolò Tommaseo e Bernardo Bellini; con oltre 100,000 giunte ai precedenti dizionarii raccolte da Nicolò Tommaseo, Gius. Campi, Gius. Meini, Pietro Fanfani e da molti altri distinti filologi e scienziati, corredato di un discorso preliminare dello stesso Nicolò Tommaseo. Turin, Unione Tipografico—Editrice Torinese, 1861–74.   4 volumes in 8.

which was reprinted in seven volumes in 1924. This is still a very useful dictionary, although its Latin etymologies can sometimes be challenged, and its arrangement and omission of variants are a definite hindrance. It is sometimes known as the *Nuovo dizionario della lingua italiana*.

Replacing Boccardo in its correspondence to the Oxford English dictionary is a new work:

> Zingarelli, Nicola. Vocabolario della lingua italiana. 7th edition. Milan, Bietti, 1938. 1723 pages. illustrated.

which has a high standard and includes variants and etymologies. Another useful work is:

> Petròcchi, Policarpo. Nòvo dizionàrio universale della lingua italiana. Milan, Fratèlli Trèves, 1900–02. 2 volumes.

which also contains etymological derivations. Like the Bellows bilingual dictionaries and Webster, it has adopted the principle of the divided page, the less common words being given in a separate alphabet on the lower half of each page. It is also valuable for its inclusion of local terms which are ascribed to their particular districts and regions. There is also a smaller edition under the title *Dizionario scolastico*.

A dictionary which is especially useful in dealing with advanced forms of Italian is:

> Rigutini, Giuseppe. Vocabolario italiano della lingua parlata. Florence, G. Barbèra, 1906–07. lii, 1296 pages.

which includes etymological derivations as well as idiomatic forms. It has been reprinted several times in this century, and there is also a shorter form under the title *Vocabolario diamante della lingua italiana* (Florence, G. Barbèra, 1935–36. vii, 811 pages).

Giulio Cappucini published a *Vocabolario* in 1916: its revision by Bruno Migliorini, the co-director of the periodical *Lingua nostra*, whose work in nineteenth and twentieth century linguistic research is well known, was published under the title:

> Cappucini, Giulio *and* Migliorini, Bruno. Vocabolario della lingua italiana. Turin, Paravia, 1945. xvi, 1820 pages. (reprinted in 1947 and 1951).

This is a valuable dictionary, rich in its apt examples from outstanding writers, its recording of new and foreign words, and its concise but excellent etymological notes. Meanings are given in historical order, and the employment of individual words is indicated, while, for the first time in an Italian dictionary, Migliorini distinguishes between hereditary and learned words in his Latin derivations. Another helpful dictionary is:

> Albertoni, A. *and* Allodoli, E.   Vocabolario della lingua italiana.
> 3rd edition. Florence, Le Monnier, 1950. viii, 1055 pages.

The Italian equivalent of the *Petit Larousse* is:

> Melzi, Gian Battista.   Il novissimo Melzi: dizionario italiana in
> due parti: linguistica-scientifica. 34th edition. Milan, Vallardi,
> 1952. 2 volumes.

This is frequently revised and reprinted, and is profusely illustrated
with line drawings, maps and plans, and a few chromolithographs.

Perhaps one of the most interesting of twentieth century dictionaries
is that compiled by a famous novelist and scholar:

> Panzini, Alfredo.   Dizionario moderno delle parole che non si
> trovano nei dizionario comuni.   Con un appendice di 5000 voci
> e gli elenchi dei forestierismi banditi dalla Reale Accademia
> d'Italia.   9a edizione, con un proemio di Alfredo Schiaffini e
> con un'appendice di 8000 voci nuovamente compilata da Bruno
> Migliorini. Milan, Hoepli, 1950. xx, 997 pages.

which has probably drawn more criticism and discussion than any of
its contemporaries.   Panzini set out to record those terms used in
conversation, politics, war, philosophy, medicine, dialect, and various
trades and professions, which he could not find in the standard dictionaries, and his discussion of their use and origin and construction makes
his dictionary delightful reading. Migliorini somewhat toned down the
brashness of Panzini's early editions and, with the assistance of many
scholars, compiled more than a hundred pages of words which have
come into common use since the late 'thirties.

Etymological Dictionaries

Many of the dictionaries already mentioned include some etymological
derivations.   It is generally agreed however that the Italian language
is not as well provided with etymological dictionaries as most of the
other important tongues.   Nevertheless, there are several dictionaries
wholly devoted to this aspect of the language.   First of all is one not
entirely concerned with the Italian tongue:

> Diez, Friedrich Christian.   Etymologisches Wörterbuch der roman-
> ischen Sprachen . . . Mit einem Anhang von August Scheler.
> 5th edition. Bonn, A. Marcus, 1887. xxvi, 866 pages.

Diez, Friedrich Christian. Neue vollständiger Index zu Diez' Etymologischen Wörterbuche der romanischen Sprachen, mit Berücksichtigung von Schelers Anhang zur 5. Ausg. von Johann Urban Jarnik. Heilbronn, Henninger, 1889. x, 382 pages.

on which should be read an important volume of criticism:

Caix, Napoleone. Studi di etimologia italiana e romanza: osservazioni ed aggiunte al *Vocabolario etimologico delle lingue romanze* di F. Diez. Florence, Sansoni, 1878. 213 pages.

and with which should be compared a more recent work of remarkable scholarship:

Meyer-Lübke, Wilhelm. Romanisches etymologisches Wörterbuch 3rd edition. Heidelberg, 1935. xxxiii, 1204 pages.

which was issued in twenty parts in the years 1930 to 1935.

Two works of the early part of this century were devoted to Italian etymology:

Pianigiani, Ottorino. Vocabolario etimologico della lingua italiana. Rome, Albrighi, 1907. 2 volumes.

which is a comprehensive account of the subject and gives cognate words in other romance languages; and:

Zambaldi, Francesco. Vocabolario etimologico italiano, con appendice dei nomi di persona. 2nd edition. Città di Castello, Lapi, 1913. 630 pages.

which gives definitions and derivatives, and includes a detailed index. Since the war, a new and greater dictionary has commenced publication:

Battisti, Carlo *and* Alessio, Giovanni. Dizionario etimologico italiano. Florence, Barbèra, 1950–   volume 1–

This is being published under the auspices of the Istituto di Glottologia of the University of Florence, and the intention is to complete it in five volumes, of which four have been issued so far. It gives derivations from the Latin, the approximate date of introduction into the Italian language, variants and similarities in other languages, as well as definitions. It includes contemporary and archaic literary terms, a selection of technical and foreign words, outstanding dialect words, prefixes and suffixes. Examples are dated wherever possible. There is also a short modern work covering the words in everyday use:

Migliorini, Bruno *and* Duro, Aldo. Prontuario etimologico della lingua italiana. Turin, Paravia, 1950. xxiv, 628 pages.

Specialist Dictionaries

Three more specialised dictionaries will be found useful by translators:

Giusto, Domenico. Dizionario degli omonimi della lingua italiana. 2nd edition. Lanciano, R. Carabba, 1937. 158 pages.

Tommaseo, Nicolò. Dizionario dei sinonimi della lingua italiana. Nuovissima edizione accuratamente corretta da Giuseppe Rigutini. Milan, Bietti, 1935. lviii, 1330 pages.

Zecchini, Stefano Pietro. Dizionario dei sinonimi della lingua italiana. 2nd edition. Turin, Unione Tipografico, 1924. 2 volumes.

Both Tommaseo and Zecchini contain detailed indexes: the 1924 edition of the latter is a stereo of an earlier issue.

Italian Dialect Dictionaries

Annovazzi, A. Nuovo vocabolario pavese-italiano (illustrato). Pavia, Bizzoni, 1935. 431 pages.

Bevilacqua, Germano. Dizionario veneto-italiano. Vicenza, Scuola tip. Istituto S. Gaetano, 1949. 122 pages.

Chiappini, F. Vocabolario romanesco. new edition. Rome, " Leonardo da Vinci ", 1945.

Malagoli, G. Vocabolario pisano. Florence, Accademia della Crusca, 1939. xix, 475 pages.

Metalaga, Marina *and* Vialardi, Enzo. Vocabulario engadinese-italiano. Milan, Ettore Padoan, 1943. 2 volumes. (Documenti sulle Alpe Centrali, vol. 4, parts 1 & 2).

Michelagnoli, A. Dizionario veneziano-italiano. Venice, Zanetti, 1935.

Rohlfs, G. Dizionario dialettale delle Tre Calabrie. Halle, Niemeyer; Milan, Hoepli, 1932–

Solinas, Giovanni. Glossario de gergo della malavita veronese. Verona, " Vita Veronese ", 1950. 55 pages.

Vellemon, Antoine. Abridged dictionary of the Ladine (or Romansh) language. With German, French and English translation. Samaden, Engadin Press, 1929. 928 pages.

Bi-Lingual Dictionaries

The interest in the Italian language in England goes back many centuries. William Thomas wrote a book entitled *Principal rules of the Italian grammer with a Dictionarie . . . gathered into this tongue by William Thomas*, which was printed by the well-known London printer Thomas Berthelet in 1550. The translator of Montaigne, John Florio, wrote *Queen Anna's new world of words* in 1611, a book which is full of obsolete English words and their Italian equivalents, and therefore a fruitful source for philological research in both languages. And the polyglot James Howell included Italian words in his *Lexicon tetraglotton* of 1660 (see page 13). In the nineteenth century the favourite reference work was:

> Baretti, Giuseppe Marco Antonio. A new dictionary of the Italian and English languages, based upon that of Baretti . . . Compiled by John Davenport . . . and Guglielmo Comelati. London, Simpkin Marshall, 1854. 2 volumes.

which has been reprinted several times. This contains the inflexions of irregular verbs, the anomalous plurals of substantives, and alphabetical lists of geographical and christian names. Diminutives and augmentatives are connected with their respective substantives and adjectives. While still a reliable work, it has been superseded by:

> Hoare, Alfred. Italian dictionary. 2nd edition. Cambridge University Press, 1925. 906 pages.

which was begun in 1906 and first issued in a small edition in 1915. The main part of the work is an Italian-English dictionary, to which is appended a brief English-Italian vocabulary. A novel feature is the translation of English geographical adjectives. Hoare based his work on that of Petròcchi and, to a less extent, on that of Tommaseo and Bellini, Rigutini and Fanfani. Words are entered in two sizes of type, the larger being reserved for words most used to-day. The volume includes a short essay on the development of the Italian language, tables of verbs and adjectives, and an outline of the metric system. A shorter version of this dictionary was issued in the years 1918 to 1926, and is now also available in one volume from the same publishers.

Hoare is generally acknowledged to be the best modern bilingual dictionary of the language; for those who need a more complete or up to date English-Italian dictionary, the following is outstanding:

> Lysle, Andrea de Roever *and* Gualtieri, Francesco Mario. Dizionario delle lingue italiana e inglese. Turin, Casanova, 1950. 2 volumes.

This is the latest edition of " the best book for an Italian student of English " as Hoare has described it. English and American slang is included, and some commercial and technical terms. Other useful modern dictionaries include:

James, William *and* Grassi, G. Dictionary of the Italian and English languages, entirely rewritten and greatly enlarged by Albert de Beaux. 18th edition. New York, Macmillan, 1930. 788 pages.

Melzi, Gian Battista. New Italian-English, English-Italian dictionary, containing the commercial, scientific, technical, military and nautical terms. Philadelphia, P. Reilly, 1922. 1186 pages.

Millhouse, John. English and Italian pronouncing and explanatory dictionary; new phototypic edition revised, corrected and enriched with an appendix containing all the words and technical terms in general use during the last twenty years in science, industry, arts, crafts, sport, etc. Edited by Francesco Bracciforti. Milan, Nicola, 1925. 2 volumes.

Orlandi, G. Dizionario italiano-inglese e inglese-italiano; voci dell'uso corrente e familiare e della lingua classica; termini commerciali, scientifici, technici; Americanismi; voci del gergo. new edition. Milan, Signorelli, 1951. xvi, 2078 pages.

Purves, John. A dictionary of modern Italian: Italian-English and English-Italian. London, Routledge, 1953. xxvii, 833 pages.

Spinelli, Nicola. Dizionario italiano-inglese, inglese-italiano. Turin, Società Editrice Internazionale, 1936. 1933. 2 volumes.

Purves's dictionary was planned by Professor Walter Bullock who died in 1942. It is a compact work confined to modern usage and including such terms as have met with general everyday acceptance. Special features of this dictionary include the recording of auxiliaries of all intransitive verbs, and the inclusion of all irregular noun plurals and irregular forms of the present tense of the commoner verbs. A smaller edition of Spinelli's dictionary, under the title *Dizionario scolastico italiano-inglese, inglese-italiano*, in 2485 pages, was published in 1939.

The subject of the Italian language and its dictionaries is especially interesting, and the articles in the *Enciclopedia italiana* under such headings as LESSICOGRAFIA, CRUSCA, ETIMOLOGIA, etc., are full of valuable information. In addition, Chapter VII: Vocabolarii, grammatiche, Retoriche, metriche, of Guido Mazzoni's *Avviamento allo studio critico delle lettere italiane* (3rd edition. Florence, Sansoni,

1923) is a useful guide, and the same author's " L'Accademia della Crusca " in the March 1928 issue of *Italica* gives a brief but good account of the Accademia which supplements the *Enciclopedia italiana's* version. Another book which can be recommended is Giacomo Devoto's *Dizionari di ieri e di domani* (Florence, Sansoni, 1944) in which are reprinted three essays from *Lingua nostra* on the latest edition of the dictionary of the Accademia, Panzini's *Dizionario moderno* as revised by Migliorini, and on etymological dictionaries.

SPANISH AND PORTUGUESE
DICTIONARIES

One of the earliest of Spanish dictionaries was Antonio de Nebrija's *Diccionarium latinum-hispanum et hispanum-latinum* (Salamanca, 1492). Nebrija was one of the most brilliant scholars of his age, and he collaborated—at the request of Cardinal Cisneros—in the revision of the Greek and Latin texts of the Complutensian Bible. Nebrija's dictionary was followed by Alonso Sánchez de la Ballesta's *Diccionario de vocablos castellanos, aplicados a la propriedad latina* (Salamanca, Renaut, 1587. 688 pages), but what was probably the next most useful source-book for the Spanish language was not published until the beginning of the seventeenth century:

> Aldrete, Bernardo José. Del origen y principio de la lengua castellana, ò romāce que oi se usa en España. Rome, Carlo Vullietto, 1606. 394 pages. (republished in Madrid, Sanchez, 1674).

His contemporary, Covarrubias y Horozco, the famous grammarian and antiquarian, wrote another work which has been used as an essential source-book by succeeding Spanish philologists:

> Covarrubias Horozco, Sebástian de. Tesoro de la lengua castellana, o española . . . Añadido por el padre Benito Remigio Noydens . . . Madrid, por M. Sanchez, a costa de G. de Leon, 1673–74. 2 volumes in 1. (first published in 1611. reprinted in Barcelona, 1944).

The Real Academia Española was founded in Madrid in 1713, and its creation and purposes were undoubtedly inspired by the examples of France and Italy. One of the chief aims of the members was the construction of a dictionary of the Spanish language which would set an example and a standard for future writers, and their work was based to a large extent on the researches of Nebrija and Covarrubias Horozco. Following the principles laid down for the compilation of the great Italian dictionary, the Spanish Academy searched the works of the greatest authors of the past, listing obsolete as well as current words, and illustrating their use by copious quotations, and citing many proverbs. Only proven etymologies were given, and some technical

terms in science and the humanities were included. The first edition
of this dictionary was published in six volumes in the years 1726 to
1739: it is of particular importance, since all later editions abandoned
the extensive use of quotations, and the size of the work was reduced to
one volume. The present numbering of the editions starts with the
first edition of the one-volume issue which was published in 1780.
Between this date and 1939 no less than sixteen editions were published,
of which the best is said to be that of 1822 (sixth edition), which incorporated the Academy's recommendations on the subject of correct orthography. Editions prior to the 15th (1925) were issued under the title
of *Diccionario de la lengua castellana*. The latest edition, which includes
rules for accentuation and for the formation of words, as well as a list
of abbreviations, is:

> Academia Española, *Madrid*. Diccionario de la lengua española.
> 17th edition. Madrid, Academia Española, 1947.

which is a provisional edition only. The sixteenth (1939) was exhausted
before the new edition could be prepared, so that the only differences
between the sixteenth and seventeenth editions are that the preliminary
pages of the latter have been subject to some changes, and a Supplement
of new words has been added. In the meantime, work proceeds on a
thorough revision. With the *Diccionario* should be noted:

> Academia Española, *Madrid*. Diccionario manual e ilustrado de la
> lengua española. 2nd edition. Madrid, Espasa-Calpe, 1950.
> xi, 1572 pages.

This, which has some four thousand illustrations, is by way of being
an abridgment of the main dictionary and a supplement to it, incorporating
many additional words intended for the seventeenth edition.

Like other great national dictionaries, the *Diccionario* has had its
critics, and one of the important works on the shortcomings of the
Academy's compilation is:

> Valbuena, Antonio de. La fe de erratas del nuevo *Diccionario* de
> la Academia. 3rd edition. Madrid, La Espasa Editorial, 1891–
> 96. 4 volumes.

The well-known philologist Ramón Menéndez Pidal undertook for
the Academy the editorship of an historical dictionary:

> Academia Española, *Madrid*. Diccionario histórico de la lengua
> española. Madrid, Hernando, 1933–   volume 1–

This was intended to bring up to date and to supplement the *Diccionario* with examples from Spanish writers of all periods. Unfortunately only two volumes (A-CEVILLA) appeared, the Spanish Civil War having brought publication to an end.

In addition, the following supplementary works should be noted:

Alba, Renato de. Suplemento de todos los diccionarios enciclo-pédicos españoles publicados hasta el día. Barcelona, Subirana, 1918. ix, 414 pages.

Toro y Gisbert, Miguel de. Enmiendas al *Diccionario* de la Academia. Paris, Ollendorff, 1909. viii, 274 pages.

Vergara y Martín, Gabriel María. Cuatro mil palabras y algunos más, de uso frecuente, no incluídas en el *Diccionario* de la Real Academia Española (décima quinta edición) o que lo están en otras acepciones o como anticuadas, . . . Madrid, Rivadeneyra, 1925. 194 pages.

of which the first includes over ten thousand words not listed in the four-teenth edition (1914) of the dictionary. The eminent and erudite Colombian scholar, Rufino Cuervo, attempted his own revision of the *Diccionario*:

Cuervo, Rufino José. Diccionario de construcción y régimen de la lengua castellana. Paris, Roger & Chernoviz, 1886-93. 2 volumes.

but unfortunately these two volumes cover only the letters A to D; further publication is however now being continued in the columns of the *Boletin del Instito Caro y Cuervo*.

Recent dictionaries of note include:

Pagés de Puig, Aniceto de *and* Pérez, Hervás José. Gran diccionario de la lengua castellana (de autoridades) con ejemplos de buenos escritores antiguos y modernos, ordenado con arreglo a la última edición de la Real Academia Española, y enriquecido con numerosas voces, acepciones, frases y refranes que no constan en ningún otro diccionario. Barcelona, Fomento Comercial del Libra, 5 volumes.

Sánchez, Luis Alberto. Diccionario enciclopédico ilustrado Ercilla . . . 2nd edition. Santiago de Chile, Ediciones Ercilla, 1942. 1510 pages.

Vox: diccionario general ilustrado de la lengua española. Prólogo de Ramón Menéndez Pidal; révision de Samuel Gili Gaya. 2nd edition. Barcelona, Spes, 1952. 1856 pages.

Nueva enciclopedia Sopena: diccionario ilustrado de la lengua
español. Barcelona, Sopena, 1953–54. 5 volumes.

The new Sopena dictionary, which was first published in 1925 in two
volumes, has more than four hundred thousand entries, and nearly
thirty thousand illustrations. Three other illustrated dictionaries are
particularly useful:

Alemany y Bolúfer, José. La fuente: diccionario enciclopédico
ilustrado de la lengua española. Barcelona, Sopena, 1945. x,
1431 pages.

González de la Rosa, Manuel. Campano ilustrado: revisión de
Miguel de Toro. Paris, Garner, 1923.

Larousse, Pierre. Pequeño Larousse ilustrado: nuevo diccionario
enciclopédico, publicado bajo la dirección de Claude Augé;
adaptación española de Miguel de Toro y Gisbert. Paris, Larousse,
1947. 1528 pages. (first published in 1912).

Etymological Dictionaries

One of the earliest Spanish etymological dictionaries was:

Cabrera y Rubio, Ramón. Diccionario de etimologías de la lengua
castellana. Madrid, Calero, 1837. 2 volumes.

This, a posthumous work by a constant contributor to the contemporary
editions of the Academy's dictionary, was followed by a larger and
sometimes inaccurate work:

Bárcia, Roque. Primer diccionario general etimológico de la lengua
español. Madrid, Alvarez, 1881–83. 5 volumes.

Another nineteenth century etymological dictionary has been kept up
to date:

Monlau y Roca, Pedra F. Diccionario etimológico de la lengua
castellana. 2nd edition. Buenos Aires, Librería " El Ateneo ",
1944. 1186 pages. (first published in Madrid, 1856).

In addition, there is also an important index to recent etymological
research:

Romera-Navarro, Miguel. Registro de lexicografía hispánica.
Madrid, Consejo Superior de Investigaciones Cientificas, 1951.
1013 pages. (Revista de Filologia Española, Anejo 54).

which is a supplementary volume to the *Revista*. It is an index to fifty thousand words in the Spanish language for which there are etymologies, linguistic explanations or studies in monographs, treatises and scholarly journals: words taken from Catalan, Gallician, and Portuguese, as well as Hispano-Americanisms, are included.

Specialist Dictionaries

For synonyms and antonyms, there are three recent dictionaries:

Benot y Rodríguez, Eduardo. Diccionario de ideas afines y elementos de tecnología. Buenos Aires, Ed. Anaconda, 1940. 1515 pages. (first published in Madrid, M. Núñez Samper, 1893).

Diccionario de sinónimos (22,000 artículos). Barcelona, Seix, 1944. 800 pages.

López Bejarano, Amós *and* Peña, Casto. Diccionario de sinónimos e ideas afines. Barcelona, Bauzá, 1941. ix, 403 pages.

In the first, the " elementos de tecnología " were not included in either edition.

Julio Casares y Sanchez, an eminent literary critic, musician and lexicographer, collaborated in the new edition of the Academy's dictionary, and has championed the purity of the Castilian language against the introduction of foreign words and expressions by contemporary writers. His new dictionary is:

Casares y Sanchez, Julio. Diccionario ideológico de la lengua española; desde la idea a la palabra: desde la palabra a la idea. 3rd impression. Barcelona, Gustavo Gili, 1951. lxxi, 597; 1124 pages. (first published in Madrid, 1942).

which is divided into three parts: I. Synoptic, II. Analogic and, III. the dictionary proper, the first two parts constituting a kind of thesaurus. Other helpful dictionaries include:

Benot y Rodríguez, Eduardo. Diccionario de asonantes; consonantes. Madrid, Sanchez, 1893. 1085 pages.

Caballero y Rubio, Ramón. Diccionario de modismos de la lengua castellana; con un prólogo de Eduardo Benot . . . Ed. Argentina presentada por Avelino Herrero Mayor. Buenos Aires, El Ateneo, 1942. 1179 pages.

Cejador y Frauca, Julio. Fraseología o estilística castellana . . . Madrid, Tip. de la " Revista de arch., bibl. y museos," 1921– volume 1–

Díaz-Retg, Enrique. Diccionario de dificultades de la lengua española. Madrid, Martorelli, 1951. 439 pages.

Sbarbi y Osuna, José María. Diccionario de refranes, adagios, proverbios, modismos, locuciones, y frases proverbiales de lengua española, recogidos y glosados . . . obra póstuma ordenada, corr. y. publ. bajo la dirección de D. Manuel José García. Madrid, Hernando, 1922. 2 volumes (reprinted in Buenos Aires, Gil, 1943, in one volume of 1028 pages).

The reader is also reminded of the great Spanish encyclopaedias which provide additional sources of information:

Diccionario enciclopédico hispano-americano de literatura, ciencias y artes. Barcelona, Montaner y Simón, 1887–1910. 28 volumes in 29.

Enciclopedia universal ilustrada Europeo-Americano. Barcelona, Espasa, 1905–   volume 1–

the latter being popularly known as the " Espasa ", and being particularly useful since it frequently gives the foreign language equivalents of the words it defines.

Special Periods

A comprehensive dictionary of Old Spanish is in preparation at the Seminar of Mediaeval Spanish Studies, at the University of Wisconsin. In the meantime, the following dictionaries are available:

Boggs, Ralph Steele *and others.* Tentative dictionary of medieval Spanish, compiled by R. S. Boggs, Lloyd Kasten, Hayward Keniston, H. B. Richardson. Chapel Hill, North Carolina, 1946. 2 volumes.

Oelschläger, Victor R. B. A medieval Spanish word-list (a preliminary dated vocabulary of first appearances up to Berceo). Madison, University of Wisconsin Press, 1940. x, 230 pages.

Gili Gaya, Samuel. Tesoro lexicográfico (1492–1726). Madrid, Consejo Superior de Investigaciones Científicas, 1947–   volume 1–

Oelschläger is, of course, the first fruits of the University of Wisconsin's project for a comprehensive dictionary, mentioned above. It covers the vocabulary of several hundred documents representing the period 900 to 1220, including those printed in Menéndez Pidal's *Orígenes del español* and his *Documentos lingüísticos*, and those literary texts (such as the *Cantar de mio Cid*) which can be safely attributed to this period. In addition, two early thirteenth century works are included: that of Berceo and the *Libro de los tres reyes de Oriente*. Texts included are limited to those in Spanish dialects—Castilian, Aragonese, Leonese, etc.—Catalan, Gallician and Portuguese being omitted. The *Tentative dictionary* was compiled by a committee, with Hayward Keniston as Chairman, appointed by the Old Spanish Group of the Modern Languages Association of America. Gili Gaya's work is planned to include all Spanish words registered in dictionaries, glossaries, phrase-books, etc., both native and foreign, from Nebrija to the first edition of the Academy's dictionary, and includes an annotated and critical bibliography of these early reference works. For each word, definitions (in the original wordings) are arranged chronologically. Some idea of the eventual size of this important new dictionary may be gained from the fact that the first fascicle, devoted to the letter A, contains 282 pages.

Spanish Dialect Dictionaries

Aguiló y Fúster, Mariano. " Diccionari Aguiló "; lexicogràfics aplegats. Barcelona, Inst. d'Estudis Catalans, 1914–34. 8 volumes.

Alcalá Venceslada, Antonio. Vocabulario andaluz. Madrid, Real Academia Española, 1951. 676 pages. (first published in 1934).

Alcover Sureda, Antonio Maria. Diccionari català-valencià-balear. Palma de Mallorca, Alcover, 1930– volume 1–

Arnal Cavero, P. Vocabulario del Alto Aragonés. Madrid, 1944. 32 pages.

Diccionari enciclopèdic de la llengua catalana, amb la correspondència castellana. new edition. Barcelona, Salvat, 1930–45. 4 volumes.

Ferraz y Castán, V. Vocabulario del dialecto que se habla en Alta Ribagorza. Madrid, 1935.

Garcia Rey, V. Vocabulario del Bierzo. Madrid, 1934.

Griera, A. Tresor de la llengua, de les tradicions i de la cultura popular de Catalunya. Barcelona, 1947. 14 volumes.

Bi-Lingual Dictionaries

Interest in the Spanish language in Britain goes back at least to Elizabethan times. Richard Perceval had a life as fully romantic as that of any hero in a light novel. Disowned by his father because of a runaway match with a penniless girl, he took refuge in Spain where he lived for the next four years. This appears to have been his only actual contact with that country, though he spent some time later in deciphering and translating captured Spanish documents for the English government.

But in 1591, he published his *Bibliotheca Hispánica*, of which a second edition—edited and enlarged by John Minsheu—was issued in 1599. The third edition was:

> Perceval, Richard.   A dictionary in Spanish and English: first published into the English tongue by Ric. Percivale Gent.   Now enlarged and amplified . . . All done by John Minsheu . . . hereunto for the further profit and pleasure of the learner or delighted in this tongue, is annexed an ample English Dictionarie, Alphabetically set downe with the Spanish words thereunto adioyned, as also an Alphabeticall Table of the Arabicke and Moorish words now commonly received and used in the Spanish tongue . . . Pr. at London by Iohn Haviland for William Aspley, 1623. c554 pages.

In the next century there were three more dictionaries:

> Connelly, Tomás.   Diccionario nuevo y completo de las lenguas española é inglesa, inglesa y española, que contiene las significaciones de sus voces, con sus diferentes usos, los términos de artes, ciencias y oficios; las construcciones, idiomas y proverbios que se usan en cada una de ellas: todo extractado de sus majores autores y considerablemente aumentado por . . . Fr. Tomas Connelly . . . y Fr. Tomas Higgins.   Madrid, en la Impr. real por P. Julian Pereyra, 1797–   volume 1–

> Giral del Pino, Hippolyto San José.   A dictionary, Spanish and English, and English and Spanish: containing the signification of words, with their different uses; the terms of arts, sciences and trades; the constructions, forms of speech, idioms used in both languages, and several thousand words more than any other dictionary; with their proper, figurative, burlesque, and cant significations, etc.   Also, the Spanish words accented and spelled according to the modern observations of the Royal Spanish Academy of Madrid . . . London, printed for A. Millar, J. Nourse, and P. Vaillant, 1763. 2 volumes in 1.

> Pineda, Pedro. Nuevo dicionario, español e ingles e ingles y español. Que contiene la etimologia, de la propria, y metaphorica significacion de las palabras, terminos de artes y sciencias: nombres de hombres, familias, lugares, y de las principales plantas, tanto en Españo, come en las Indias-Occidentales. Junto con las palabras arabigas y moriscas recebidas en la lengua española. Con la explicacion de las palabras dificiles, proverbios, y frases

en Don Quixote, y en los otros graves autores de dicha lengua ...
London, Gyles, 1740. 772 pages.

One of the basic dictionaries of the modern Spanish language was:

Neuman, Henry *and* Baretti, Giuseppe Mario Antonio. Neuman
and Baretti's Dictionary of the Spanish and English languages.
9th edition by M. Seoane. London, Longman, Brown, 1850.
2 volumes.

on which was based one of the best modern dictionaries of the Spanish
tongue:

Velázquez de la Cadena, Mariano. Pronouncing dictionary of the
Spanish and English languages. New edition, revised and
enlarged by Edward Gray and J. L. Iribas, with a supplement
of new words by Carlos Toral. Chicago, Wilcox & Follett,
1942. 2 volumes. (first published in 1852).

of which the last major revision was carried out in 1901—but a reprint
edition (in one volume of 1486 pages) was published in 1952, with a
supplement of new words in both languages. This dictionary includes
synopses of the Spanish and English languages, lists of abbreviations,
and tables of currency, weights and measures. Other more modern
dictionaries include:

Casares y Sánchez, Julio. Novísimo diccionario inglés-español y
español-inglés. Madrid, Ed. " Saturnino Calleja ", 1925. 2 volumes
in 1.

Castillo, Carlos *and* Bond, Otto Ferdinand. The University of
Chicago Spanish dictionary; a new concise Spanish-English
and English-Spanish dictionary of words and phrases basic to
the written and spoken languages of to-day. Chicago, University
of Chicago Press, 1948. xxxvi, 226; xvii, 251 pages.

Corona Bustamente, Francisco. Nuevo diccionario inglés-español
y español-inglés . . . new edition. La Plata, Ed. " Mundo
Científico ", 1942. 2 volumes in 1.

Cuyás, Arturo. Appleton's new English-Spanish and Spanish-
English dictionary, containing more than six thousand modern
words and twenty-five thousand acceptations, idioms and technical
terms. revised edition. New York & London, Appleton-Century,
1953. 2 volumes.

This last dictionary is compiled for the general use of the American
learner of Spanish and the Spanish learner of English, with special

reference in either case to New World uses as found in the United States and in Latin America. About thirty thousand of the words most commonly used are included. Introductory material to each section includes pronunciation, parts of speech, suffixes, lists of irregular verbs, etc. Three other recent dictionaries are:

> Fucilla, Joseph G. Concise Spanish dictionary: Spanish-English and English-Spanish. London, Harrap, 1948. viii, 306; 332 pages.

> Martínez Amador, Emilio M. Diccionario inglés-español y español-inglés. 2nd edition. Barcelona, Sopena, 1951. 2066 pages. (first published in 1946).

> Raventós, Margaret H. A modern Spanish dictionary. London, English Universities Press, 1953. xii, 1241 pages.

Fucilla is designed for beginners and includes recent words. Each part of Martínez Amador includes colloquialisms, idioms, Americanisms and technical terms, geographical and personal names, and lists of abbreviations. Raventós covers both Spanish-English and English-Spanish, and includes modern general and technical and scientific words, but does not attempt to cover highly-specialised words or purely localised linguistic variants of Spanish America. In the same way, Raventós omits obsolete and regional words for the most part, and allows idioms to take precedence over proverbs.

There are also two more specialised dictionaries:

> Santamaría, Francisco Javier. Diccionario general de americanismos .... 1. ed. ... Mexico, Robredo, 1942 (actually published in 1943). 3 volumes.

> Nunn, Marshall Elbert *and* Van Scoy, Herbert. Glossary of related Spanish-English words. Talahassee, University of Alabama Press, 1949. 68 pages.

Santamaría includes common and scientific equivalents for flora and fauna. Nunn's book is an enlarged edition of his *A list of related Spanish-English words*, published in 1944.

Portuguese Dictionaries

One of the earliest Portuguese dictionaries was bilingual: Bishop Agostinho Barbosa's *Dictionarium Lusitanico-Latinum: juxta seriem alphabeticam, optimis probatisque doctissimorum auctorum testimonijs perutili quadam expositione locupletatum, cum copiosissimo Latini sermonis indici, etc.*, was published in two parts at Braga as early as 1611.   His work was followed by Raphael Bluteau who compiled an eight-volume *Vocabulario portuguez, e latino . . . autorizado com exemplos dos melhores escritores portuguezes, e latinos*, with a *Diccionario castellano, y portuguez* as an appendix, which was issued by the Jesuits at Coimbra during the years 1712–21, and which was quickly followed by a two-volume Supplement (Lisbon, Sylva, 1727–28).

The effort of the national academy in this case had little effect on the future of the language.   The Academia das Ciências at Lisbon issued the first volume of its *Diccionario da lingoa portugueza*—which was largely the work of Pedro José da Fonseco—in 1793.   This devoted more than five hundred pages to the letter A, but as it was the only volume to be issued, its use to-day is confined to the 150-page " Catalogo dos autores e obras, que se lérão, e de que se tomárão as autoridades para a composição do diccionario ".

At the end of the same century the most influential of all Portuguese dictionaries was already in universal use: António de Moraes e Silva's *Diccionario da lingua portugueza* was first published in 1789, and was remarkable for its skilful choice of quotations as examples of the use of the more important words.   Second, third and fourth editions followed in 1813, 1823 and 1831 respectively, and are all worthy of preservation for their contributions to this feature.   The current edition is:

> Moraes e Silva, António de. Grande dicionário da língua portuguesa. 10a edição revista, corrigida, muito aumentada e actualizada segundo as regras do Acordo Ortográfico Luso-Brasileiro de 10 Agosto de 1945, por Augusto Moreno, Cardoso Júnior e José Pedro Machado. Lisbon, Editorial Confluência, 1949– volume 1–

which is to be completed in eight volumes, and which is generally considered to be the best current dictionary. As almost invariably happens when any major dictionary is issued, an independent supplementary work was published very soon after Moraes e Silva's first edition:

> Santa Rosa de Viterbo, Joaquim de. Elucidario das palavras, termos e frases que em Portugal antiguamente se usarão e que hoje regularmente se ignorão; obra indispensavel para entender sem erro os documentos mais raros e preciosas que entre nós se conservão. Publicado em beneficio da litteratura portugueza. Lisbon, Ferreira, 1798–99. 2 volumes.

of which a second edition was edited by Innocencio Francisco da Silva in 1865 (Lisbon, Fernandes Lopes. 2 volumes in 1). Other nineteenth century dictionaries of importance included:

> Fonseca, José da. Diccionario da lingua portugueza . . . feito inteiramente de novo e consideravelmente augmentado por J. I. Roquette. Paris, Guillard, Aillaud, 1848. xxxv, 971 pages.

> Vieira, Domingos. Grande diccionario portuguez; ou, Thesouro da lingua portugueza. Oporto, Chardron & Moraes, 1871–74. 5 volumes.

the latter still being of use at the present time for all but the purely contemporary language.

Reference has already been made in the entry for the current edition of Moraes e Silva's *Grande dicionário* to the Acordo Ortografico Luso-Brasileiro de 10 Agosto de 1945, which was brought about by the recognition of Portuguese-speaking peoples on both sides of the Atlantic of the urgent need for agreement on general principles, if the two versions of the Portuguese language were not to grow hopelessly apart. A little before, both national academies had published dictionaries which concerned themselves with the spelling of the language:

> Academia Brasileira de Letras. Pequeno vocabulário ortográfico da língua portuguesa. Rio de Janeiro, Imprensa Nacional, 1943. xlvii, 1342 pages. (edited by José de Sá Nunes).

> Academia das Ciências de Lisboa. Vocabulário ortografico da língua portuguesa. Lisbon, Imprensa Nacional, 1940. xcii, 821 pages.

and after the Acordo, the Portuguese Academy soon issued its *Vocabulário ortográfico, resumido da língua portuguesa* (Lisbon, Imprensa Nacional de Lisboa, 1947. xli, 475 pages). The Acordo also stimulated the publication of new editions of some old dictionaries, and the compilation of some new dictionaries as well, including the following:

> Bivar, Artur. Dicionário geral e analógico da língua portuguesa. Coordenaçáo de M. dos Santos Ferreira e M. V. dos Santos Ferreira. Oporto, Ed. Douro, 1948– volume 1– (to be completed in two volumes of over 3200 pages, the first volume being a general dictionary, and the second to be devoted to a " Dizionário analógico " in classified form).

> Caldas Aulete, Francisco Julio. Dicionário contemporâneo da lingua portuguesa. 3ª edição muito aumentada e actualizada por Vasco Botelho de Amaral e D. Margarida de Brito Botelho de Amaral

. . . e por Jorge Guimarães Daupiás . . . Lisbon, Pereira, 1947. (a remarkable fact about this excellent dictionary is, that while Caldas Aulete was born in 1740 and died in 1800, the first edition of his work was not published until 1881).

Correia, Carlos Alberto. Dicionário geral da lingua portuguesa com a etimologia e as principais noções e leis fonéticas; . . . Lisbon, Ed. Império, 194–   volume 1–

Lello popular: novo dicionário ilustrado da língua portuguesa . . . Oporto, Lello & Irmão, 1948. 1343 pages. (a popular encyclopaedic type of work, with small illustrations in the text).

Subtil, Manuel. Pequeno dicionário escolar, com ilustraçoes de Eduardo Romero e Rocha Vieira. 6th edition. Lisbon, Sá da Costa, 1946. xlviii, 624 pages.

Torrinha, Francisco. Novo dicionário da língua portuguesa, para os estudantes e para o povo . . . Oporto, Barreira, 1947. 1303 pages.

Of those published prior to the Acordo, the following are worthy of note:

Freire, Laudelino de Oliveira. Grande e novíssimo dicionário da língua portuguesa . . . com a colaboração técnica do J. L. de Campos. Rio de Janeiro, " A Noite ", 1939–44. 5 volumes.

Montenegro, J. Peres. Vocabulário ortográfico, prosódico e remissivo da língua portuguesa. Lisbon, Ed. Sociedade Industrial de Tipográfia, 1938. xx, 688 pages.

Seguier, Jayme de. Diccionario prático illustrado: novo diccionário encyclopédico luso-brasileiro . . . Oporto, Lello & Irmão, 1941. 1812 pages.

There are also some works devoted specifically to Brazilian Portuguese, in spite of the fact that almost all modern Portuguese dictionaries have paid special attention to the inclusion of the language and style of both countries. Among the more outstanding items are the following:

Brown, Charles B. *and* Shane, Milton L. Brazilian Portuguese idiom list. Nashville, Tennessee, Vanderbilt University Press, 1951. xiii, 118 pages.

Escragnolle Taunay, Affonso de. Lexico de lacunas [subsidios para os diccionarios da lingua portugueza. Lexico de termos vulgares, correntes no Brazil, sobretudo no estado de São Paulo, e de accepções de numeros vocabulos, ainda não apontados nos grandes diccionarios da lingua portugueza]. Tours, Arrault, 1914. 223 pages. (Rev. do Inst. Hist. de São Paulo, volume 16).

Lima, Hildebrando *and* Barroso, Gustavo.   Pequeno dicionário brasileiro da língua portuguesa . . . revisto na parte geral por Manuel Bandeira e José Baptista da Luz.   9ª ediçao inteiramente revista e considerávelmente aumentada—sobretudo na parte de brasileirismos—por Aureliano Buarque de Hollanda Ferreira. Rio de Janeiro, Editora Civilizaçao Brasileira, 1951. xxxii, 1310 pages.

Mesquita de Carvalho, José.   Dicionário prático da língua nacional. Porto Alegre, Livraria do Globo, 1945. 1119 pages. (Enciclopedias e Dicionários Globo).

For historical Portuguese, in addition to the older dictionaries— especially Santa Rosa de Viterbo's *Elucidario*—mentioned above, the following work now in course of publication is of great importance:

Magne, Augusto.   Dicionário da língua portuguesa, especialmente dos períodos medieval e clássico.   Rio de Janeiro, Ministério da Educação e Saúde, Instituto Nacional do Livro, 1950– volume 1–

Of the etymological dictionaries, the best is one which is not specifically devoted to this subject:

Figueiredo, Cândido de.   Dicionário da lingua portuguesa.   10ª edição actualizada segundo as regras do Acordo Ortográfico . . . e em perfeita harmonia com o " Vocabulário resumido " de 1947 da Academia das Ciências . . . Lisbon, Bertrand, 1949–50. 2 volumes.

and there are also three etymological dictionaries of great merit:

Coelho, Francisco Adolpho.   Diccionário manual etymológico da língua portugueza, contendo a significação e prosódia.   Lisbon, Plantier, 1897. xii, 1248 pages.

Nascentes, Antenor.   Dicionário etimológico da língua portuguesa . . . com prefácio de W. Meyer Lübke . . . 1. e única ed. Rio de Janeiro, Alves, 1932. 829 pages.

—— (Volume 2): Nomes proprios: com pref. de Serafim Silvio Neto. Rio de Janeiro, Alves, 1952. xxvii, 389 pages.

Silva Bastos, José Thimoteo da.   Diccionário etymológico, prosódico e orthográphico da língua portugueza. 2nd edition. Lisbon, Parceria Antónia Maria Pereira, 1928. xiv, 1434 pages.

The Portuguese language is remarkably well provided with dictionaries of synonyms and antonyms, among which the following should be specially noted:

Costa, Agenor. Dicionário de sinonimos e locuções de língua portuguesa. Rio de Janeiro, Imprensa Nacional, 1950. 2 volumes.

Fernandes, Francisco. Dicionário de sinônimos e antônimos da língua portuguêsa. 2nd edition. Rio de Janeiro, Livraria do Globo, 1946. 919 pages.

Mendes de Morais, Orlando. Dicionário de sinônimos. Rio de Janeiro, Getúlio Costa, 1944. 259 pages.

Pereira, Manuel José. Dicionário de sinónimos da língua portuguesa. Cucujáis, Escola Tipográfica, 1940. 798 pages.

Pinheiro, Eduardo. Dicionário da língua portuguesa. Oporto, Livraria Figueirinhas, 1948. viii, 1438 pages.

Roquete, J. I. and Fonseca, Josè da. Dicionário dos sinónimos, poético e de epítetos, da língua portuguesa . . . segundo as bases do último Acordo . . . Oporto, Lello & Irmão, 1949. xx, 785 pages.

There is also a number of dictionaries which help with various difficulties in the use of the Portuguese language:

Botelho de Amaral, Vasco. Novo dicionário de dificuldades da língua portuguesa. Formação. Ortografia. Ortoepia. Morfologia. Sintaxe. Solecismos. Semantologia. Neologismos. Estilística. Vernaculidade. Estrangeirismos. Oporto, Ed. Educaçao Nacional, 1943 [i.e. 1945]. 1046 pages.

Fernandes, Francisco. Dicionário de verbos e regimes, . . . Mais de 10,000 verbos em suas diversas acepções e regências. 6th edition. Rio de Janeiro, Livraria do Globo, 1947. 623 pages.

Glossário crítico de dificuldades do idioma português. Lisbon, Lopes, 1947. 631 pages.

Moreno, Augusto. Dicionário complementar da língua portuguesa (ortoépico, ortográfico e etimológico) com um glossário de arcaísmos e uma lista das principais locuções estrangeiras, aplicáveis em português. 5ª edição, melhorada e em rigorosa harmonia com as Bases do Acordo . . . Oporto, Liv. Ed. Educação Nacional, 1948. ix, 1412 pages.

Of the bilingual dictionaries, the best and most scholarly is:

Ferreira, Júlio Albino.   Dicionário inglês-português nova edição
revista e aumentada por James Machin. Oporto, Barreira, 1948.
2 volumes in 1.

and another important dictionary—though somewhat out-of-date—
is one which has been a standard work in both countries for more than
fifty years:

Michaelis, Henriette.   Novo diccionario da lingua portugueza e
ingleza, enriquecido com os termos technicos do comercio e
da industria, das sciencias e das artes e da linguagem familiar.
8th edition. Leipzig, Brockhaus, 1932. 2 volumes. (this, itself
a reprint of the 7th edition of 1923, was itself reprinted: New
York, Ungar, 1943). (first published 1893).

Other useful bilingual dictionaries include the following:

Almeida e Araujo Corrêa de Lacerda, José Maria de. Novo diccionario
geral das linguas ingleza e portugueza, augmentado com multos
mil vocabulos de uso commum ou litterario . . . Lisbon, Imprensa
Nacional, 1866–71. 2 volumes.

Doria, António Alvaro.   Dicionário português-inglês, elaborado
segundo os melhores dicionários e gramáticas . . . Oporto,
Figueirinhas, 1940. 618 pages.

Elwes, Alfred. A dictionary of the Portuguese language in two parts:
1. Portuguese-English.   2. English-Portuguese; including a
large number of technical terms used in mining engineering.
11th impression. London, Technical Press, 1942. 606 pages.

Franco, Alvaro.   Dicionário: inglês-português, português-inglês.
new edition. Porto Alegre, Livraria do Globo, 1952. 955 pages.

Richardson, Elbert L. *and others*.   Modern Portuguese-English,
English-Portuguese dictionary.   Philadelphia, McKay, 1943;
London, Harrap, 1945. 347 pages.

Serpa, Oswaldo. Dicionário inglês-português. São Paulo, Ed. do
Brasil, 1945. 545 pages.

Vieyra, Antonio. Novo diccionario portatil das linguas portugueza
e ingleza, em duas partes: portugueza e ingleza—ingleza e
portugueza; resumida do diccionario de Vieyra. Nova edição,
revista e consideravelmente augmentada por J. P. Aillaud. Paris,
Aillaud, 1860. 2 volumes.

The last-mentioned dictionary was based on the work of the great
eighteenth-century philologist, Antonio Vieyra, who died in 1797.

Basque Dictionaries

The classic dictionary of Basque retains its position to-day:

*Azkue, Resurrección María de.   Diccionario vasco-español-francés.
Bilbao & Paris, 1905–06.   2 volumes.

—— Diccionario español y vasco.   Bilbao, 1916–   volume 1–

A new work, which has made use of more recent material and investigations, may—when it is completed—supersede Azkue:

Lhande, Pierre.   Dictionnaire basque-français et français-basque
(dialectes labourdin, bas-navarrais et souletin) d'après le Dictionnaire basque-espagnol-français de R. M. de Askué et les dictionnaires manuscrits de M. Harriet, M. Hirribarren et Pierre Foix.
Paris, Beauchesne, 1926–   volume 1–

There is also a pocket-size Spanish-Basque, Basque-Spanish
dictionary:

Bera'tar'. Er'oman Mirena Aba burunur'duna.   Diccionario castellano-
euzkera.   Tolosa, 1916.   514 pages.

Mendizabal' dar' Ixaka, Lopez.   Euzkel-Er'del-iztegia.   Tolosa, 1916.
654 pages.

---

* In connection with Azkue's work, note should be taken of H. E. M. Schuchardt's *Baskisch
und romanisch: zu dem Azkues Baskischem Wörterbuch.* 1. Band.   1906.   (Zeitschrift für
Romanische Philologie.   Beiheft 6).

RUSSIAN DICTIONARIES

The first edition of the Russian Academy's dictionary was published in the years 1789 to 1794 in six volumes and was arranged in etymological order.   But, as in the case of the dictionary of the Académie Française, this arrangement was abandoned in the second edition, and a six-volume edition in alphabetical order was published during the years 1806 to 1823.   At the end of the nineteenth century a new edition was begun:

> Akademīia Nauk.   Slovar' russkago iazyka sostavlemnnii Vtorym otdieleniyem Imperatorskoi Akademīi Nauk. Petrograd, 1895–1930. volumes 1–9.

but this was abandoned, the nine volumes having reached only as far as OBKAT in more than thirty years.   Two years later, another edition commenced publication and is still in progress:

> Akademīia Nauk.   Institut Iazyka i myshleniia imeni N. Ia. Marra.   Slovar' russkogo iazyka.   Novoe pererabotannoe i dopolnennoe, izdanie.   Leningrad, Akademīia Nauk, 1932–   volume 1–

In addition to this effort, which is of the same style as those of the other national academies, the Russian Academy has recently started work on a new dictionary:

> Akademīia Nauk.   Institut Russkogo Iazyka.   Slovar' sovremennogo russkogo literaturnogo iazyka. 2nd edition. Moscow, Akademīia Nauk, 1950–   volume 1–

which is planned to be completed in fifteen volumes.   This dictionary is somewhat similar to the Oxford English dictionary in its method, although it is confined to the modern language from the time of Pushkin onwards.   Words are grouped together under basic words, the philological background of each word is given with references to other dictionaries and to original research, while the meanings and use are illustrated by quotations from literary and scientific works of the past hundred years or so.   Dialect and technical words are omitted for the most part.

An earlier work which also resembles the Oxford English dictionary in its treatment, though it is by no means on such a vast scale, was first published in 1863.   The latest edition is:

Dal', Vladimir Ivanovich.   Tolkovyi slovar zhivago velikorusskago yazyka Vladimira Dalya . . . chetvertoe ispravlennoe i znachitel'no dopolnennoe izdanïe pod redaktsieyu I. A. Boduéna-de-Kurtené. St. Petersburg, Wolf, 1913.   4 volumes.   (reprinted, Tokio, Tachibana Tsioten, 1934. Also reprinted, Moscow, 1935).

This includes many dialect and colloquial words, and makes extensive use of synonyms to explain the meanings of words.   An additional advantage is the frequent use of proverbs, idiomatic sayings and other examples to illustrate the use of individual words.

Contemporary dictionaries of note include:

Ozhegov, S. I.   Slovar' russkogo iazyka.   2nd edition.   Moscow, Gos. izd-vo inostrannykh i natsional'nykh slovareĭ, 1952.   848 pages.

Tolkovyi slovar' russkogo iazyka.   Sostavili: G. O. Vinokur, B. A. Larin, S. I. Ozhegov, B. V. Tomashevskii, D. N. Ushakov. Moscow, Sovet Entsiklopedïia, 1935–40.   4 volumes. (reprinted Ann Arbor, Mich., Edwards Brothers, 1948. 4 volumes. American Council of Learned Societies. Reprints. Russian Series, no. 1).

Ozhegov is, it will be noticed, also a contributor to the larger compilation which, for the most part, omits vernacular, dialect, scientific and technical terms.   It classifies words according to their use (literary, conversational, etc.), and gives their pronunciation, meaning and use.

Etymological Dictionaries

The first attempt at an etymological dictionary of the Russian language came fairly late:

Goryaef, N. V.   Sravnitel'nii etimologicheskii slovar' literaturnago russkago iazika.   2nd edition.   Tiflis, 1896.   451 pages.

This, however, was not a success, and at the beginning of this century work was commenced on a dictionary whose extraordinary fate is graphically described by Professor Roman Jakobson in a recent review of the completed work (*Word*, volume VII, pages 187 to 188. August, 1951).

Preobrazhensky, Aleksandr G.   Etymological dictionary of the Russian language. New York, Columbia University Press, 1951. 3 volumes in 1. (Columbia Slavic Studies).

This is a facsimile reprint of the first and second volumes printed originally in Moscow in the years 1910 and 1916 respectively, plus the recently-discovered fragments of the third volume, first printed in Moscow more than thirty years after the death of the author. " All the influences," says the American preface, " of neighbouring peoples and cultures are reflected in the linguistic borrowings and in the highly interesting loan translation, where the foreign word is not taken over in its original form but translated literally and element by element into native garb, from various linguistic groupings and languages . . . Each entry contains, in addition to examples from all the Slavic languages, comparative linguistic material drawn from other branches of the Indo-European family of languages . . . Scholarly articles and dictionaries treating the origin of a given word are consistently cited and evaluated."

But, as Professor Jakobson points out, a new work bids fair to supersede Preobrazhensky's great pioneer effort altogether:

Vasmer, Max. Russisches etymologisches Wörterbuch. Heidelberg, Carl Winter, Universitätsverlag, 1950– volume 1–

publication of which is proceeding energetically at the present time. This work includes proper and geographical names, argot and dialectical variants; and Old Russian, Church Slavonic, Ukrainian, West and South Slavic variants are cited in roman transliteration. As one critic puts it, this " when completed will be one of the foremost aids to Slavistics " (*Language*, volume XXVII, pages 577 to 581. October to December, 1951). Another dictionary, Erich Karl Berneker's *Slavisches etymologisches Wörterbuch* (Heidelberg, Winter, 1908. reprinted 1924), unfortunately reached only to the end of the first two volumes—i.e. to the letter M—the project being abandoned in 1913.

Specialist Dictionaries

Four recent works on Soviet abbreviations are available:

Bahder, Egon von. Russkie sokrashchenia. Russische Abkürzungen und ihre Auflösung aus dem Gebiet von Staat, Verwaltung, Wirtschaft, Wissenschaft, Wehrwesen und Sprachgebrauch. 2nd edition. Leipzig, Birnbach, 1943. 182 pages. (first published in 1942).

Patrick, George Zinovei. A list of abbreviations commonly used in the USSR. Berkeley, Calif., University of California, 1937. 124 pages.

Svešnikov, A. *and* Hoch, A. A. Slovníček sovětských zkratek. Prague, Orbis, 1948.

U.S. Library of Congress. Reference Department. Russian

abbreviations: a selective list. Compiled by Alexander Rosenberg. Washington, Library of Congress, 1952. vii, 128 pages.

There are also two other specialist dictionaries of particular interest to translators:

Lechin, I. V. *and* Petrov, F. N. Slovar' inostrannych slov. Pod redakcijej I. V. Lechina i F. N. Petrova. 3rd edition. Moscow, G.I.S., 1949. 808 pages. (first published 1937).

Ushakov, D. N. *and* Krjuckov, S. E. Orfograficeskij slovar' dlya nachal'noi i srednei shkoli, izd. sed'moe, ispravlennoe i dopolnennoe. Moscow, Uchpedgiz, 1951. 190 pages. (first published 1934).

Lechin and Petrov is a dictionary of foreign words in the Russian language—incidentally, the first such dictionary, *Lexikon vokabulam novym po alfavitu*, was compiled in the times of Peter the Great.

Special Periods

Little work has been done so far on historical lexicography, although a comprehensive dictionary of the Russian language, covering the eleventh to the eighteenth century, is planned by the Akademīia Nauk. The following are of some use meanwhile:

Duvernya, A. Materiali dlya slovarya drevnerusskago yazika. Moscow, 1894. iv, 236 pages.

Sreznevski, I. I. Materiali dlya slovarya drevnerusskago yazika po pismennim pamyatnikam, I-III, dopolnennoe. St. Petersburg, 1893–1909, 1912.

of which the second is of use for the eleventh to the fifteenth century, and the second for the sixteenth and seventeenth centuries.

Russian Dialect Dictionaries

Abayev, V. I. Russko-osetinskiy slovar'. Moscow, Gosudarstvennoye Izdatel'stvo Inostrannykh i Natsional'nykh Slovarei, 1950. 624 pages.

Abdurakhmanov, R. Russko-Uzbeksky slovar'. Tashkent, Akademiya Nauk Uzbekskoi SSR, 1954.

Cherkesi, E. Georgian-English dictionary. Hertford, Stephen Austin & Sons (for the Trustees of the Marjory Wardrop Fund, University of Oxford), 1950. ii, 275 pages.

Dojacek, Frank. A pocket dictionary of the English and Ukrainian languages, giving the pronunciation of English words in Ukrainian characters and Ukrainian sounds. New revised edition. Winnipeg, Ukrainian Booksellers and Publishers, 1949.

Kluge, Th. Georgisch-deutsches Wörterbuch. Leipzig, Harrassowitz, 1919– volume 1–

Koliadenkov, M. N. *and* Tsyganov, N. F. Russko-Erzianskii [Erziansko-Russkii] slovar'. Moscow, 1948–49. 2 volumes.

Marr, N. Abxazsko-russkii slovar'. Leningrad, 1926. lv, 152 pages (Izdanie Akedemii Abxazskovo jazyka i literatury).

Miller, Vs. Ossetisch-russisch-deutsches Wörterbuch: herausgegeben und ergänzt von A. Freiman. Leningrad, Académie des Sciences, 1927– volume 1–

Bi-Lingual Dictionaries

One of the very early English-Russian dictionaries was compiled for the use of midshipmen at the Naval Academy at St. Petersburg, and it contained nearly forty thousand words:

Zhdanov, Prokhor. A new dictionary, English and Russian. St. Petersburg, 1784. 778 pages.

Since then, interest in Britain in the Russian language has grown and, stimulated by the tremendous literary output in Russia in the nineteenth century, and by the political, literary and economic developments of the twentieth, has resulted in a large number of excellent dictionaries, of which the following are the most important:

Akhmanova, O. S. Anglo-russkii slovar' . . . okolo 20,000 slov. Moscow, OGIZ, izd-vo inostr. i. nats. slovarei, 1944. 543 pages.

Aleksandrov, A. *pseudonym*. Complete Russian-English [and English-Russian] dictionary. 6th–7th editions. Petrograd; New York, Maisel, and Hebrew Publishing Company, 1916–23. 2 volumes.

Müller, Vladimir Karlovich *and* Boianus, Semen Karlovich. English-Russian and Russian-English dictionary. 3rd edition. Philadelphia & New York, Blakiston & Dutton, 1944. (reprinted 1951). 2 volumes.

Segal, Louis. New complete English-Russia and Russian-English dictionary (new orthography). 4th edition. London, Lund Humphries; New York, British Book Centre, 1951. 2 volumes. (reprint of Russian-English, 1953).

Smirnitskii, Alexksandr Ivanovich. Russko-angliiskii slovar'. Sostavili: O. S. Achmanov. Okolo 50,000 slov. Moscow, Gos. izd-vo inostr. i nats. slovarei, 1949. 987 pages.

Zaimovskii, Semen Grigorevich. English-Russian dictionary. 2nd edition. Moscow, 1932. 1084 pages. (first published, Berlin, 1923).

Aleksandrov is still of value for its scholarly treatment, in spite of its being out of date, but in combination with Müller and Boianus it can prove a very useful aid. The latter covers some sixty thousand words and is based chiefly on Wyld's *Universal dictionary of the English language*, English and American idiomatic expressions being included. Segal, which is based on Aleksandrov, includes both literary and scientific and technical terms, and covers idioms, proper and geographical names, and abbreviations. A shortened version of Zaimovskii, covering both English-Russian and Russian-English, was published recently (Moscow, Gos. izd-vo inostr. i nats. slovarei, 1949. 364 pages).

Much useful information and evaluation of Russian dictionaries— and a detailed account of the Academy's dictionaries—will be found in a new work, B. O. Unbegaun and J. S. G. Simmons's *A bibliographical guide to the Russian language*. (Oxford, Clarendon Press, 1953. xiv, 174 pages).

DICTIONARIES OF THE SCANDINAVIAN LANGUAGES

Richard Cleasby, an Englishman of independent means, had already acquired a profound knowledge of German dialects when—with the encouragement, among others, of Jacob Grimm—he embarked in 1840 on the task of compiling the first Icelandic-English dictionary. In spite of constant ill-health he managed to amass, in the eight years left to him, a vast amount of valuable material. His death however threw everything into confusion, and it was not until some twenty-seven years later that his dictionary was eventually published, and this largely through the efforts of the Icelandic scholar Sir George Webbe Dasent, who also contributed a vivid sketch of Cleasby's remarkable life as a preface. To-day, the three main dictionaries for the study of Old Norse are:

Cleasby, Richard. An Icelandic dictionary based on the MS. collections of the late Richard Cleasby, enlarged and completed by Gudbrand Vigfusson, with an introduction and life of Richard Cleasby by George Webbe Dasent. Oxford, Clarendon Press, 1874. cviii, 779 pages. (reprinted Heidelberg, 1954).

Fritzner, Johan. Ordbog over det gamle norsk sprog. new edition. Christiania, Norske Forlagsforening; Chicago, Relling, 1886-96. 3 volumes in 4. (reprinted in 3 volumes, Oslo, Møller, 1954-55).

—— Tillegg til Fritzner's Ordbog, ved Didrik Arup Seip og Trygve Knudsen. Oslo, Møller, 1955. 150 pages.

Heggstad, Leif. Gamalnorsk ordbok med nynorsk tyding. Oslo, Det Norske Samlaget, 1930. xii, 837 pages.

Fritzner, who was a theologian by education and for many years a dean by occupation, had made a thorough study throughout his long life of all the available material, so that his work with all its quotations, its references and its explanations of the real meanings of words, is still unsurpassed, and a committee of eminent philologists under the Chairmanship of Professor Didrik Arup Seip has made itself responsible for preparing an authoritative supplement of additions and corrections.

Heggstad's dictionary—which supersedes an older work by Kristofer Marius H. Haegstad and Alf Torp—covers the vocabulary of Old Norse up to the middle of the fourteenth century.

Three dictionaries deal specifically with the poetic Edda:

Egilsson, Sveinbjörn.   Lexicon poëticum antiquae linguae septentrionalis.   Edidit Societas Regia Antiquariorum Septentrionalium [i.e. Nordiske Oldskrift Selskab, Copenhagen].   Copenhagen, Quist, 1854–60. lii, 937 pages. (another edition, edited by Finnur Jónson. 2nd edition. Copenhagen, 1931. xvi, 667 pages).

Gering, Hugo. Glossar zu den Liedern der Edda (Saemundar Edda). 5th edition. Paderborn, Schöningh, 1923. ix, 231 pages. (first published 1887).

Gering, Hugo. Vollständiges Wörterbuch zu den Liedern der Edda. Halle, Buchhandlung des Waisenhauses, 1903. xiii, 1404 columns. (issued in 2 parts, 1901–03).

Cleasby made a considerable financial contribution towards the cost of producing Egilsson's dictionary. There are also three other works which are of help:

Holmboe, Christopher Andreas.   Det norske sprogs vaesentligste ordforraad, sammenlignet med Sanskrit og andre sprog af samme aet.   Bidrag til en norsk etymologisk ordbog af Christopher Andreas Holmboe . . . Udg. ved understöttelse af det Kgl. Norske Videnskabsselskab.   Vienna, Keiserlig-kongelige Hof- og Statstrykkerie, 1852. xx, 496 pages.

Möbius, Theodor.   Altnordisches Glossar: Wörterbuch zu einer Auswahl alt-isländischer und alt-norwegischer Prosatexte . . . Leipzig, Teubner, 1866. xii, 532 pages.

Zoëga, Geir Tómasson. A concise dictionary of old Icelandic . . . Oxford, Clarendon Press, 1910. vii, 551 pages. (reprinted 1926).

of which the last was founded on Cleasby and Vigfusson's dictionary. In Zoëga's dictionary the purely poetic vocabulary—with the exception of the Edda poems—has largely been omitted, together with a number of compounds occurring only in legal, theological or technical works. Holmboe, who was an orientalist and a numismatist as well as a philologist, provides the etymology of most Scandinavian words.

On Icelandic in general, and on modern Icelandic, there are the following works:

Blöndal, Sigfús. Islandsk-dansk ordbog. Hovedmedarbejdere: Björg Thorláksson Blöndal, Jón Ofeigsson, Holgar Wiehe. Reykjavík, Thorláksson, 1920–24. 1052 pages.

Jóhannesson, Alexander. Isländisches etymologisches Wörterbuch. Berne, Francke, 1951– part 1–

Olafsson, Jón. Orðabók íslenzkrar tungu að fornu og nýju. Reykjavík, Gutenberg, 1912–15. volumes 1 and 2 (A-Brynn, only. No more published).

þorkelsson, Jón. Supplement til islandske ordbøger. [1.–4. Samling]. Reykjavík, Pórdarsón, 1876–99. 4 volumes.

þorkelsson, Jón. Supplement til islandske ordbøger. Anden samling, ny udgave. Copenhagen, Forlagt af Skandinavisk Antiquariat, 1895. xx, 639 pages.

Zoëga, Geir Tómasson. Islensk-ensk [ensk–islensk] orðabók. 3rd edition. Reykjavík, Kristjánsson, 1932–51. 2 volumes. (first published 1904).

Blöndal's dictionary includes dialect and colloquial words. Jóhannesson is to be completed in nine parts in approximately six years. A new dictionary of Old Norse, covering Old Icelandic monuments until about 1550 and Old Norwegian documents until 1370, is in preparation at the present time at the University in Copenhagen, and a dictionary of modern Icelandic (1550 to 1950) is being compiled under similar circumstances at Reykjavík.

Scandinavian Dialect Dictionaries

Christie, Wilhelm F. K. Norsk dialect-lexicon og nokre folkeminne og brev. Gustav Indrebø gav ut. Bergen, Grieg, 1938. 261; 374 pages. (Bergens Museums Aarbog, 1937. Historisk-antiquarisk rekke, nr. 1).

Danell, G. Ordbok över Nuckömålet. Uppsala, 1951. (Skr. utg. Kungl. Gustav Adolfs Akad. XXVII).

Danell, G. *and others*. Gotländsk ordbok. På grundval av C. och P. A. Säves samlingar redigerad av G. Danell, A. Schagerström och H. Gustavson. Uppsala, Lundequist, 1918–45. viii, 1271, liii pages.

Jørgensen, J. Lollandsk ordbog (Thoreby-Maalet). Copenhagen, Schultz, 1943. 671 columns.

Lindgren, J. V.   Ordbok över Burträskmålet, utg. av D. O. och M. Zetterholm. Uppsala, Lundequist, 1940. viii, 168 pages.

Ljunggren, K. G.   Svenska dialektordböcker: en oversikt. (*in* Vetensk.-Soc. i Lund Årsbok, 1938 (1939), pages 19 to 37).

Peterson, P. N.   Ordbok över Valldamålet. Lund, Gleerup, 1935–46. 10 volumes.

Rietz, Johan Ernst.   Svenskt dialekt-lexikon. Malmö, Cronholm, 1867. 2 volumes.

Skyvm, A. C.   Morsingmålets ordforråd, I.1.   Århus, Universitetsforlaget, 1948. 144 pages.

Norwegian

Two of Norway's earliest dictionaries have recently been reprinted:

Jensen, Christen (died 1653).   Den norske dictionarium eller glosebog. Utgj. paa nyom av Den norske historske kildeskriftkommission ved Torleiv Hannaas. Christiania, Grøndahl, 1914.   99 pages.

Leem, Knud (1697–1774).   Norske maalsamlingar fraa 1740–aari (håndskr. nr. 597.4 to i Kallske samling). Utg. for Kjeldeskriftfondet ved Torleiv Hannaas.   Christiania, Dybwad, 1923. xix, 354 pages.

The original title of the MS. of the latter—reproduced in this edition—was *Een liden glose-bog*.   Another early dictionary of the Norwegian language was:

Hallager, Laurents.   Norsk ordsamling eller prøve af norske ord og talemaader.   Tilligemed et anhang indeholdende endeel viser, som ere skrevne i det norske bondesprog . . . Copenhagen, Popp, 1802. xxiv, 197 pages.

The history of the present confusion in Norwegian linguistic matters has been summarised by Mr. Anthony Curwen, of Westminster Central Reference Library, a keen student of Scandinavian affairs.   Twentieth century doubts and controversies derive from the original colonisation of Iceland by Vikings from Norway and from subsequent events. No inhabitants had preceded them, and no other race has since been present for any length of time, apart from a few Danish officials, so that Modern Icelandic is still very close to Old Norse.   From the Union of Kalmar in 1397 Norway remained under Danish rule until 1814 when it was lost to Sweden at the end of the Napoleonic wars.   During this long period Danish—with modifications—was the language of administration and education, and is referred to as Dano-Norwegian or, in its

modern form, as Riksmål (the " State language ") or Bokmål (the " literary language "). Old Norse or Old Norwegian was driven into the valleys and, since there are no easy communications between them, the common language soon developed into a number of dialects. During the nineteenth century, Norwegian nationalism under the inspired leadership of the gifted writer Ivar Aasen and Arne Garborg turned to these dialects as the real " Norwegian" language and created Landsmål (the " country language ")—often referred to as Nynorsk, Neo-Norwegian or New Norwegian—from elements taken from all the dialects. At the present time efforts are being made to combine the two as Samnorsk (" together-Norwegian "). Skåne, the southernmost province of Sweden, was under Danish rule as well until 1676 and therefore speaks Skånsk, a Danish-Swedish dialect all of its own. A diagram may help to show the relationships of the various Scandinavian languages:

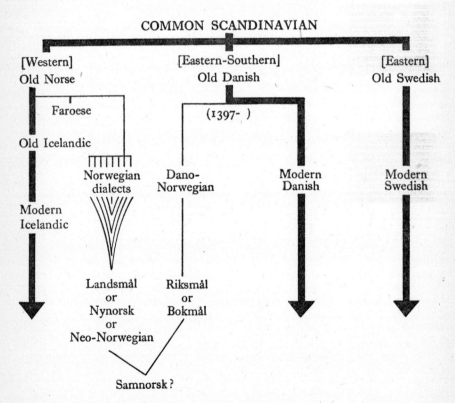

COMMON SCANDINAVIAN

[Western]
Old Norse

[Eastern-Southern]
Old Danish

[Eastern]
Old Swedish

Faroese

(1397-)

Old Icelandic

Norwegian
dialects

Dano-
Norwegian

Modern
Danish

Modern
Swedish

Modern
Icelandic

Landsmål
or
Nynorsk
or
Neo-Norwegian

Riksmål
or
Bokmål

Samnorsk?

It is not possible to go into more detail concerning this fascinating philological problem, but readers desiring to pursue the subject further could not do better than study the brilliant chapter on Language contributed by the eminent philologist, Professor Alf Sommerfelt, to the current edition of the *Norway year book* (Oslo, Tanum), Dr. Bjarne Berulfsen's illuminating summary of " The language situation in Norway " (in *The Norseman*, volume 10, 1952: pages 183 to 192), Ingvald Torvik's "A survey of the language situation in Norway " (*Revue des langues vivantes*, volume XIX, No. 5), and Philip Boardman's entertaining and instructive *Nuggets of Norse: a skirmish with sounds, words and language feuds in Norway* (Oslo, Aschehoug, 1952)—more especially parts IV and V, pages 48 to 101. It will be seen therefore that dictionaries of both types of Norwegian—Riksmål and Landsmål—are necessary if current books and periodicals and newspapers are to be dealt with, and the following are among the more recent and comprehensive examples:

> Alnaes, Ivar. Norsk uttale-ordbok. Utgitt av Bymaalslaget. 2nd edition. Oslo, Aschehoug, 1925. 270 pages. (first published 1910). (Riksmål).
>
> Heggstad, Leiv. Fornorskingsordbok, bokmål-nyorsk: obligatoriske former. 3rd edition. Oslo, Norli, 1950. 281 pages.
>
> Hellevik, A. Norsk ordbok. Oslo, det norske Samlaget, 1950– volume 1–
>
> Knudsen, Knud Anton. Unorsk og norsk: eller, Fremmedords avløsning . . . Christiania, Cammermeyer, 1881. xxxiv, 992 pages.
>
> Krogsrud, Torgeir *and* Seip, Didrik Arup. Norsk riksmåls-ordbok for rettskrivning og ordbøining . . . Godkjent av Kirke- og Undervisningsdepartementet. Christiania, Steen, 1924. 222 pages.
>
> Norsk riksmålsordbok, utarbeidet av Trygve Knudsen og Alf Sommerfelt, under medvirkning av K. E. Bödtker, Ulrik Mörk, J. Mörland, R. Ullmann. Oslo, Aschehoug, 1930– volume 1–
>
> Skard, Matias Olsen. Nynorsk ordbog for rettskrivning og literaturlesnad. Christiania, Aschehoug, 1912. xv, 249 pages.
>
> Sverdrup, Jakob *and* Sandvei, Marius. Norsk rettskrivningsordbok, bokmål; godkjent av Kirke- og Undervisningsdepartementet til offentlig bruk og som hjelpebok i skolen. Oslo, Tanum, 1940. xv, 520 pages.

Alnaes's dictionary is an excellent phonetic lexicon of riksmål. Heggstad's work is devoted to landsmål. Hellevik is a comprehensive Nynorsk dictionary. Knudsen and Sommerfelt commenced work on their grea dictionary as early as 1918—i.e. almost immediately after the new orthography introduced in the previous year. It is hardly an historical dictionary, for no examples are given from works appearing before 1870, but rather a dictionary of the usage of the language employed by the majority of educated people. Precise definitions are given, and emphasis is given to words in current use. In addition, the resources of the well-known encyclopaedic dictionary *Aschehougs Konversasjons-leksikon* (4th edition. Oslo, Aschehoug, 1954– volume 1–) should not be overlooked.

There are two important etymological dictionaries:

Falk, Hjalmar Sejersted *and* Torp, Alf. Etymologisk ordbog over det norske og det danske sprog. Christiania, Aschehoug, 1903–06. 2 volumes.

of which the German edition is considered by some to be the better:

Falk, Hjalmar Sejersted *and* Torp, Alf. Norwegisch-dänisches etymologisches Wörterbuch. Auf Grund der Übersetzung von H. Davidson neu bearb. deutsche Ausg., mit literaturnachweisen strittiger Etymologien, sowie deutschen und altnordischen Wörterverzeichnis . . . Heidelberg, Winter, 1910–11. 2 volumes.

and:

Torp, Alf. Nynorsk etymologisk ordbog. Christiania, Aschehoug, 1919. 886 pages.

Attention is also drawn to two recent slang and dialect dictionaries; it must be noted however that the author of the first lived from 1778 to 1849:

Christie, Wilhelm F. K. Norsk dialect-lexikon og nokre folkeminne og brev. Gustav Indrebø gav ut. Bergen, Grieg, 1938. 635 pages. (Bergens Museums Aarbog, 1937. Historisk-antiquarisk rekke, nr. 1).

Gleditsch, Ulf. Det får'n si: norsk slangordbok. Oslo, Nasjonal-forlaget, 1952. 119 pages.

Modern bilingual dictionaries include the following:

Berulfsen, B. *and* Scavenius, H. Gyldendal's English-Norwegian and Norwegian-English dictionary. Oxford, Blackwell; New York, McKay, 1951. 2 volumes in 1.

Brynildsen, John. Norsk-engelsk ordbog. 3rd edition. Oslo, Aschehoug, 1927. 1228 pages.

Gleditsch, Theodor *and others*.   English-Norwegian dictionary, by Theodor Gleditsch, Margit Sahlgaard Borresen and Birger Krogh Johanssen. London, Allen & Unwin, 1950. vii, 855 pages.

Jorgenson, Theodore. Norwegian-English school dictionary. Northfield, Minn., St. Olaf College Press, 1943. 460 pages.

Larsen, Anton Laurentius. Dansk-norsk-engelsk ordbog. Gennemset af Johannes Magnussen. 4th edition. Copenhagen, Gyldendal, 1910 (i.e. 1918). vii, 687 pages.

Raknes, Ola. Engelsk-norsk ordbok, med grunnlag i Engelsk-norsk ordbog af Th. Gleditsch. Oslo, Aschehoug, 1927. 1049 pages. (Landsmål).

Swedish

One of the earliest Swedish dictionaries has recently been reprinted :

Schroderus, E. Lexicon Latino-Scondicum, 1637. Utg. med alfabetiska register över de svenska och de finska orden av Bengt Hesselman. Uppsala, 1942. 269 pages.

Two other early Swedish dictionaries are important for their contributions to later studies :

Sahlstedt, Abraham. Svensk ordbok, med Latinsk uttolkning . . . Dictionarium Svecicum cum interpretatione Latina. Stockholm, 1773.

Spegel, Haquin. Glossarium Sueo-Gothicum, eller Swensk Ordabook . . . Lund, 1712.

Spegel subsequently became Archbishop of Uppsala. Sahlstedt, whom Bergman* describes as " the most influential grammarian and lexicographer of the eighteenth century ", was also the author of the *Swensk grammatica* (1769) which helped to set a standard for modern Swedish, a standard which was further maintained by the Swedish Academy which was founded by Gustavus III in 1906.

For the Swedish language of modern times the following dictionaries are available :

Dalin, Anders Fredrik. Ordbok öfver svenska språket. Stockholm, Beckman, 1850–53. 2 volumes.

---

* Bergman, Gösta. A short history of the Swedish language. Stockholm, Swedish Institute for Cultural Relations, 1947.

Dalin, Anders Fredrik. Svensk handordbok. Med tillägg af ordens etymologi, jemte ett bihang, innehållande de i svensk skrift allmännast brukliga främmande ord. Stockholm, Beckman, 1868. iv, 800 pages.

Ekbohrn, Carl Magnus. Förklaringar öfver 100,000 främmande ord och namn m.m. i svenska språket, tillika med deras härdledning och uttal. new edition. Stockholm, Bonnier, 1936. 2 volumes.

Lundell, Johan August. Svensk ordlista, med reformstavning ock uttalsbeteckning, under medvärkan av Hilda Lundell ock Elise Zetterquist samt flere fackmän. Stockholm, Geber, 1893. xxxii, 384 pages.

Lundström, J. B. Svensk ordbok, med angifvande af ordens härledning. Stockholm, Hierta, 1870. 256 pages.

Lyttkens, Ivar Adolf *and* Wulff, F. A. Svensk ordlista med uttalsbeteckning, i enlighet med Svenska akademiens ordbok, och med stavning enligt 1906 års cirkulär, samt vägledning till riksspråksuttal. Lund, Gleerup, 1911. 515 pages.

Morén, C. G. *and others*. Uppslagsbok för stafning och böjning af svenska språkets ordförråd jämte vanliga främmande ord och egennamn stafning och böjning efter 7:e uppl. af Akademiens ordlista. Stockholm, Skoglund, 1903. 356 pages.

Ordbok över svenska språket, utgiven af Svenska Akademien. Lund, Lindstedt, 1898– volume 1–

—— Källförteckning. 1939. 296 columns.

Ordlista över svenska språket, utgiven av Svenska Akademien. 8th edition, 11th impression. Stockholm, Svenska Bokförlaget, 1945. vii, 378 pages. (this edition originally issued in 1923).

Östergren, Olof. Nusvensk ordbok. Stockholm, Wahlström & Widstrand, 1918– volume 1–

Sundén, Daniel Anton. Ordbok öfver svenska språket. Stockholm, Beckman, 1892. 2 volumes. (issued in 6 parts, 1885–92).

Wenström, Oscar Edmund *and* Jeurling, Ossian. Svenska språkets ordförråd, eller 80,000 inhemska och främmande ord och namn, med öfversättningar och förklaringar jämte uttalsbeteckning och accentuering, enligt Sv. Akademiens ljudenligaste stafsätt. Gottland, Visby, 1891. 598 pages.

For the study of the older texts, the following two dictionaries are of use:

Bergroth, Hugo. Högsvenska: kortfattad hjälpreda vid undervisningen i modersmålet. 2nd edition. Helsinki, Söderström, 1924. 105 pages.

Söderwall, Knut Fredrik. Ordbok öfver svenska medeltidsspråket. Stockholm, Svenska Fornskriftsällskapet, 1884–1918. 2 volumes in 3. (issued in 24 parts).

—— Supplement, av K. G. Ljunggren. Lund, 1925–

Elof Hellquist, who was also responsible for *Det svenska ordforrådets ålder och ursprung*: *en översikt* (Lund, Gleerup, 1929–32. xv, 1101 pages) which Bergman (*op. cit.*) has described as " an exhaustive work on the native and foreign element in the modern Swedish vocabulary ", wrote an important etymological dictionary:

Hellquist, Elof. Svensk etymologisk ordbok. 3rd edition. Lund, Gleerup, 1948. 2 volumes. (first published in 16 parts, 1920–22).

a compilation which includes the cognate forms of Germanic words in both old and modern western languages, and which also contributes much useful information on Old Norse. Two other works give additional assistance in this field:

Levander, Lars *and* Wessén, Elias. Våra ord: deras uttal och ursprung. Populär etymologisk ordbok. Ɩ ockholm, Bonnier, 1932. 345 pages.

Tamm, Fredrik August. Etymologisk svensk ordbok. Uppsala, Berling, 1890–1905. volume 1–

—— Bidrag till en Svensk etymologisk ordbok . . . Uppsala, Berling, 1874– volume 1–

The first dictionary, which makes critical use of Hellquist's findings, includes modern borrowings from foreign languages. Tamm's work reached only the word Karsk by the time of his death, at the age of 59, in 1905.

The most important dialect dictionary of the Swedish language is:

Rietz, Johan Ernst. Svenskt dialekt-lexikon. Malmö, Cronholm, 1867. 2 volumes.

and further information on the present position may be obtained from Elias Wessén's *Våra folkmål* (2nd edition. Stockholm, 1945. 96 pages),

and from K. G. Ljunggren's " Svenska dialektordböcker: en oversikt "
(*Vetensk.-Soc. i Lund Årsbok*, 1938, pages 19 to 37).
One other recent specialist dictionary should be noted:

Odhner, Einar.   Svenskt rimlexikon.   Stockholm, Forum, 1952.
280 pages.

An early dictionary reflects the interest of the British and the Swedish
in each other:

Serenius, Jakob.   Dictionarium suethico-anglo-latinum, quo singulae
voces suethicae, secundum proprias et metaphoricas signifi-
cationes, anglice ac latine redduntur, et phrases magis usitatae,
communia utriusque gentis proverbia, locutiones vulgares, non
nunquam etjam vocabula obsoleta, exhibentur, ut harum lingua-
rum indagini et cognationi, haud ita pridem tentatae, sua paretur
auctoritas, adjecto indice terminorum in mercatura, et re navale.
Stockholm, Momma, 1741. 284 pages.

and among the more important bilingual dictionaries for use at the
present day are the following:

Afzelius, J. A.   Svensk-engelsk synonymbok.   Stockholm, 1911.
740 pages.

Björkman, Carl Gustaf.   Svensk-engelsk ordbok.   Stockholm,
Norstedt, 1889. 1360 pages. (reprinted 1902).

Buergel-Goodwin, Heinrich Karl Hugo.   Svenskt-engelskt parlör-
lexikon. Stockholm, Norstedt, 1928. 356 pages.

Harlock, Walter Ernest.   Svensk-engelsk ordbok, skolupplaga,
under medverkan av Arvid Gabrielson, John Holmberg och
Margareta Angström. 2nd edition. Stockholm, Svenska Bokförlaget, 1947. viii, 1048 pages. (earlier editions were by O. E. Wenström and W. E. Harlock.)   (first published 1944).

Harlock, Walter Ernest *and others*. Svensk-engelsk ordbok. Stockholm, Svenska Bokförlaget, 1936–51. 2 volumes.

Kärre, Karl *and others*. Engelsk-svensk ordbok, skolupplaga. 2nd
edition. Stockholm, Svenska Bokförlaget, 1949. (first published
1935).

Nöjd, Ruben. Engelsk-svensk och svensk-engelsk ordbok. Stockholm, Bonnier, 1942. 2 volumes in 1.

Wenström, Oscar Edmund. Engelsk-svensk ordbok. Fullständigt
omarbetad av Ruben Nöjd och Anna C. Petterson. Stockholm,
Norstedt, 1941. viii, 648 pages.

Wessely, Ignaz Emanuel. Swedish-English dictionary. In two parts: Swedish-English, English-Swedish. new edition. Philadelphia, McKay, 1941. 735 pages.

Danish

The standard Danish dictionary was the work of a Commission set up under the Danish Academy of Sciences. Although their work is by no means the largest of the national dictionaries, it took more than one hundred years to produce:

Dansk ordbog, udgiven under Videnskabernes Selskabs Bestyrelse. Copenhagen, Moller, 1793–1905. 8 volumes.

One of the members of the Commission was Christian Molbech. Molbech, who was originally destined for the Navy, had by the accident of ill-health become librarian and was also an historian and a prolific man of letters. A constant traveller, he reported favourably on the early nineteenth century British libraries and himself published a treatise on the organisation and administration of public libraries. Eventually he produced his own short dictionary:

Molbech, Christian. Dansk haand-ordbog til retskrivnings og sprogrigtigheds fremme med grundtraek af den danske retskriv-nings-laere . . . Copenhagen, Brummer, 1813. xxi, 563 pages.

His major work—which set a high standard for later Danish lexicographers —did not appear until he was fifty:

Molbech, Christian. Dansk ordbog indeholdende det danske sprogs stammeord, tilligemed afledede og samensatte ord, efter den nuaerende sprogbrug forklarede i deres forskiellige betydninger, og ved talemaader og exempler oplyste. 2nd edition. Copenhagen, Gyldendal, 1859. 2 volumes. (first published 1833).

More recent dictionaries of importance include:

Dahl, Bendt Treschov. Dansk ordbog for folket, udarbejdet af B. T. Dahl . . . H. Hammer . . . under medvirkning af Hans Dahl . . . Copenhagen, Gyldendal, 1907–14. 2 volumes.

Glahder, Jørgen. Dansk retskrivningsordbog. Udg. af Under-visningsministeriets Retskrivningsudvalg. Med en retskrivnings-vejledning af Henrik Bertelsen. 3rd edition, 5th impression. Copenhagen, Gyldendal, 1947. 238 pages.

Grundtvig, Svend Hersleb.   Dansk haandordbog, med den af Kultusministeriet anbefalede retskrivning . . . Copenhagen, Reitzel, 1872. xv, 144 pages.

—— Tillaeg til dansk haandordbog . . . Copenhagen, Reitzel, 1882. 59 pages.

Holst, Hans Peter.   Dansk retskrivningsordbog . . . Copenhagen, Philipsen, 1863. 760 pages.

Såby, Viggo Alfred Emil.   Saabys Retskrivnings ordbog, udgivet af P. K. Thorsen . . . 5th edition.   Copenhagen, Gyldendal, 1909. vi, 261 pages.

Holst was the well-known Danish poet.   Grundtvig was the son of the Danish poet, Bishop N. F. S. Grundtvig (the moving spirit behind the Danish Folk High School movement), and himself an historian and antiquarian.   His work and that of Såby, though compiled in the nineteenth century, retain their position in the front rank of Danish lexicography.

The original *Dansk ordbog* is now being superseded by the work of the leading Danish society (which was founded as late as 1911):

Ordbog over det danske sprog, grundlagt af Verner Dahlerup; med understøttelse af Undervisningsministeriet og Carlsbergfondet udg. af Det Danske Sprog- og Litteraturselskab. Copenhagen, Gyldendal, 1919–54.   27 volumes.

—— Liste over forkortelser i bind I-XII, med en lydskrifttavle. Copenhagen, 1931. 69 pages.

In preparing this great work, this Society—whose purpose is to study Danish language and literature—attempts to include all Danish words since 1700, in addition to those of the previous century which have had any considerable influence on the language.   Dialect and foreign loanwords are covered, special attention is given to pronunciation, and the different meanings of words are given in strict logical order.

For the study of Old Danish, there is the standard reference work:

Kalkar, Karl Otto Herman Tryde.   Ordbog til det aeldre dansk sprog (1300–1700) . . . Copenhagen, Thiele, 1881–1918. 5 volumes. (Universitets Jubileets danske Samfund. Publikation nr. 1).

—— Kilde-fortegnelse og forkortelses-liste til 1.-5. bd. Copenhagen, Thiele, 1925. xxviii pages.

which, with the *Ordbog over det danske sprog*, gives a comprehensive survey of the language for seven centuries.

Etymology is covered by the classic:

> Falk, Hjalmar Sehersted *and* Torp, Alf. Etymologisk ordbog over det norske og det danske sprog. Christiania, Aschehoug, 1903–06. 2 volumes. (issued in parts, 1901–06).

of which the German edition is considered by some to be the better (see page 75): and by:

> Jessen, Carl Arnold Edwin. Dansk etymologisk ordbog. Copenhagen, Gyldendal, 1893. 291 pages.

For synonyms in the Danish language there is:

> Albeck, Ulla. Dansk synonym-ordbog. 3rd edition, 2nd impression. Copenhagen, Schultz, 1951. 307 pages. (this edition first issued in 1948. First published in 1941).

In 1784, Christian Fredrik Bay issued his *Compleat vocabulary, English and Danish,* of which the fourth and last edition was:

> Bay, Christian Fredrik. Fulstaendig dansk og engelsk haandordbog. 4th edition. Copenhagen, Gyldendal, 1820. 614 pages.

On this pioneer work all later bilingual dictionaries of the language have drawn extensively. One of the best of the modern bilingual dictionaries—in spite of its age—is still:

> Brynildsen, John. Dictionary of the English and Dano-Norwegian languages. Danisms supervised by Johannes Magnussen: English pronunciation by Otto Jespersen. Copenhagen, Gyldendal, 1902–07. 2 volumes.

Other modern dictionaries include:

> Bolbjerg, Alfred. Dansk-engelsk ordbog. Copenhagen, Berlingske Forlag, 1947. 365 pages.

> Gleditsch, Theodor *and* Rathsack, E. Engelsk-dansk ordbog. Copenhagen, Gyldendal, 1912. 1200 pages.

> Haislund, Niels *and* Salling, Aage. Engelsk-dansk [og dansk-engelsk] ordbog; med autoriseret anvendelse af Otto Jespersens Lydskrift. new edition. Copenhagen, Berlingske Forlag, 1950. 2 volumes. (first published in 1937).

> Larsen, Anton Laurentius. Dictionary of the Dano-Norwegian and English languages, revised by Johannes Magnussen. 4th edition. Copenhagen, Gyldendal, 1910. 687 pages. (first published 1880).

Magnussen, Johannes Julius Claudi *and others*.   Danish-English [and English-Danish] dictionary. By Johannes Magnussen, Otto Madsen, Hermann Vinterberg, Knud Herløv, and Bodil Ladgaard. Copenhagen, Gyldendal: London, Allen & Unwin, 1944–54. 2 volumes. (5th and 6th editions respectively).

Rosing, Svend.   Engelsk-dansk ordbog.   7th edition.   Copenhagen, Gyldendal, 1899.   541 pages.   (first published in 1853).

A recent work of particular interest to translators is:

Naestad, Henning.   Engelsk-dansk synonym-ordbog: engelske synonymer forklaret paa dansk . . . Copenhagen, Grafisk Forlag, 1946.   531 pages.   (Indexes of both English *and* Danish words enable this work to be used also as a Danish-English dictionary).

GREEK AND LATIN DICTIONARIES

The history of lexicography in the classical tongues covers more than two thousand years: even at the commencement of the second century B.C. the Librarian of the Alexandrine Library, Aristophanes of Byzantium, was compiling a dictionary of Greek words, and interest in the subject increased throughout the classical period. The results of the research of the many Greek and Roman philologists into the origins of their languages were crystallised and recorded about the year one thousand A.D. in the great lexicon known as *Suidas*, a compilation which included some thirty thousand articles on language, literature and history. In part it drew on the work of Hesychius, a fifth or sixth century lexicographer of Miletus or Alexandria, but it incorporated much new material and also quoted copiously from the works of the Greek writers. Two editions of this work have been edited and issued in recent years:

> Suidae Lexicon, ex recognitione Immanuelis Bekkeri. Berlin, G. Reimer, 1854. 1158 pages.

> Suidae lexicon, edidit Ada Adler . . . Leipzig, Teubner, 1928– volume 1–

In the sixteenth century two Greek dictionaries were published which are still of considerable interest. The first may have been used for the translation of the New Testament into English:

> Crespin, Jean. Lexicon graecolatinum Ioannis Crispini operá tredecim abhinc annis ex R. Constantini aliorumque scriptis, qui in hoc commentandi genere excelluerunt, utili compendio collectum . . . operâ et studio E. G. London, Henry Bynneman, 1581.

which was dedicated to Edward Grant. Henri Estienne (whose name is sometimes written in its Latin form, Henricus Stephanus), a member of the famous firm of publishers, issued his *Thesaurus graecae linguae* after twelve years of continuous work at Geneva in 1572, in five folio volumes. This edition remained unrivalled for nearly three centuries. Only in 1831 did the renowned Parisian printer and publisher, Ambroise Firmin Didot—himself an outstanding Hellenist—commence to issue, with the aid of the best scholars of his time, a new edition which took thirty-four years to complete (in nine folio volumes):

> Estienne, Henri.   Thesaurus graecae linguae, ab Henrico Stephano constructus. Post editionem anglicam novis additamentis auctum, ordineque alphabetico digestum tertio ediderunt Carolus Benedictus Hase . . . Gulielmus Dindorfus et Ludovicus Dindorfus . . . Paris, Firmin Didot, 1831–65. 8 volumes in 9. (reprinted, Graz, Akademische Druck & Verlagsanstalt, 1954).

Another work which served as a foundation for later lexicons is:

> Schneider, Johann Gottlob.   Griechisch-deutsches Wörterbuch beym Lesen der griechischen profanen Scribenten zugebrauchen. 3rd edition. Leipzig, Hahn, 1819. Supplement, 1821.

which was first published in 1797-98 at Züllichau. It was on this work that one of the greatest lexicons still in current use was based:

> Passow, Franz Ludwig Carl Friedrich.   Handwörterbuch der griechischen Sprache . . . neu bearbeitet und zeitgemäss umgestaltet von Valentine Christian Friedrich Rost und Friedrich Palm . . . 5th edition. Leipzig, Vogel, 1841–57. 2 volumes in 4.

of which Wilhelm Crönert started to compile a revised edition (Göttingen, 1912–13); this project was however abandoned owing to the first World War. On this effort, in turn, was based the principal lexicon of this century:

> Liddell, Henry George *and* Scott, Robert. A Greek-English lexicon . . . a new edition revised and augmented throughout by Sir Henry Stuart Jones . . . with the assistance of Roderick McKenzie . . . and with the co-operation of many scholars . . . Oxford, Clarendon Press, 1925–40. 2 volumes.

of which the first edition was issued in 1843. This is essentially a conservative dictionary, and has drawn some criticism from scholars on the grounds that not enough notice has been taken of recent discoveries. Etymological comment was deliberately reduced to a minimum—no doubt to save space—and for the same reason, place names and many proper names were omitted, so that it is necessary to use Passow for this purpose. In a similar fashion, words beginning with the same element were usually grouped together, an arrangement which may impede reference from time to time. Latin and Semitic words in Greek form were included, but Byzantine and Patristic literature were not covered, the dictionary limiting its period to roughly A.D. 600. New words and new meanings were included in an Addendum of nearly seventy pages.

Recent dictionaries include:

Bernardakes, Grēgorios N. Lexikòn hermeneutikòn . . . Athens, Petrakos, 1918. xxiv, 1283 pages.

Kretschmer, P. Rückläufiges Wörterbuch der griechischen Sprache . . . ausgearbeitet von E. Locker. Göttingen, Vandenhoeck & Ruprecht, 1944. 688 pages.

Zervos, J. Mega lexikon tes hellenikes glosses. Athens, Dimitrakos, 1933–50. 9 volumes.

The last named covers all periods from ancient to modern Greek, with examples arranged historically, but only indications are given of the language of the original term.

There has always been a certain amount of hesitation on the part of scholars to provide English-Greek lexicons—mainly because the compilation of an adequate reference work of this nature is thought to be impossible, but three small dictionaries are available for the use of students:

Edwards, Gerald Maclean. An English-Greek lexicon. 2nd edition. Cambridge University Press, 1914. xxxi, 338 pages. (reprinted in 1938).

Woodhouse, Sidney Chawner. English-Greek dictionary: a vocabulary of the Attic language. London, Routledge, 1910. viii, 1029 pages. (reprinted in 1932).

Yonge, Charles Duke. An English-Greek lexicon: edited by Henry Drisler. New York, American Book Company, 1870. 663, cxv pages. (reprinted in 1890).

The last named is of use mainly for its inclusion of dialect words.

Research into the etymology of the Greek language is recorded in a work originally compiled between 1100 and 1250, printed at Venice in 1499, and still being issued in the nineteenth century:

Etymologicon magnum, seu Magnum grammaticae penu: in quo et originum et analogie doctrina ex veterum sententia copiossisime proponitur historiae item et antiquitatis monumenta passim attinguntur; superiorum editionum variorumque auctorum collatione a multis ac foedis mendis repurgatum perpetuis notis illustratum utilissimisque indicibus verborum rerum atque auctorum numero

pene infinitorum nunc recens adauctum opera Friderici Sylburgii
. . . Editio nova correctior. Leipzig, Weigel, 1816. xv, 1092
columns.

on which, among other lexicons, was based:

Etymologicon magnum . . . Ad codd. mss. recensuit et notis
variorum instruxit Thomas Gaisford . . . Oxford University Press,
1848. 2308 columns, 2309–2470 pages.

Two more recent works are:

Prellwitz, Walther. Etymologisches Wörterbuch der griechischen
Sprache. 2nd edition. Göttingen, Vandenhoeck & Ruprecht,
1905. xxiv, 524 pages.

which contains some bibliographical references, and:

Uhle, H. Griechisches Vokabular in etymologischer Ordnung.
3rd edition. Gotha, Perthes, 1915. xiv, 107 pages.

But the most important work in this field is:

Boisacq, Emile. Dictionnaire étymologique de la langue grecque,
étudiée dans ses rapports avec les autres langues indo-européennes.
Augmentée d'un index par Helmut Rix. 4th edition. Heidelberg,
Winter, 1950. xxxii, 1256 pages.

which was first issued in 1916. The extensive index—some 130 pages—
covers all the languages cited in the text and thus gives the book additional
value for comparative philological research. Another recent but smaller
work, which includes the results of twentieth-century research, is:

Hofmann, Johann Baptist. Etymologisches Wörterbuch des Griechischen. Munich, Oldenbourg, 1949–50. 433 pages.

The compiler, who is revising the latest edition of Walde's *Lateinisches
etymologisches Wörterbuch*, is conservative in his choice of etymologies,
but more up to date than Boisacq. The latter, now out of print and
rather dated—it was first published in fascicles in 1907 and revision in
the later editions consisted mainly in the provision of new indexes—
may eventually be superseded by:

Frisk, Hjalmer. Griechisches etymologisches Wörterbuch. Heidelberg, Winter, 1954–   volume 1–

The intention of this new work (which will be completed in about
thirteen fascicles) is to avoid restricting itself to comparisons of Greek

words with cognates and corresponding words in other languages, and to trace the developments in the several dialects of classical Greek.

Four more specialised Greek dictionaries are:

Buck, Carl Darling *and* Petersen, Walter. A reverse index of Greek nouns and adjectives, arranged by terminations, with brief historical introductions. Chicago, University of Chicago Press, 1945. xvii, 765 pages.

which has over one hundred thousand entries arranged in about one hundred groups under main headings of vowel and diphthong stems, and nasal, liquid, labial, dental, guttural and palatal terminations, in reverse alphabetical order within each group. Proper names are mostly omitted. The work covers literature, inscriptions, papyri, commentators, grammarians, and lexicographers up to the Byzantine age. Some historical surveys of the more important formations are included.

Dufour, Médéric. Traité élémentaire des synonymes grecs. Paris, Colin, 1910. xvi, 208 pages.

Guethling, O. Griechisches Namenwörterbuch. Berlin, Langenscheidt, 1913. viii, 460 pages.

Schmidt, Johann Hermann Heinrich. Synonymik der griechischen Sprache. Leipzig, Teubner, 1876-86. 4 volumes.

There are a number of dictionaries devoted to the Greek of various periods. Those which are concerned with single authors, etc., are included in Hermann Schöne's *Repertorium griechischer Wörterverzeichnisse und Speziallexika* (Leipzig, Teubner, 1907. iv, 28 pages). For the Greek of the papyri and of the inscriptions, there are two dictionaries:

Herwerden, Henricus van. Lexicon graecum suppletorium et dialecticum ... revised edition. Leyden, Sijthoff, 1910. 2 volumes.

which is somewhat antiquated and not always reliable: and:

Preisigke, Friedrich. Wörterbuch der griechischen Papyrusurkunden mit Einschluss der griechischen Inschriften, Aufschriften, Ostraka, Mumienschilder, usw., aus Ägypten bearbeitet und herausgegeben von Emil Kiessling. Heidelberg, Preisigke, 1924– volume 1–

Preisigke, who was honorary Professor of Papyrology at Heidelberg, set himself to list as many references as possible to all the words which have appeared in papyrus documents, and he included many lists of

technical terms as well. There is also an index classified by topics.
For the later classical Greek, there are:

> Sophocles, Evangelinus Apostolides. Greek lexicon of the Roman
> and Byzantine periods (from 146 B.C. to A.D. 1100). Memorial
> edition. New York, Scribner, 1900. 1188 pages.

which was reprinted, under the editorship of Joseph Henry Thayer,
by Harvard University Press in 1914: and:

> Du Cange, Charles de Fresne, *Sieur*. Glossarium ad scriptores mediae
> et infimae graecitatis . . . réimp. du Collège de France. Paris,
> Geuthner, 1943. 1250 pages.

which is a reprint of the original seventeenth century work by the
compiler of the standard dictionary of mediaeval Latin (see page 94).

For the New Testament many guides have been issued, from Edward
Leigh's *Critica sacra: or, Philologicall and Theologicall Observations
upon all the Greek Words of the New Testament, in order alphabeticall:
wherein usually the etymon of the word is given, its force and emphasis
observed, and the several acceptions of it in Scripture, and versions by
Expositors are set down* (London, George Lathum, 1639. 683 pages),
to such modern works as:

> Abbott-Smith, George. A manual Greek lexicon of the New Testa-
> ment. 2nd edition. Edinburgh, Clark, 1923. xvi, 512 pages.
>
> Moulton, James Hope *and* Milligan, George. The vocabulary of the
> Greek New Testament, illustrated from the papyri and other
> non-literary sources. London, Hodder, 1930. xxxii, 705 pages.

The latter was issued in eight parts during the years 1914 to 1929.
Two other helpful works are:

> Andriotes, N. P. Etumologiko lexiko tes koines neohellenikes. Athens,
> 1951. xvi, 312 pages. (Collection de l'Institut Français
> d'Athènes, XXIV).
>
> Bauer, Walter. Griechisch-deutsches Wörterbuch zu den Schriften
> des Neuen Testaments . . . 4th edition. Berlin, Töpelmann,
> 1949– volume 1–
>
> Zorell, F. Lexicon graecum Novi Testamenti. 2nd edition. Paris,
> Lethielleux, 1931. xxiv pages, 1502 columns.

There are also plans for a comprehensive dictionary of Patristic Greek
(see *Actes du VIe Congrès International d'Etudes Byzantines*, pages 389
to 392).

For the study of modern Greek, there are a number of small dictionaries:

Jannaris, Anthony Nicholas. A concise dictionary of the English and modern Greek languages as actually written and spoken. English-Greek. New York, American Book Company, 1919. xvi, 436 pages. (a reprint of the first edition of 1895).

Kontopoulos, Nikolaos. English-modern Greek dictionary. 9th edition. Athens, Constantinides, 1928. 695 pages.

Kykkotes, Hierotheos. English-Greek and Greek-English dictionary, including English and Greek grammar, geographical and proper names and abbreviations. London, Lund Humphries, 1942. 704 pages. (reprinted 1951).

Kyriakides, A. Modern Greek-English dictionary with a Cypriote vocabulary. 2nd edition. Athens, Constantinides, 1909. 908 pages. (first published in 1892).

Missir, Emile. Dictionnaire français-roméique. 2nd edition. Paris, Klincksieck, 1952–   volume 1–

The first edition of Missir's dictionary (Smyrna, 1933) was never completed. The second, which will be in two volumes, is devoted to current written and spoken colloquial Greek, excluding its dialects.

Latin Dictionaries

The interest of the Romans in their own language was always great, and the pages of the classical authors contain many discussions and speculations concerning the origins of particular words and the changes in their meanings. Marcus Verrius Flaccus, tutor to the grandsons of Augustus, wrote a treatise devoted to this subject, *De verborum significatu*, but unfortunately this was lost. Luckily, a second-century writer, Sextus Pompeius Festus, abridged this work and, although only the second portion of his version has survived, there is also an epitome by the eighth-century author Paulus Diaconus of the complete abridgment. Both of these have been edited and reprinted in recent years:

Festus, Sextus Pompeius. Sexti Pompei Festi De verborum significatu quae supersunt cum Pauli epitome: Thewrewkianis copiis usus edidit Wallace M. Lindsay. Leipzig, Teubner, 1933. xxviii, 573 pages.

Research into the Latin language continued throughout the later centuries. The work of Jean Crespin has been mentioned at the beginning of this chapter, and in the same century that Henri Estienne published his great *Thesaurus graecae linguae* (see page 86), the elder Robert Estienne compiled:

> Estienne, Robert.   Thesaurus linguae latinae: seu, Promptuarium dictionum et loquendi formularum omnium ad latini sermonis perfectam notitiam assequendam pertinentium: ex optimis auctoribus concinnatum . . . Lyons, 1573.

In the late eighteenth century Jacopo Facciolati set his pupil Egidio Forcellini to compile a new Latin lexicon, and took most of the credit for this substantial work which was to serve as the basis for so many later dictionaries. The lexicon was first published at Padua in four volumes in 1771, and was many times reprinted with corrections and additions. The latest edition is:

> Forcellini, Egidio.   Lexicon totius latinatis, ab. Ae. Forcellini lucubratum, deinde a I. Furnalettu emendatum et auctum, nunc vero curantibus F. Corradini et I. Perrin emendatius et auctius melioremque in formam redactum. Padua, Casa ed. del Seminario, 1940. 6 volumes.

A few years later, Immanuel Johann Gerhard Scheller published his *Lexicon totius latinatis*, which J. E. Riddle revised and translated into English in the next century (Oxford University Press, 1835. viii, 1469 pages).   It was Riddle who also, with John Tahourdin White, revised Wilhelm Freund's 4-volume *Wörterbuch der lateinischen Sprache*, 1834–45, which has contributed to many modern dictionaries. A new edition of this dictionary has been published in this century:

> Freund, Wilhelm.   Grand dictionnaire de la langue latine: traduit en français et augmenté par N. Theil. réimpression. Paris, Didot, 1929. xxxii, 2729 pages.

But the greatest and the most important of modern dictionaries of the Latin language is that prepared by five great German universities:

> Thesaurus linguae latinae, editus auctoritate et consilio academiarum quinque Germanicarum Berolinensis, Gottingensis, Lipsiensis, Monacensis, Vindobonensis. Leipzig, Teubner, 1900–volume 1–

> —— Supplementum: nomina propria (onomasticon). Leipzig, Teubner, 1909–   volume 1–

—— Index librorum scriptorum inscriptionum ex quibus exempla adferuntur. Leipzig, 1904. 109 pages.

which is illustrated by copious quotations from the classical authors, and is planned to include every word used by them. Vollmer, who wrote the preface to the *Index*, started to epitomise the great *Thesaurus* into a seventh of its size in his *Epitome thesauri latini* (Leipzig, Teubner, 1912. 159 pages), but abandoned the project after the publication of the first fascicle.

The first English-Latin dictionary was Galfridus Grammaticus's *Promptorium parvulorum*, 1440, which has twice been reprinted in recent times: first, under the editorship of Albert Way, by the Camden Society (1843–65. 3 volumes); and, secondly, under the editorship of A. L. Mayhew, by the Early English Text Society (1908). One of the most influential of the early English dictionaries of the Latin language was the *Thesaurus linguae latinae compendarius*, published by Robert Ainsworth in 1736. This was reprinted in many revised editions and abridgments in the nineteenth century.* But the modern English dictionaries of the language are for the most part based on the researches of Forcellini, Freund and Scheller, and the most important of these include:

Cassell's Latin dictionary (Latin-English and English-Latin) revised by J. R. V. Marchant and Joseph F. Charles. London, Cassell, 1944. xiv, 927 pages. (frequently reprinted).

Lewis, Charlton Thomas *and* Short, Charles. Latin dictionary. new edition. Oxford, Clarendon Press, 1907. 2019 pages.

Smith, *Sir* William. A Latin-English dictionary; with tables of the Roman calendar, measures, weights, and money, and a dictionary of proper names. London, Murray, 1926. xii, 1265 pages.

Smith, *Sir* William *and* Hall, Theophilus Dwight. A copious and critical English-Latin dictionary, to which is added a dictionary of proper names. New York, Harper, 1871. xi, 1009 pages.

Woodhouse, Sidney Chawner. The Englishman's pocket Latin-English and English-Latin dictionary. London, Routledge, 1925. 491 pages.

Shorter versions have been published of Lewis and Short, and of Sir

---

* A recent scholarly study is well worth consulting: De Witt T. Starnes's *Renaissance dictionaries: English-Latin and Latin-English* (Austin, University of Texas Press; London, Nelson, 1954. xii, 428 pages).

William Smith's dictionaries. Two modern French dictionaries of the Latin language are also of importance to translators:

> Benoist, Eugène *and* Goelzer, Henri. Nouveau dictionnaire latin-français ... 11th edition. Paris, Garnier, 1934. xxxvi, 1682 pages.

> Gaffiot, Félix. Dictionnaire illustré latin-français. Paris, Hachette, 1934. 1702 pages.

At the present time there is in preparation the *Oxford Latin dictionary* which, like Liddell and Scott, will include the results of the latest researches in the classical field.

The Latin of the first part of the Christian era is covered in part by the great dictionaries of mediaeval Latin, and specifically by:

> Souter, Alexander. A glossary of later Latin to A.D. 600. Oxford, Clarendon Press, 1949. xxxii, 454 pages.

which has nearly forty thousand entries, covering the literature from A.D. 180, and will serve as a supplement to the projected *Oxford Latin dictionary* from which Christian authors are being excluded.

The standard dictionary of mediaeval Latin is:

> Du Cange, Charles du Fresne, *Sieur*. Glossarium mediae et infimae Latinatis . . . auctum a monachis ordinis S. Benedicti; cum supplementis integris D. P. Carpenterii, Adelungii, aliorum, suisque digessit G. A. L. Henschel. Sequunter glossarium gallicum, tabulae, indices auctorum et rerum, dissertationes. Editio nova, aucta pluribus verbis aliorum scriptorum a Léopold Favre. Niort, Favre, 1883–87. 10 volumes. (reprinted in five volumes, Graz, Akademische Druck- & Verlagsanstalt, 1954).

> —— Petit supplément au Dictionnaire de Du Cange, par C. Schmidt. 1906. 71 pages.

Du Cange published his great dictionary in Paris in 1678, and there have been many later and revised editions, but little has been added since the nineteenth century, and the International Union of Academies is now preparing its *Dictionnaire du latin médiéval*, of which the first volume is almost ready. The British Academy felt that the projected work would not sufficiently cover mediaeval British Latin, and it is therefore preparing its own dictionary, of which the first fruits are:

> Baxter, James Houston *and* Johnson, Charles. Mediaeval Latin word-list from British and Irish sources, prepared . . . with the assistance of Phyllis Abrahams . . . under the direction of a

committee appointed by the British Academy. Oxford University Press, 1934. xiii, 466 pages. (reprinted in 1947).

Similarly, Professor Niermeyer, forseeing that the great dictionary would take many years to complete, has compiled:

Niermeyer, J. F. Mediae latinatis lexicon minus: a medieval Latin-French/English dictionary. Leiden, Brill, 1954– volume 1–

which is to be completed in six to eight fascicles of 96 pages each. It is designed to act as "a compendious lexicon for rapid information", and provides copious brief quotations from charters, histories, specialist dictionaries, etc., mainly of the period 550 to 1150, with dates and places of origin given wherever possible. The vocabulary of later Latin, insofar as it appears in mediaeval writings, is incorporated, with quotations in exceptional cases. "Syntax as well as grammatical matter has been deliberately neglected," and etymology only indicated.

Other useful dictionaries of mediaeval Latin include:

Arnaldi, Francesco. Latinitatis italicae medii aevi inde ab a. CDLXXVI usque ad a. MXXII lexicon imperfectum . . . cura et studio Mariae Turriani . . . Brussels, 1936– volume 1– (Union Académique International. Bulletin Du Cange Archivium latinitatis medii aevi, volume 10).

Castro, Américo. Glosarios latino-españoles de la edad media. Madrid, Hernando, 1936. 378 pages. (Revista de filología española, anejo XXII).

Habel, E. Mittellateinisches Glossar: unter Mitwirking von F. Groebel. Paderborn, Schöningh, 1931. viii, 432 columns.

Maigne d'Arnis, W. H. Lexicon manuale ad scriptores mediae et infimae latinatis ex glossariis Caroli Dufresne, D. Ducangii, D. P. Carpenterii, Adelungii, et aliorum, in compendium accuratissime redactum; ou, Recueil de mots de la basse latinité, dressé pour servir à l'intelligence des auteurs, soit sacrés, soit profanes, du moyên âge. Paris, Migne, 1866. 2336 columns. (reprinted in 1890).

Most of the important research into the etymology of the Latin language was carried out in the nineteenth century. Johann Matthias had published his *Index etymologicus latinitatis* as early as 1749: it was undertaken as a new edition of Estienne, but it was in effect a new work. The most outstanding work on this subject was until recently:

Walde, Alois. Lateinisches etymologisches Wörterbuch. 3rd edition. Heidelberg, Winter, 1938– volume 1–

which was originally published in 1906. Edited by J. B. Hofmann, it lays practically all its emphasis on the etymology of Latin words as related to Indo-European, giving the first appearance of each Latin word in the ancient documents, and stating whether it survived into the Romance period. Many Greek and other loan words are included for the first time. Derivatives are listed under the primitives.

Frederik Müller originally planned to contribute an Italic volume to the proposed continuation of Fick's *Vergleichendes Wörterbuch der indogermanischen Sprachen*, the fourth edition of which (Göttingen, 1890–1909) was never completed. Out of this project grew:

> Müller, Frederik. Altitalisches Wörterbuch. Göttingen, Vanden-hoeck & Ruprecht, 1926. vii, 583 pages.

Müller did not intend to include every Latin word, but only those which might justly be termed 'old Italic'. The material is arranged under reconstructed Primitive Italic captions, and earliest meanings and place of first appearance are given together with any survivals in the Romance languages. Müller pays greater attention to the history of Italic words than does Walde, but omits words subsequently borrowed by Latin, Oscan or Umbrian.

The most important recent etymological dictionary of the Latin language is:

> Ernout, Alfred *and* Meillet, Antoine. Dictionnaire étymologique de la langue latine: histoire des mots. new edition. Paris, Klinck-sieck, 1951. 2 volumes.

Ernout was primarily responsible for the history within Latin, and Meillet for the comparative material. Their work does not attempt to replace Walde or Müller, their aim being to give an historical account of the Latin vocabulary by demonstrating the morphological and sema-siological development from the time of the earliest inscriptions down to the Romance period, and the development of the Latin vocabulary from the time of the common Indo-European language until the period when Latin had established itself as a separate language. Copious references are given to the works of the classical authors, and to inscriptions and glosses, borrowed words being included.

Other etymological dictionaries of the Latin language include:

> Bréal, Michel Jules Alfred *and* Bailly, Anatole. Dictionnaire étymologique latin: les mots latins groupés d'après le sens et l'étymologie. Paris, Hachette, 1855. viii, 463 pages.

Körting, Gustav. Lateinisch-romanisches Wörterbuch (etymologisches Wörterbuch der romanischen Hauptsprachen). 3rd edition. Paderborn, Schöningh, 1907. vi, 1374 columns. (reprinted, New York, Stechert, 1923).

For the use of students of records and inscriptions, there are several important aids:

Capelli, Adriano. Lexicon abbreviaturarum . . . 4th edition. Milan, Hoepli, 1949. lxxiii, 531 pages.

This includes about fourteen thousand Latin and Italian abbreviations, with special reference to the Middle Ages, roman and arabic numerals, and signs referring to money, the calendar, and measures. Probably the most valuable part of the work is its reproduction of the abbreviations in manuscript form. A nineteenth century Assistant Keeper of the Public Records prepared:

Martin, Charles Trice. The record interpreter: a collection of abbreviations, Latin words and names used in English historical manuscripts and records. 2nd edition. London, Stevens, 1910. xv, 464 pages.

which includes abbreviations of French words as well as the Latin forms of British place and personal names. Another outstanding work is:

Olcott, George N. Thesaurus linguae latinae epigraphicae: a dictionary of the Latin inscriptions.

The first twenty-two fascicles of this work were published by the firm of Loescher in Rome during the years 1904 to 1912. After Olcott's death, publication was suspended until 1935 when Columbia University Press in New York took over the handling of the original fascicles and started the completion of the work. Olcott includes proper names, and gives valuable information concerning the dates of different words. His work is sometimes known as the *Olcott dictionary of Latin inscriptions*.

For a more detailed listing of dictionaries of the classical languages, and more especially for information relating to dictionaries devoted to particular authors, the following will be found of use:

Faider, Paul. Répertoire des index et des lexiques d'auteurs latins. Paris, Société d'édition " Belles-Lettres ", 1926. (Société des Etudes Latines. Collection d'Etudes Latines, no. III).

Rowald, Paul. Repertorium lateinischer Wörterverzeichnisse und Speziallexika. Supplementum auctorum latinorum. Leipzig, Teubner, 1913. 22 pages.

Rowald includes etymological dictionaries and onomastica and diction-aries of the Italic dialects, mediaeval Latin and inscriptions. In addition, the important annual bibliography, *L'Année philologique*, records new dictionaries, and new editions of classical dictionaries, as soon as they appear. An English aid, the Classical Association's *Year's work in classical studies*, was unfortunately discontinued soon after the war, but the new *Linguistic bibliography* (*see* Bibliography, page 191) pays much attention to new work and criticism in the classics.

DICTIONARIES OF THE LANGUAGES OF THE BALTIC, THE BALKANS AND CENTRAL EUROPE

One of the characteristics which the languages in this chapter have in common is that they are each an example of the struggle for nationhood in Europe during the past centuries. Language is in fact one of the principal features in the struggle for power, and the rise or survival of a national tongue is clear evidence of the decline in control of the ruling country. That the great powers realised this is shown in their constant attempts to suppress all evidence of the languages and dialects of the countries over which they had sway, and there is much testimony to prove that their measures were so thorough and so effective that many tongues—such as Serbian—only survived through the tenacity of oral tradition. Thus Latvia, which suffered from numerous occupations, might not have had a distinctive language of its own had it not been for the efforts of the seventeenth century German Lutheran pastors who, without any idea that they were helping to foster a nationalistic spirit, compiled vocabularies and dictionaries of the Latvian language for the use of their newer colleagues. The harm which was wrought by foreign invaders is shown too in the difficulty which the philologists experienced in freeing themselves from the insidious influence of their rulers—even as late as 1904, when Gérov and Pánchev completed the first Bulgarian dictionary, their work showed evidence of strong Russian influence: and after Alexander II of Russia, when opening the new Diet, had granted a decree in 1863 awarding equal place to Finnish and Swedish in Finland, that country had great difficulty in ridding itself of Swedish idiom, owing to the use which had previously been made of the Swedish language in official circles.

Partly for the same reasons, in most of the languages lexicographical development was late: in Albania there was no written literature earlier than Don Gjon Buzuku's Litany of 1555 (of which a single manuscript survives in the Vatican); and the first Albanian dictionary, Father Francesco Blanco's *Dictionarium latino-epiroticum*—a five thousand word vocabulary with grammatical rules compiled for the use of the clergy—was not published in Rome until 1635. The first Latvian vocabularies were not issued until after 1685; and in Poland it was only

99

the intervention of Bishop Józef Zaluski which made possible the publications of the first Polish dictionary in 1744.

The action of the clergy in promoting the compilation of vocabularies and grammars was inspired by their desire to furnish their newly-arrived brethren with the means of communicating with the people of the country, and was therefore a missionary effort on the part of a colonising power. Quite different is the type of dictionary compiled by the first nationalists when they in their turn began to publish their own lexicons. In contrast to the lexicographical history of most of the larger countries of Europe, the countries dealt with in this chapter rarely achieved the compilation of any substantial dictionary before the nineteenth century: a fact which is hardly surprising when it is remembered, for instance, that Croatia only adopted the use of its own language, instead of Latin, in its communications with the Habsburgs, in 1843, that Slovak was not revived as a literary language until 1844, and that officials were not required to use the Czech language in answer to Czech requests until 1886. Add to this that the universities ignored these languages until very recent times, that local philologists had little communication with their colleagues in other countries, and that they lacked experience, and the reasons for lexicographical lacunae become painfully apparent.

As far as the Slav countries are concerned, much of the lexicographical work of the nineteenth century is due to the pioneer efforts of the great Czech priest Father Joseph Dobrovsky (1753–1829), who urged the necessity for undertaking the serious study of Slav culture and laid the foundations of Slavic philological investigation with his *Institutiones linguae slavica veteris dialecti*, 1821, a study of Old Church Slavonic. His friend, Jérnej Kopîtar (1780–1844), a Slovene, a member of the staff of the Hofbibliothek at Vienna and chief censor for the Slavic languages, was responsible for the encouragement of the greatest of the philologists, the patriot Vuk Stefanović Karadžić (1787–1864). The latter was the father of the modern Serbo-Croat tongue; lacking any formal education of his own, but steeped in the folklore of his country, and aided by the all-powerful Kopîtar, he introduced the use of the Cyrillic alphabet for Serbian and published his *Lexicon serbico-germanico-latinum* in 1818 (3rd edition, issued in 1898, is still a very useful work).

Then there was Stanislaw Staszyc (1755–1826) who, with a group of friends, started at the beginning of the nineteenth century a Society for the Promotion of Learning in Warsaw, which in turn gave birth to the first dictionary of Polish in modern times, compiled by the German Samuel Bogumil Linde; and Teodoro di Elbasàn who compiled an Albanian dictionary at the end of the eighteenth century. But other countries were not so fortunate: for instance, in the case of Latvia, it was not until the foundation of the Latvian State University in 1919 that Latvian philology really came into its own.

Among other influences must be mentioned that of the youthful Sreznevsky during his linguistic odyssey in Istria and Dalmatia, and that of three great philologists: Miklosich, Jungmann and Daničić. Franz Miklosich (1813-1891), a Slovene and a friend of Kopîtar, inherited Dobrovsky's mantle and by his grammars and in particular his *Lexicon linguae palaeo-slovenicae*, 1865, exerted a welcome influence on the paths which Slavic studies were then taking. Josef Jungmann (1773–1847), the literary historian, compiled the great dictionary of the Czech language, and George Daničić continued Karadžić's work and laid the foundations of the great Serbo-Croat dictionary.

Albanian

Christophoridis, Konstantin. Lexikon tes albanikes glosses. Athens, Sakellarious, 1904. iv, 504 pages. (Albanian-Greek only. The best and most scholarly Albanian dictionary. Slav borrowings relegated to an appendix; Turkish omitted).

Drizari, Nelo. Fjalór Shquip-Inglisht dhe Inglisht-Shqip: Albanian-English and English-Albanian dictionary. New York, Nassy, 1934. v, 313 pages.

Godin, Marie Amelie, *Freiin von*. Wörterbuch der albanischen und deutschen Sprache. Leipzig, Harrassowitz, 1930. (volume 1 only: deutsch-albanisch).

Leotti, Angelo. Dizionario albanese-italiano. Rome, Istituto per l'Europa Orientale, 1937. 1710 pages.

Mann, Stuart Edward. An historical Albanian and English dictionary (1496–1938). London, Longmans, for the British Council, 1948. ix, 601 pages.

Meyer, Gustav. Etymologisches Wörterbuch der albanesischen Sprache. Strasbourg, Trübner, 1891. xiii, 526 pages.

Roques, Mario. Le dictionnaire albanais de 1635 édité, avec introduction et index complet. Paris, Geuthner, 1932. 224 pages. (a reprint of Bianchi's *Dictionarium Latino-Epiroticum* of 1635, the first volume to contain specimens of the Albanian language).

Bulgarian

Andrejčin, Liubomir D. Dictionnaire orthographique de la langue bulgare. Sofia, Hemus, 1945. 168 pages.

Balabanov, Al. *and* Rusev, Rusi. Dzheben anglo-bŭlgarski rechnik. 3rd edition. Sofia, Dŭrzhavno izd-vo, 1946. 374 pages.

Bogorov, Ivan A.   Frensko-bulgarski, bulgarski-frenski riechnik. Vienna, Sommerov, 1869-71. 2 volumes.

Chakalov, G'ocho G. English-Bulgarian dictionary. Sofia, Military Publishing Fund, 1948. 1229 pages.

Derzhavin, Nikolai Sevast'ianovich.   Bolgarsko-russkiĭ slovar'; sostavili; S. B. Bernshteĭn, T. S. Lukanov, E. P. Tineva. Moscow, Gos. izd-vo inostr. i. nats. slovareĭ, 1947. 495 pages.

Gerov, Nayden.   Riechnik na bl''garskyi iazyk s tl''kuvanie riechi-ty na bl''garsky i na russky. S''bral, nariadil i na sviet izvazhda Naiden Gerov.   Plovdiv, Druzhestvena pechat S''glasie, 1895– 1904. 5 volumes.

—— Supplement. 1908. 336 pages.

Ghennadiew, Chariton. Grand dictionnaire français-bulgare. Philippopoli, Danoff, 1910. 1134 pages.

Miladinov, Ivan An.   Deutsch-bulgarisches [bulgarisch-deutsches] Wörterbuch. 2nd edition. Sofia, the author, 1912–15. 2 volumes.

Mladenov, Stefan. Bălgarski tălkoven rečnik. Sofia, Stefanov, 1939– volume 1–

Mladenov, Stefan. Etimologičeski i pravopisen rečnik na bălgarskija knižoven ezik. Sofia, Danov, 1941. xviii, 704 pages.

Mladenov, Stefan. Rečnik na čuždite dumi v bălgarskija ezik. 3rd edition. Sofia, Chemus, 1947. 491 pages. (a dictionary of foreign words in the Bulgarian language).

Nanov, L. Bălgarski sinonimen rečnik. 2nd edition. Sofia, Mauka i Izkustva, 1950. 684 pages.

Pavlov, Ch. Pravopisnik na balgarskija knizoven ezik s objasnitelen rečnik. 8th edition. Sofia, Narodna Prosveta, 1947 (published in 1949). 217 pages.

Rusev, Rusi. Bŭlgaro-angliĭski rechnik. Sofia, Dŭrzhavno izd-vo, 1947. 235 pages. (reprinted 1953).

Stephanove, Constantine. Complete Bulgarian-English [and English-Bulgarian] dictionary. Sofia, Nickoloff, 1914; Haemus, 1929. 2 volumes.

Czech

Čermák, Alois. Nový kapesní slovník anglicko-český a česko-anglický. 2nd edition. Trebíč, Lorenzi; Milwaukee, Caspar, 1932. 2 volumes in 1.

Cheshire, Harold T. *and others.* Česko-anglický slovník . . . Czech-English dictionary . . . compiled by H. T. Cheshire, V. Jung, L. Klozner and others. Prague, Nakladatelství J. Otto, 1933–35. 2 volumes.

Gebauer, Jan. Slovník staročeský. Vidávají Česka Akademie Císare Františka Josefa pro vědy, slovesnost a uměnií a Česká grafická společnost "Unie." Prague, 1901–13. (2 volumes in 17 parts, never completed. A dictionary of Old Czech).

Holub, Josef *and* Kopecny, Frantisek. Etymologický slovník jazyka českého. Prague, Státní Nakladatelství Učebnic, 1952. 575 pages. (based on Holub's *Stručný slovník etymologický jazyka československého*, 1933, of which a second edition was published in 1937).

Janko, J. *and* Siebenschein, H. Příruční slovník německo-česky. Prague, Státní Nakladatelství, 1938–48. 4 volumes. (comprehensive German-Czech dictionary).

Jonas, Karel. Slovník česko-anglický s úplnou anglickou výslovností. A Bohemian and English dictionary. Vydáni se všeobecným doplňkem. 5th edition. Chicago, Pancner, 1946. 621 pages. (first published in 1918).

Jung, Vaclav Alois. Slovník-anglicko-český. Dictionary of the English and Bohemian languages. 2nd edition. Prague, Otto, 1923. 1564 pages.

Kott, František Štěpán. Česko-německý slovník zvláště grammaticko-fraseologický. Prague, Kolář, 1878–93. 7 volumes.

Krupička, František *and* Procházka, Jindřich. A dictionary of the English and Czech languages, giving pronunciation of all words, with special regard to idiomatic phrases and phraseology of commercial correspondence. 11th–13th editions. Prague, Kvasnička & Hampl, 1946. 2 volumes in 1.

Mašín, J. *and* Bečka, J. V. Malý slovník českých synonym. 1947.

Mourek, Václav Emanuel. Kapesní slovník-jazyka českého i anglického. 3rd edition. Leipzig, Holtze, 1920. 2 volumes.

Pech, Vilém. Velký slovník cizích slov, rčení a zkratek v jazyce psaném i mluveném ze všech oborů lidskeho vědění a konání. Prague, Kvasnicka & Hampl, 1948. x, 809 pages.

Příruční slovník jazyka českého: vydává třetí třída České Akademie věd a umění. Sestavuje ústav pro jazyk český. Redigují: B. Havránek, V. Šmilauer, A. Získal. Prague, Státní Nakladatelství,

1947–   volume 1–   (the dictionary of the Czech Academy, first published in 1935).

Procházka, Jindřich *and* Hokeš, Jaroslav. Kapesní slovník anglicko-český a česko-anglický s připojenou výslovností. 14th edition. Prague, Kvasnička & Hampl, 1950. 2 volumes. (cf. Krupička & Procházka *supra*).

Šimek, F. Slovníček staré češtiny. 1947. (a dictionary of mediaeval Czech).

Trávníček, František. Slovník jazyka českého. Čtvrte, přepracované a dopelněné vydání. Prague, Slovanské Nakladatelství, 1952. xvi, 1801 pages. (a revised edition of Pavel Váša and F. Trávníček's *Slovník jazyka českého*, 1935–36. 3rd edition, 1946).

Zaorálek, J. Lidová rčení. Prague, Borový, 1947. xxiv, 741 pages. (idioms and proverbial phrases).

Estonian

Grenzstein, A. Eesti sõnaraamat. 1600 uut ja wôerast sôna korjanud ja (Saksa sôna lisandusega) eesti keeles selgitanud . . . Tartu, Oma Trükk ja Kirjastus, 1884. 90, xiv pages.

Muuk, Elmar. Väike õigekeelsus-sõnaraamat. 9th edition. Stockholm, Eesti Raamat, 1947. 459 pages.

Neumann, Minkel. Sistematikaline eesti-inglise sõnaraamat. Tallinn, Zwetkow & Kitzel, 1924. viii, 191 pages. (cover date 1925).

Pöhl, Hans. Inglise-eesti sõnaraamat. Tallinn, Pihlakas, 1927. xxv, 732 pages.

Silvet, J. Inglise-eesti sõnaraamat. Vadstena, Eesti Kirjastus Orto, 1949. 1207 pages.

Vrangel', M. Dictionnaire estonien-français. Revu par Joh. Aavik et Oskar Peters. Tallinn, Istandik, 1932. 350 pages.

Villecourt, Louis. Dictionnaire français-estonien. Tartu, 1930. lxx, 577 pages.

Wiedemann, Ferdinand Johann. Eesti-saksa sõnaraamat . . . Estnisch-deutsches Wörterbuch. 2nd edition, 3rd impression. Tartu, Eesti Kirjanduse Seltsi Kirjastus, 1923. xxxix, 703, clx pages. (first published in 1865).

Finnish

N.B.—An interesting but brief account of the development of Finnish dictionaries is given in W. R. Mead's " Anglo-Finnish cultural relations " (*Norseman*, volume 6, 1948. page 377).

Alanne, Severi. Suomalais-englantilainen sanakirja. Finnish-English dictionary. Superior, Wisconsin, Työmies Kustannusyhtiön Kustannuksella, 1919. 957 pages.

Cannelin, Knut Leopold. Suomalais-ruotsalainen sanakirja. Finskt-svenskt lexikon. 6th–8th editions. Poorvoo, Söderström, 1943–47. viii, 960 pages.

Nyksuomen sanakirja. Helsinki, Söderström, 1951– volume 1– (contemporary Finnish. Published with the aid of the Finnish government. To be completed in 6 volumes. Numerous examples given).

Perret, Jean Louis *and* Nurmela, T. Suomalais-franskalainen sanakirja. Dictionnaire finnois-français. Helsinki, Suomalaisen Kirjallisuuden Seura, 1944. x, 1016 pages.

Schreck, Inez. English-Finnish dictionary. Poorvoo, 1921.

Swan, Carl Gustaf *and* Granström, Hanna. English and Finnish dictionary. Helsinki, Suomalais Kirjallis. Seuran Kirjapainon Osakeyhtiö, 1904. ix, 1218 pages. (the first English-Finnish dictionary).

Tuomikoski, Aune *and* Slöör, Anna. Englantilais-suomalainen sanakirja. 2nd edition. Helsinki, Suomalaisen Kirjallisuuden Seura,* 1948. xiii, 1100 pages. (first published 1939).

Vuolle, Aino. Finnish-English, English-Finnish dictionary. Helsinki, Söderström, 1951–52. 2 volumes. (first published in 1940). (Author's surname given as Wuolle on title-page).

Hungarian

Balassa, József. A magyar nyelv szótára. Budapest, Grill, 1940. 2 volumes.

Ballagi, Mór. Neues vollständiges ungarisches und deutsches Wörterbuch. Új teljes magyar és német szótár. 7th edition. Budapest, Franklin-Társulat, 1905. 2 volumes.

Bárczi, Géza. Magyar szófejtö szótár. Budapest, Magyar Egyetemi Nyomda, 1941. 371 pages. (concise etymological dictionary).

* i.e. The Finnish Literary Society.

Biró, Lajos Pál *and* Willer, József. Angol-magyar és magyar-angol iskolai és kéziszótár. 10th edition. Budapest, Athenaeum, 194 . 663 pages.

Bizonfy, Ferencz de Paula. English-Hungarian and Hungarian-English dictionary. Budapest, Franklin-Társulat, 1886. 971 pages.

Czuczor, Gergely István *and* Fogarasi, János. A magyar nyelv szótára. A magyar tudományos akadémia megbiszásából. Pest, Magyar Akademiai Nyomdásznál, 1862–74. 6 volumes.

Gombocz, Zoltán *and* Melich, John. Magyar etymologiai szótár. (Lexicon critico-etymologicum linguae hungaricae). Budapest, Académie des Sciences Hongroises, 1914–   volume 1–

James, E. W. New dictionary of the English and Hungarian languages. Budapest, Stampfel-Féle Könyvkia-dóhivatal, 1914. (volume 1 only: English-Hungarian).

Országh, László. Angol-magyar kéziszótár. Budapest, Franklin-Társulat, 1948. xi, 791 pages.

Országh, László. Magyar-angol szótár. Budapest, Franklin-Társulat, 1953. 1350 pages.

Szarvas, Gábor *and* Simonyi, Zsigmond. Magyar nyelv-történeti szótár a legrégibb nyelvemlékektöl a nyelvújításig. A Magyar Tudományos Akadémia Megbizásából szerkesztették . . . Budapest, Hornyánsky, 1890–93. 3 volumes.

Welsh, T. E. *and others*. English-Hungarian [and Hungarian-English] dictionary, by T. E. Welsh, L. Joó and D. Lee de Lisle. Debrecen, " Méliusz " Könyukereskedés, 1948. 2 volumes.

Yolland, Arthur Battishall. A dictionary of the Hungarian and English languages. Budapest, Franklin-Társulat, 1937. 2 volumes in 3. (first published in 1905).

Latvian

Blese, E. Batgalve: dictionnaire lette-français. Riga, 1941. lxxx, 876 pages.

Brants, Kārlis *and* Matthews, William K. A Latvian-English dictionary edited by P. Schmidt. Riga, Gulbis, 1930. 420 pages.

Lusis, J. Dictionary of Latvian, English and German languages. I: Latvian-English-German. Kempten (Allgäu), Volkswirtschaftlicher Verlag, 1946. 321 pages.

Mülenbachs, Kārlis. Latviešu valodas vārdnīca. Redigējis, papil-
dinājis, turpinājis J. Endzelīns . . . Izdevusi Izglītības ministrija.
Riga, Kultura Fonda Izdevums, 1923–32. 4 volumes.

—— Papildinājumi un labojumi K. Mülenbacha Latviešu valodas
vārdnīcai. Riga, 1934– volume 1–

Roze, Klaudija. An English-Latvian [and Latvian-English] dictionary. Riga, the author, 1946. 2 volumes. (first published in 1931).

Rūke, V. Latviešu valodas pareizrakstības vārdnīca. Papildināts un
pārlabots otrs izdevums. 2nd edition. Riga, Latvju Gramata,
1944. 107 pages.

Turkina, Eiženija. Angliski-latviska vārdnīca. Ar fonetisku izrunu,
grammatiku, īpatnējiem izteicieniem izteicieniem un saīsinājumu
paskaidrojumiem. Vārdnīcā ir ap 30,000 vārdu. Riga, Latvijas
Valsts Izdevniecība, 1948. 1062 pages.

Turkina, Eiženija. Latviska-angliska vārdnīca. Riga, Latvijas
Valsts Izdevniecība, 1948. 392 pages.

Ulmann, Carl Christian *and* Braschke, G. Lettisches Wörterbuch.
Riga, Brutzer, 1872–80. 2 volumes.

Lithuanian

Balčikonis, J. Lietuvos kalbos žodynas. Vilna, Institut de Langue
Lituanienne de l'Académie Lituanienne des Sciences et des
Lettres, 1941. xxiv, 1008 pages.

Lalis, Anthony. Dictionary of the Lithuanian and English languages.
3rd edition. Chicago, Lietuvos, 1910–15. 2 volumes in 1. (first
published in 1903).

Niedermann, Max *and others*. Wörterbuch der litauischen Schriftsprache: litauisch-deutsch, bearbeitet von Max Niedermann,
Alfred Senn, Franz Brender, Anton Salys . . . Heidelberg, Winter,
1926– volume 1– (current literary language with carefully
chosen examples. No historical, etymological or dialectical
treatment).

Peteraitis, Vilius. Lithuanian-English dictionary. Brooklyn, N.Y.,
Gabija, 1948. xv, 579 pages. (concise edition, 1949).

Pewtress, Harry Howard *and* Gerikas, T. Marlborough's English-
Lithuanian and Lithuanian-English dictionary. London, Marlborough, 1939. 333 pages.

Polish

Booch-Arkossy, Friedrich Wilhelm. Neues vollständiges polnisch-deutsches und deutsch-polnisches Wörterbuch. Leipzig, Haessel, 1913. 2 volumes.

Brückner, Alexander. Slownik etymologiczny języka polskiego. Cracow, 1927.

Chodzko, Aleksandr Borejko. Dokładny słownik polsko-angielski i angielsko-polski, czerpany z najlepszych zródeł krajowych i obcych a mianowicie ze słowników polskich . . . Chicago, Polish American Book Publishing Company, 191 . 2 volumes in 1. (first published 1874).

Karłowicz, Jan Aleksandr Ludwik August *and others.* Słownik języka polskiego: utożony pod redakcją Jana Karłowicza, Adama Kryńskiego i Władysławo Niedźwiedzkiego. Warsaw, Nakładem Prenumeratorów i Kasy Im. Mianowskiego, 1900–27. 8 volumes. (republished in 1952 by the Państwowy Instytut Wydawniczy of Warsaw).

Kierst, Władysław *and* Callier, Oskar. A new pronouncing English-Polish and Polish-English dictionary. Philadelphia, McKay, 1942. 2 volumes in 1.

Konarski, Franciszek *and others.* Vollständiges Handwörterbuch der deutschen und polnischen Sprache, bearbeitet von Franz Konarski, Adolf Inlender, Felix Goldscheider und Albert Zipper. Vienna, Perles, 1897–1908. 4 volumes.

Lam, Stanisław. Trzaski, Everta i Michalskiego encyklopedyczny słownik wyrazów obcych pochodzenie wyrazów, wymowa, objaśnienia pojęć, skroty, przyslowia, cytaty. Warsaw, Trzaski, Everta i Michalskiego, 1939. 2445 columns.

Lilien, Ernest. Lilien's dictionary . . . Buffalo, N.Y., Wydawnictwa słownika Liliena, 1944–   volume 1–

Linde, Samuel Bogumił. Słownik języka polskiego . . . Wydanie drugie, poprawne i pomnozone, staraniem i nakładem Zakładu Narodowego Imienia Ossolińskich. Lwów, 1854–60. 6 volumes. (first published 1807–14; reprinted, Warsaw, Państwowy Instytut Wydawniczy, 1951).

Rykaczewski, Erazm. A complete dictionary, English and Polish and Polish and English. Berlin, Behr; London, Barthès & Lowell, 1849–51. 2 volumes.

Stanisławski, Jan. English-Polish and Polish-English dictionary, Philadelphia, McKay, 1940. 2 volumes in 1. (reprinted 1945 and 1947).

Sławski, F. Słownik etymologiczny języka polskiego. Cracow, Nakl. Tow. Milosnikov Jezika Polskiego, 1952– volume 1–

Szober, Stanisław. Słownik poprawnej polszczyzny. Warsaw, Wiedza, 1948. xvi, 662 pages. (first edition published in 1938 under the title: *Słownik ortoepiczny*).

Rumanian

Academia Română, *Bucharest*. Dictionarul limbiĭ române, întocmit şi publicat dupa îndemnul maiestătii Sale Regelui Carol I. Bucharest, Impr. Nationala, 1913– volume 1– (includes archaic, regional and literary forms, gives etymological explanations, and many examples to illustrate different meanings and use).

Axelrad, Philip. Complete Roumanian-English dictionary. Philadelphia, McKay, 1942. xxxvi, 532 pages. (reprint of first edition of 1918).

Cihac, Alexandru. Dictionnaire d'étymologie daco-romane, éléments slaves, magyars, turcs, grecs-moderne et albanaic. Frankfurt, St. Goar, 1879. xxiv, 816 pages.

Damé, Frédéric. Nouveau dictionnaire roumain-français. Bucharest, Impr. de l'Etat, 1893. 4 volumes.

Halaceanu, Virgil Em. The great dictionary of the Roumanian and English languages. Jassy, Typ. " Dacia ", Iliescu & Grossu, 19–. volume 1–.

Lolliot, Henry L. Dicţionar englez-român . . . Opera tiparita cu cheltuiala statului. Bucharest, Impr. Statului, 19 . 2 volumes.

Schönkron, Marcel. Rumanian-English and English-Rumanian dictionary. With supplement of new words, English-Rumanian. New York, Ungar, 1952. 2 volumes in 1.

Titkin, H. Rumänisch-deutsches Wörterbuch. Bucharest, 1903–25. 3 volumes.

Serbian and Serbo-Croatian

Barić, H. Rečnik srpskoga ili hrvatskoga i arabanaskoga jezika. Zagreb, Izdavački Zavod Jugoslavenske Akad., 1950– volume 1–

Bogadek, Francis Aloysius. English-Croatian and Croatian-English dictionary. London, Allen & Unwin, 1950. vii, 497 pages. (published as 3rd edition. New York, 1949).

Cvetanović, Ratimir J. Rečnik englesko-srpskohrvatski i srpskohrvatsko-engleski sa engleskom gramatikom. A pocket dictionary, English-Serbocroatian and Serbocroatian-English, with English grammar. Sarajevo, 1952. 751 pages.

Drvodelić, Milan. Hrvatsko-engleski [englesko-hrvatski] rječnik. Zagreb, 1953–54. 2 volumes.

Lochmer, Alexander. Englesko-hrvatski rječnik. Senj, Hreljanovic, 1906. 1112 pages.

Petrović, Ilija M. Praktičan englesko-srpski rečnik. 2nd edition. Belgrade, Prosveta, 1951. xxx, 770 pages. (first published in 1933).

Popović, Georg. Wörterbuch der serbischen und deutschen Sprache. 2nd edition. Pancova, Jovanovic, 1886–95. 2 volumes.

Rječnik hrvatskoga ili srpskoga jezika, na svijet izdaje Jugoslavenska Akademija znanosti i umjetnosti. Obraduje D. Daničić. Zagreb, Hartman, 1880– volume 1– (the great dictionary of the Academy at Zagreb).

Ristic, Svetomir and Kangrga, Jowan. Wörterbuch der serbokroatischen und deutschen Sprache. Belgrade, Rajkovic & Cukovic, 1928. (volume 2 only: Serbokroatisch-deutsch. 1263 pages).

Slovak

Hrobak, Philip A. Hrobak's English-Slovak dictionary. Middletown, Pa., Jednota Printery, 1944. xxx, 702 pages.

Jánošík, A. and Jóna, E. Slovník spisovného jazyka slovenského. Turčiánsky, Sv. Martin, Matica Slovenská, 1949.

Kálal, Miroslav. Slovenský slovník z literatúry aj nárečí. Banská Bystrica, Tlačou Slovenskeygrafie, 1924–26. ciii, 1012 pages.

Slovene

Glonar, Joža. Slovar slovenskega jezika. Ljubljana, Umetniška Propaganda, 1936. 496 pages.

Isačenko, A. V. Slovensko-ruský prekladový slovník. 1951– volume 1–

Kern, Frank Jauhi.   A pronouncing English-Slovene dictionary for general use. Cleveland, American Home Publishing Company, 1944. 273 pages. (first published in 1919).

Kotnik, Janko. Slovensko-angleski slovar. revised edition. Ljubljana, Državna založba Slovenije, 1952. 697 pages. (first published in 1945).

Škerlj, Ružena. English-Slovene dictionary. 3rd edition.   Ljubljana, Državna založba Slovenije, 1953. viii, 695 pages.

Slovenski pravopis. Ljubljana, Slovenska Akad. Znanosti in umetnosti, 1950. 935 pages.

LANGUAGES OF THE NEAR AND MIDDLE EAST

From the earliest times there has been considerable interest in the languages of the various countries of the Near and Middle East, both among the inhabitants of those countries and among the Westerners who came to trade or do battle in those regions. Arabic, for instance, has a long history of dictionary-making and vocabulary-compiling for well over a thousand years, and it was on the best of these compilations that Lane was one day to base his own work. Indeed, it is surprising that no comprehensive dictionary of English and Arabic or of French and Arabic was forthcoming from the Crusaders' long stay in the Levant. Nor were two later travellers—Lady Hester Stanhope or Sir Richard Burton—more helpful, though the latter contributed perhaps even more handsomely by the vast amount of philological material included in his magnificent translation of the Arabian Nights Entertainments.

In the field of Hebrew there has naturally been a constant effort on the part of Western scholars to analyse the language to a degree accorded to few others. In any account of their endeavours, pride of place must be given to the astonishing family of Buxtorfs who, throughout some four generations, laid the foundations of modern knowledge of the language of the Bible. Johann Buxtorf, who was born in Westphalia in 1564, was Professor of Hebrew at Basle for nearly forty years. It was his habit to entertain the most distinguished Hebrew scholars of the day, and from the unremitting discussions and researches with his friends he was able to compile his great lexicon, which was first published in 1607. It was his son, Johann (who succeeded him at the University of Basle) who published a *Lexicon chaldaicum et syriacum* at Basle in 1622, and other members of his family contributed further to the study of these and related tongues. Reineccius, who was born in Saxony and became Professor of Languages and Philosophy at Leipzig, compiled a great quadrilingual New Testament (Leipzig, 1713) and an Old Testament (Leipzig, 1718), as well as his *Janua hebrāeāe linguāe Veteris Testamenti*, which was first published in Leipzig in 1704, and of which numerous subsequent editions have been issued. Another interesting character was Edwin Norris, the compiler of an Assyrian dictionary, who was born in Taunton in 1795 and served in India with the East

India Company, later becoming Secretary of the Royal Asiatic Society in London.

Perhaps the most remarkable story of all is the history of the researches into the real nature and meaning of the Egyptian language, commencing with the complete lack of comprehension and curiosity on the part of the earliest travellers, and proceeding through the many learned but misguided efforts of later philologists to apply Western principles to a tongue which was so much older than any European language. In it is the story of the discovery of the Rosetta stone, the circulation of copies of it to the leading scholars and the rivalry between the British and the French for the honour of first mastering its secrets, and the eventual triumph of Champollion. But with him in the glory of explaining and recording an exceptionally difficult language, must now be placed the courageous Wallis Budge, who, in spite of the handicap of the poorest beginnings and an early education which consisted of no more than the barest essentials, won his way to university, to a post at the British Museum—in which he was still subject to much academic criticism and opposition—and eventually brought forth his *Egyptian hieroglyphic dictionary*, one of the most impressive of one-man efforts.

Many of the dictionary-makers have been travellers and have lived for years in the countries which they studied. Edward Lane was such a one. After a valuable apprenticeship in the service of the merchants at Aleppo, he returned to the Near East to merge himself almost completely in the life of the people of Cairo, living in practically every way as one of them and gaining a knowledge of the Cairenes of those days—at a time when they were scarcely affected by Western ways—which only a few travellers since that time have been able to rival. From this, in addition to his *Arabic-English lexicon*, he was inspired to write his important work on the ways and manners of the Egyptians which is still a storehouse of useful information for the modern student of Egypt. Then there was the considerable contribution to Middle Eastern studies made by Sir William Jones (1746–94) who was responsible for the initiation and development of Persian studies in Europe—a movement which was greatly strengthened by his early translation of the lyrics of Hāfiz—and for stimulating new interest in the study of Sanskrit both in England and on the Continent.

But many of the lexicographers never went anywhere near the countries whose languages they were studying. None of the Buxtorfs appears to have visited Palestine or any of its neighbouring countries. And, in a safer age, even a man like Gesenius, who was born at Nordhausen and became Professor of Theology at Halle in 1811, seems to have stayed in his home country. Yet from Gesenius came one of the most erudite of all works on Hebrew etymology, and his Hebrew-German dictionary which was first published in Leipzig in 2 volumes in 1810–12.

In a few languages of this area, it will be noticed that the part played by the English-speaking peoples is astonishingly small: nowhere is this more evident than in the Armenian and Assyro-Babylonian languages. In the first, the work has been left almost entirely to the Armenian people, and in the latter most of the research has been done in Germany. Valuable as the result has been in both cases, it is evident that there is room for additional dictionaries in which special attention is paid to the point of view of the English language.

Below, in alphabetical order of language, is given a list of the outstanding dictionaries in each language of the Near and Middle East, and some idea of the growing interest and effort in this field will be gained from the number of works which are in progress at the present time.

ARABIC

One of the very early dictionaries of Arabic was discovered in a library in Florence and was published there in the last century:

Schiaparelli, Celestino. Vocabulista in arábico, pubblicato per la prima volta sopra un codice della Biblioteca Riccardiana di Firenze. Florence, Tip. dei successori Le Monnier, 1871. xxxv, 641 pages.

Of the more general dictionaries of classical and modern Arabic, the following are the best known:

Badger, George Percy. An English-Arabic lexicon, in which the equivalents for English words and idiomatic sentences are rendered into literary and colloquial Arabic. London, Paul, 1881. xii, 1244 pages.

Catafago, Joseph. An English and Arabic dictionary . . . in two parts, Arabic and English, and English and Arabic, in which the Arabic words are represented in their oriental character, as well as their correct pronunciation and accentuation shown in English letters. 2nd edition. London, Quaritch, 1873. 1096 pages.

Elias, Elias Antoon. Elias' modern dictionary, English-Arabic [and Arabic-English]. Cairo, Elias Modern Press, 1953 and 1947. 2 volumes. (9th and 4th editions respectively).

Hava, J. G. Arabic-English dictionary for the use of students. new edition. Beirut, Catholic Press, 1921. 916 pages.

Lane, Edward William. An Arabic-English lexicon, derived from the best and most copious Eastern sources. In two books: the first containing all the classical words and significations commonly known to the learned among the Arabs: the second, those that are of rare occurrence and not commonly known. Book I. London, Williams & Norgate, 1863–93. 1 volume in 8 parts. (Book II never published).

Salmoné, Habib Anthony. Arabic-English dictionary on a new system. London, Trübner, 1890. 2 volumes. (includes an English-Arabic index).

Spiro, Socrates, *Bey*. Arabic-English and English-Arabic vocabulary of the modern and colloquial Arabic of Egypt. Cairo, Elias, 1923–29. 2 volumes. (2nd and 3rd editions respectively).

Yūhannā Abkāriyūs. English-Arabic dictionary. 3rd edition. London, Probsthain, 1906. 1061 pages.

Three dictionaries deal specifically with colloquial Arabic:

Brille, Moshe, *and others*. The basic word list of the Arabic daily newspaper. Jerusalem, Hebrew University Press Association, 1940. 202 pages.

Elias, Edward E. Elias' practical dictionary of the colloquial Arabic: English-Arabic. Cairo, Elias, 1942. viii, 252 pages.

Pellat, Charles. L'Arabe vivant: mots arabes groupés d'après le sens et vocabulaire fondamental de l'arabe moderne. Paris, Adrien-Maisonneuve, 1952. v, 617 pages.

Since the war a comprehensive dictionary of modern literary Arabic, based on the vocabulary of contemporary writers—especially those in Egypt—and on current newspaper idiom, has been published:

Wehr, Hans. Arabisches Wörterbuch für die Schriftsprache der Gegenwart. Leipzig, Harrassowitz, 1952. 2 volumes.

Dictionaries which add to the vocabulary supplied in the more usual works include the monumental:

Dozy, R. P. A. Supplément aux dictionnaires arabes. 2nd edition. Paris, Maisonneuve, 1927. 2 volumes. (first published in 1881).

and:

Fagnan, E. Additions aux dictionnaires arabes. Algiers, Soubiron, 1923. 193 pages.

These include the Arabic of North Africa which is more specifically dealt with in the following:

Bercher, Léon.   Lexique arabe-français, avec un index français-arabe correspondant;   contribution à l'étude de l'arabe moderne. 2nd edition. Algiers, Carbonel, 1942. 351 pages.

Mercier, Henry.   Dictionnaire arabe-français [et français-arabe]. Rabat, Ed. La Porte, 1951.   2 volumes.

Bercher's *Lexique*, whose words and phrases are arranged under their roots, is supplementary to Jean Baptiste Belot's *Dictionnaire français-arabe; nouvelle édition entièrement refondue sous la direction du R. P. R. Nakhla* (Beirut, Catholic Press, 1952. 745 pages. first published 1889, and itself continuing and revising an earlier work by the R. P. Henry, published in 1857), which includes many classical poetic words little used to-day. Mercier's *Dictionnaire* deals with contemporary Moroccan Arabic, and gives transliterations into the roman alphabet.

For the Arabic of the Levant, the following will be found of assistance:

Barthélemy, Adrien.   Dictionnaire arabe-français.   Dialectes de Syrie: Alep, Damas, Liban, Jérusalem. Paris, Geuthner, 1935– volume 1–

Khalil Saad, *Bey*.   Centennial English-Arabic dictionary. . . . Beirut, American Mission Press, 1926.   1058 pages.

Tabet, Checri Antoine.   Tabet's English-Arabic dictionary.   Beirut, Catholic Press, 1930.   636 pages.

Wortabet, William Thomson, *and others*.   Arabic-English dictionary. 3rd edition.   Beirut, American Press, 1913.   802 pages.   (first published in 1888).

Attention must also be drawn to two other dictionaries of regional Arabic:

Hillelson, S. Sudan-Arabic: English-Arabic vocabulary. London, published by the Sudan Government, 1925. xxvii, 341 pages.

Leslau, Wolf.   Lexique Soqotri (Sudarabique moderne); avec comparaisons et explications étymologiques. Paris, Klincksieck, 1938. viii, 503 pages. (Société Linguistique de Paris. Collection Linguistique, LXI).

ARAMAIC

Davies, Benjamin.   A compendious and complete Hebrew and Chaldee lexicon to the Old Testament, with an English-Hebrew index. Revised by Edward C. Mitchell. Andover, Draper, 1879. 752 pages.

Jastrow, Marcus. A dictionary of the Targumim, the Talmud Babli and Yerushalmi, and the Midrashic literature. London, Luzac; New York, Putnam, 1903. 2 volumes. (reprinted London, Shapiro, Vallentine, 1926).

ARMENIAN

There are two early dictionaries of Armenian which are still of use to-day:

Aukerian, Haroutiun *and* Brand, John. A dictionary, English and Armenian. Venice, Armenian Academy of St. Lazarus, 1821–25. 2 volumes.

Bedrosian, Madatia. New dictionary, Armenian-English. Venice, S. Lazarus Armenian Academy, 1875–79. 786 pages.

Two works in Armenian are noted for their scholarship:

Adjarean, H. Hayerēn kavaṙagan paṙaran. Tiflis, 1913. xviii, 1141 pages. (Eminskij etnografičeskij sbornik, édité par l'Institut Lazarev de Moscou, t. IX).

Adjarean, H. Hayerēn aṙmatakan baṙavan. Erivan, the author, 1933. 1626 pages.

the latter being a comprehensive etymological dictionary, rich in information and examples, and in comparable derivative words in other languages, as well as in modern dialectical forms.

The most important dictionary of recent times, and one which includes many general and technical terms not listed elsewhere, is:

Froundjian, Dirair. Armenisch-deutsches Wörterbuch. Munich, Oldenbourg, 1952. xvi, 505 pages.

and another outstanding dictionary is:

Kouyoumdjian, Mesrob G. A comprehensive dictionary, Armenian-English. Cairo, Sahag-Mesrob Press; London, Safrastion, 1951. 1159 pages.

There are also the following twentieth century dictionaries which cover both classical and modern words:

Chakmakjian, Haroutioun Hovanes. A comprehensive dictionary, English-Armenian. Boston, Mass., Yeran, 1922. 1424 pages.

Hagopian, V. H. A dictionary, English-Armenian. Constantinople, Matteosian, 1907. vii, 949 pages. (reprinted New York, Stechert, 1912).

Papasian, Thoros. A practical dictionary: Armenian-English [and, Illustrated practical dictionary, English-Armenian]. New York, Stechert, 1905–10. 2 volumes.

ASSYRO-BABYLONIAN

Bezold, Carl. Babylonisch-assyrisches Glossar: nach dem Tode des Verfassers unter Mitwirkung von Adele Bezold zum Druck gebracht von Albrecht Götze. Heidelberg, Winter, 1926. 343 pages.

Delitzsch, Friedrich. Assyrisches Handwörterbuch. Leipzig, Hinrichs; Baltimore, Johns Hopkins Press, 1894–96. xx, 730 pages.

Ebeling, Erich *and* Meissner, Bruno. Reallexikon der Assyrologie. Berlin, de Gruyter, 1931–   volume 1–

Gelb, I. J. Materials for the Assyrian dictionary. No. I: Sargonic texts from the Diyala region. No. II: Old Akkadian writing and grammar. Chicago, University of Chicago Press; Cambridge University Press, 1953. 2 volumes. (to be completed with No. III: Glossary of Old Akkadian. These are preliminary volumes prepared in connection with the projected great Assyrian dictionary now in preparation at the University of Chicago).

Muss-Arnolt, William. A concise dictionary of the Assyrian languages. Berlin, Reuther; New York, Lemcke, 1905. 1202 pages. (issued in 19 parts, 1895–1905).

Norris, Edwin. Assyrian dictionary: intended to further the study of the cuneiform inscriptions of Assyria and Babylonia. London, Williams & Norgate, 1868–72. Parts 1–3 (A–Nst) only: no more published.

COPTIC

Crum, Walter Ewing. A Coptic dictionary. Oxford, Clarendon Press, 1929–39. parts 1–6. (Numerous examples for each word. Greek and Arabic equivalents given, but Greek loan words not included. For most part includes only those etymologies not given in Spiegelberg).

Spiegelberg, Wilhelm. Koptisches Handwörterbuch. Heidelberg, Winter, 1921. xvi, 339 pages. (largely etymological. Gives Egyptian prototypes in hieroglyphics and transcription. Based on Amadeo Peyron's dictionary of 1835).

EGYPTIAN

Budge, *Sir* Ernest Alfred Thompson Wallis. An Egyptian hieroglyphic dictionary. With an index of English words, king list and geographical list with indexes, list of hieroglyphic characters, Coptic and Semitic alphabets, etc. London, Murray, 1920. cliv, 1356 pages.

Erman, Adolf *and* Grapow, Hermann. Wörterbuch der aegyptischen Sprache; in Auftrage der deutschen Akademien. Berlin, Akademie-Verlag; Leipzig, Hinrichs, 1926–50. 6 volumes.

—— Die Belegstellen, bearb. von H. Grapow und W. Erichsen. 1935–51. 3 volumes. (This dictionary covers both the hieroglyphic and the hieratic vocabulary. For each word is given the epoch, and an enumeration of the principal orthographic variants arranged chronologically).

Lambert, R. Lexique hiéroglyphique. Paris, Geuthner, 1925. ii, 445 pages.

HEBREW

There are three early dictionaries of the Hebrew tongue which still have interest for the historians of that language:

Buxtorf, Johann. Lexicon hebraicum et chaldaicum. Basle, Richter, 1710. 1052 pages.

Reineccius, Christian. Janua hebräeäe linguäe Veteris Testamenti. Leipzig, 1733. 1446 pages.

Stock, Christian. Clavis linguae sanctae aditum aperiens. Jena, Bielck, 1717. 1554 pages.

Of the more modern dictionaries, the following are among the more important:

Arnold-Kellner, Paula *and* Gross, M. D. Complete Hebrew-English dictionary, containing a list of Hebrew abbreviations. London, Shapiro, Vallentine, 1926. 487 pages.

Ben Judah, Eliezer. Thesaurus totius hebraitatis et veteris et recentioris. Berlin-Schöneberg, Langenscheidt, 1908–28. volumes 1–8.

Blackman, Philip. English-Hebrew dictionary. 2nd edition. London, Pordes, 1929. 500 pages.

Gesenius, Friedrich Heinrich Wilhelm. A Hebrew and English lexicon of the Old Testament, with an appendix containing the Biblical Aramaic. Boston, Mass., Houghton, 1906. 1127 pages.

Gesenius, Friedrich Heinrich Wilhelm. Hebraïsches und aramaïsches Handwörterbuch über des Alte Testament . . . 17th edition. Leipzig, Vogel, 1921. 1013 pages.

Glenn, Mendel Gershon. Hamillon hamaasi: practical Hebrew-English dictionary for use in school and home. New York, 1947. 564 pages.

Grossman, Reuben *and* Sachs, H. Compendious Hebrew-English dictionary: comprising a complete vocabulary of Biblical, Mishnaic, medieval and modern Hebrew. Revised and edited by M. H. Segal. Tel-Aviv, Dvir, 1946. 426 pages.

Harkavy, Alexander. Student's Hebrew and Chaldee dictionary to the Old Testament with supplement: Neo-Hebrew vocabulary. New York, Hebrew Publishing Company, 1914. 888 pages.

Kaufman, Judah Ibn-Shmuel, *editor*. English-Hebrew dictionary, by Israel Efros, Judah Ibn Shmuel Kaufman, Benjamin Silk. 9th edition. Tel-Aviv, Dvir, 1950. xxxii, 751 pages.

Koehler, Ludwig Hugo. Lexicon in Veteris Testamenti libros . . ., a dictionary of the Hebrew Old Testament in English and German . . . Leiden, Brill, 1948-54. 2 volumes.

Levy, Jacob. Wörterbuch über die Talmudim und Midraschim. 2nd edition. Berlin, Harz, 1924. 4 volumes. (first issued in 1876-89).

Waldstein, Abraham Solomon. Hebrew-English [and English-Hebrew] dictionary. 6th edition. Tel-Aviv, 1939. 2 volumes in 1.

Zorell, Francesco. Lexicon Hebraicum et Aramaicum Veteris Testamenti, quod aliis collaborantibus edidit. Rome, 1940-46.

MALTESE

Barbera, B. G. Dizionario maltese-arabo-italiano con un grammatica comparata arabo-maltese. Rome, 1939– volume 1–

Dessoulavy, Charles Louis. A Maltese-Arabic word-list: showing which of the corresponding Arabic roots are shared by other Semitic tongues or used in the Quran. London, Luzac, 1938. iv, 146 pages.

PERSIAN

Bartholomae, Christian.   Altiranisches Wörterbuch.   Strasbourg, Trübner, 1904. xxxii, 1000 pages.

—— Zum altiranischen Wörterbuch: Nacharbeiten und Vorarbeiten. 1906. xiii, 287 pages. (Indogermanische Forschungen, XIX. Beiheft.)

Boyle, John Andrew. A practical dictionary of the Persian language. (Persian-English). London, Luzac, 1949. 199 pages.

Desmaisons, *Baron* Jean Jacques Pierre.   Dictionnaire persan-français. Rome, Imprimerie Vaticane, 1908–14. 4 volumes.

Dikhudā, Alī Akbar. Lughat nāmah. Tehran, 1946–   volume 1–   (in Persian throughout).

Fazl-i-Ali, *Maulavi*.   A dictionary of the Persian and English languages, designed for the use of military and civil officers and schools. Bombay, Education Society's Press, 1885. iv, 668 pages.

Haïm, Sulaimān. The larger English-Persian dictionary. Tehran, Béroukhim, 1941–43. 2 volumes.

Haïm, Sulaimān. New Persian-English dictionary, complete and modern . . . English meanings of over 50,000 words, terms, idioms, and proverbs in the Persian language as well as the transliteration of the words in English characters.   Tehran, Béroukhim, 1934–36. 2 volumes.

Palmer, Edward Henry. A concise dictionary of the Persian language. London, Kegan Paul, 1944. 363 pages. (first published 1876).

Steingass, Francis Joseph.   A comprehensive Persian-English dictionary, including the Arabic words and phrases to be met with in Persian literature; being Johnson and Richardson's Persian, Arabic and English dictionary revised, enlarged and entirely reconstructed . . . 2nd impression. London, Kegan Paul, 1930. viii, 1539 pages. (first published in 1892).

Tolman, Herbert Cushing. Ancient Persian lexicon, and the texts of the Achaemenidan inscriptions transliterated and translated, with special reference to their recent re-examination. New York, American Book Company, for Vanderbilt University, 1908. xii, 134 pages. (Vanderbilt Oriental Series, VI).

—— Cuneiform supplement (autographed) . . . 1910. xxv, 71; iv, 51 pages. (Vanderbilt Oriental Series, VII).

Wollaston, *Sir* Arthur Naylor. A complete English-Persian dictionary, compiled from original sources. London, W. H. Allen, 1889. viii, 1491 pages.

Wollaston, *Sir* Arthur Naylor. An English-Persian dictionary, compiled from original sources. 2nd edition reprinted. London, Murray, 1922. xv, 462 pages.

SYRIAC

Brockelmann, Carl. Lexicon Syriacum. 2nd edition. Halle, Niemeyer, 1928. 930 pages.

Brun, J. Dictionarium syriaco-latinum. 2nd edition. Beirut, Tip. PP. Soc. Jesu, 1911. xii, 765 pages.

Oraham, Alexander Joseph. Oraham's dictionary of the stabilised and enriched Assyrian language and English. Chicago, Consolidated Press, 1943. v, 576 pages. (covering Nestorian Syriac).

Smith, Robert Payne. Thesaurus syriacus. Oxford, Clarendon Press, 1879–1901. 2 volumes.

—— Supplement. 1927. 345 pages.

Smith, Robert Payne. Compendious Syriac dictionary, founded upon the *Thesaurus syriacus* . . . edited by J. Payne Smith (Mrs. Margoliouth). Oxford, Clarendon Press, 1903. 626 pages.

TURKISH

Brockelmann, Carl. Mitteltürkischer Wortschatz nach Mahmûd al Kašgarīs Dīvan lugāt at-Turk. Budapest, Leipzig, 1928. (Bibliotheca Orientalis Hungarica, no. 1).

Fahrettin, İskender. Ingilizce-Türkçe yeni lûgat. Istanbul, Kanaat Kütüphanesi, 1931. 671 pages. (revised edition, 1954. 694 pages).

Gövsa, İbrahim Alaettin. Resimli yeni lûgat ve ansiklopedi (ansiklopedik sözlük). Istanbul, Yedigün Basimevi, 1947– volume 1–

Hony, Henry Charles *and* Fahir İz. A Turkish-English [and English-Turkish] dictionary. Oxford, Clarendon Press, 1947–52. 2 volumes.

Moran, A. Vahid. Türkçe-ingilizce sözlük. Istanbul, Şirketi, 1945. xix, 1462 pages. (published by the Turkish Ministry of Public Instruction).

Okçugil, Vâsif. Yeni türkçe-ingilizce okul lûgati. Istanbul, Kanaat Kitabevi, 1945. iv, 694 pages. (etymological).

Okçugil, Vâsif. İngilizce türkçe büyük lûgat. Istanbul, Kanaat Kitabevi, 1941-43. 2 volumes.

Kadri, Hüseyin Kâzim. Türk lûgati: Türk dillerinin istikakive edebî lûgatlar. Istanbul, Maarif Matbaasi, 1927-45. 4 volumes.

Redhouse, *Sir* James William. Yeni Redhouse lûgati: ingilizce-türkçe. Revised Redhouse dictionary: English-Turkish. Istanbul, American Board of Missions, 1950. xx, 1196 pages. (companion Turkish-English volume now in preparation).

Taner, Ali Haydar. Yabanci kelimeler lûgati. Istanbul, Kanaat Kitabevi, 1941. vii, 640 pages. (foreign words in Turkish).

Taniklariyle Tamara Sözlügü. Istanbul, Cumhuriyet Basimevi, 1943– volume 1–

Thomson, H. M. Turkish-English dictionary, with supplement of new words by John L. Mish. New York, Ungar, 1954. 580 pages. (first published, Istanbul, Kanaat Kütüphanesi, 1932).

Tolun Haydar. Yabanci kelimeler lûgati. Bursa, Yeni Basimevi, 1939. 224 pages. (foreign words in Turkish).

Türk Dil Kurumu. Tûrkiyede halk ağzindan söz derleme dergisi. Istanbul, Maarif Matbaasi, 1939–47. 3 volumes. (continues the tradition of the collection and publication of dialectical vocabularies in Turkey, inaugurated by Hamit Zübeyr and Ishak Refet's *Anadilden derlemeler* (Istanbul, 1932. 448 pages), and the Türk Dil Kurumu's *Tarama dergisi* (Istanbul, 1934. 1310 pages).

Türk Dil Kurumu. Türkçe sözlük. Türk Dil Kurumu lûgat kolu çalişmalariyle hazirlanmiştir. Istanbul, Cumhuriyet Basimevi, 1945. xi, 669 pages.

Türk Dil Kurumu. Imlâ kilavuzu. Istanbul, Millî Eğitim Basimevi, 1948. 223 pages.

N.B. The Latin alphabet was adopted by Turkey on 1st December, 1928.

THE LANGUAGES OF AFRICA SOUTH OF THE SAHARA

" When the first Europeans made contact with Moshesh and his tribe about the year 1833, the language which is now called Southern or Basutoland Sotho had not yet been written down.   Therefore it is quite obvious that there could be no written dictionary or vocabulary or list of words of any kind relating to it.   Every Mosotho carried his dictionary about with him in his own mind, and little-known words were transmitted from man to man or woman to woman at the chiefs' courts, in conversation at the fountain, at initiation schools, or in the evenings when a grandmother would recite tales to her grand-children.   Chiefs and their warriors would chant praise-songs learned by heart, and tell stories of ancient times, which the memory of hearers would preserve with remarkable accuracy.   The first missionaries, bent on the herculean task of providing the illiterate Basotho with first the Gospels, the New Testament, and then the complete Bible, besides hymns, readers and numerous other books, were rather late in publishing a list of Sotho words."

Thus wrote R. A. Paroz in Mabille and Dieterlin's *Southern Sotho-English dictionary* (Morija, 1950) in describing a situation which matches almost word for word that which faced the first-comers in many other parts of Africa.   In her graphic account of the very great work done by her father, Miss Dorothea Frances Bleek tells how the Bushmen " had been almost completely proof against any efforts by missionaries. Whereas almost every other tribe in Africa had been in some measure influenced by these workers for the Gospel, they had repelled all advances. Apart from the religious aspect, it had thus been almost impossible to prepare any kind of grammar or dictionary of their language." (Eric Rosenthal. *Cave artists of South Africa*. Cape Town, Balkema, 1953. page 9).   While most of the philologists did not have to run the same dangers which threatened Dr. Bleek, there were others which were sometimes even more frightening.   What inner power, for instance, could have confirmed Ludwig Krapf in his determination to continue his magnificent work after the loss of his young family immediately following his arrival in Kenya?   And how was it that Bishop Colenso pursued his valuable researches into the Zulu tongue when his whole career was jeopardised by the misunderstandings and jealousy which arose both in South Africa and in Britain? The whole story of Africa is one of astonishing personal effort against seemingly insuperable odds, and of all the problems with which Africa has confronted her visitors in each generation, that of language has always been among the most difficult and the most elusive. As H. L. M. Butcher puts it when describing how a committee was formed to standardise the writing of the Bini language, " the first step in making a literature in any hitherto unwritten language " is to ensure " that what one man writes another can read ". (*Africa*, volume 11, 1938: page 372).

For the most part, then, the difficulties derive directly from the fact that almost all African languages are oral and not written tongues. There was therefore no Rosetta stone to seek, and the collective memory of the tribe did not stretch as far as etymologies and derivations. There is, of course, a certain amount of circumstantial evidence—for instance, the words for table and for tea are foreign introductions in most African languages—but it is of such a nature that it is more likely to give rise to speculation rather than to throw any really helpful light on the growth of a language. Even where the language was written down, as in the case of the semi-artificial tongue, Swahili, which the Arabs had taught their African servants and slaves to write in Arabic characters, the medium chosen was more of a hindrance than a help.

The first philologists in Africa in the great majority of cases were missionaries. Philology was to them a hobby to pursue in their scanty leisure for, as Mr. Paroz has pointed out, they had many other more urgent duties to perform. By the very nature of their work they were also amateurs in the field of languages for the most part, and the fact that so many of them were successful in preparing efficient and accurate pioneer grammars and dictionaries is a tribute to their early training and to their perseverance under very difficult conditions. " It is no disparagement," says Professor Lucy Mair of the early missionary lexicologists, " to point out that their work suffers from the inherent disadvantages of the circumstances in which it was done." (" Linguistics without sociology." *Bulletin of the School of Oriental and African Studies*, volume 7, 1933–35; pages 913 to 921). Some of these early efforts are, in fact, in need of substantial revision: philology has advanced considerably in its technique and its possibilities during the past hundred years, and with the aid of recordings and of an effective phonetic system nuances and variations hardly suspected by the western ear have gradually become apparent and have assumed an importance unrealised by the pioneers. In the field of spelling comparison of any old and modern dictionaries of the same African language will reveal how far our knowledge of true African speech has advanced and, incidentally, how far the " kitchen " variety is from the correct form! Under the auspices of such bodies as the International Institute of African Languages and Cultures, the Institut d'Ethnologie in Paris, the Commission Belge d'Ethnologie, the Instituto de Estudios Africanos in Madrid and the Centre IFAN, much has been done to produce good modern dictionaries, but there are still many African languages where there is little or nothing in published form which is of help to the newcomer. Despite the fact, for instance, that much has been written on the Masai and the Nandi tribes, there are no dictionaries or grammars of their languages comparable to those available for the Acholi or the Hausa.

From the English-speaking point of view there is one difficulty which does not arise in any other continent: not every African language has a bilingual dictionary in which the foreign language is English. The reason for this is easily found in the fact that much of Africa is owned or controlled by the French, the Belgians, the Portuguese and the Spaniards, and that English philological exploration in these territories is necessarily still in its infancy. The reader therefore who is interested in many an African language is thus faced with the problem of using a foreign-language dictionary or of going without—a situation which has existed from the earliest times for the first Bantu dictionary (which survives in manuscript in the Vittorio-Emmanuele Library in Rome) consists of a Latin-Spanish-Congo vocabulary compiled in the middle of the seventeenth century by a Capuchin monk, Georges de Gheel, who subsequently suffered martyrdom at the hands of tribesmen (*Le plus ancien dictionnaire bantu; edité par J. van Wing et C. Penders, S. J.* Louvain, Kuyl-Otto, 1928. xxv, 365 pages). It is thus to the credit of European settlers that this has been a circumstance which they have invariably overcome, and it is a pity that much of the valuable and curious philological material which many an upland farmer must have acquired from day to day concerning the local language or dialect will die with him.

High up in the hills, some thirty miles north of Kisumu and the shores of Lake Victoria, on the famous mission station of Kaimosi of the American Friends, two great American missionaries compiled years ago their own brief dictionary of the local language. This they printed on their own hand-press, and it is doubtful whether there are more than a very few copies outside Kenya, though it is well enough known and used in its own territory. This is a typical situation with many of the African languages where the philological research into the language of a tribe is unknown beyond the radius of a hundred miles or so. Owing to the lack of libraries in Africa practically no effort is being made to preserve this elusive material, which has usually been published in very small editions. From many points of view a more determined effort should be made before it is too late to collect all the diverse material on African linguistics and to make it available wherever it can really be of service to the many people who are now interested in it.

No one knows with certainty how many distinct languages there are in Africa, but their number certainly runs into several hundreds. " There are at least 150, e.g., between the Atlantic Ocean and Lake Chad in French West Africa alone, some of them spoken by only a few thousand people " (*Africa*, volume 4, 1931: page 56). From these have been selected the more usual, and below are listed the principal dictionaries in each of them. It should be noted, however, that dictionaries of Afrikaans are included in the chapter on German, Dutch and Afrikaans dictionaries, and that dictionaries of Arabic-speaking countries in North Africa are included in the chapter on the Near and Middle East.

In perusing the lists of recent dictionaries of African languages it is encouraging to note the part now being played in modern African lexicography by the Africans themselves, such as the eminent poet Benedict Wallet Vilakazi, Moussa Travélé and the remarkable African Bishop, Samuel Adjai Crowther. The contribution of the African philologist is to be welcomed for it will help to prevent recurrences of the situations mentioned by Professor Mair in which " the efficacy of further studies has been hampered by the complete absence of such sociological knowledge as would point the way, where necessary, to some context of institutions taken for granted by the native informant but non-existent to the European translator ". (*op. cit.*)

ACHOLI (Southern Sudan—South and South-East Mongalla Province— and the Lwoo people of Northern Uganda)

Crazzolara, J. Pasquale. A study of the Acooli language, grammar and vocabulary. London, published for the International Institute of African Languages and Cultures, by Oxford University Press, 1938. xix, 426 pages.

Muratori, C. English-Bari-Lotuxo-Acoli vocabulary. Okaru, Catholic Mission Printing Press, 1948. vii, 270 pages.

AMHARIC (Ethiopia)

Armbruster, Carl Hubert. Initia amharica: an introduction to spoken Amharic. Cambridge University Press, 1908–20. volumes 1–3 (no more published).

Baeteman, Joseph. Dictionnaire amarigna-français, suivi d'un vocabulaire français-amarigna. Dire Dawa, Imp. Saint Lazare, 1929. xxi, 433 pages.

Grébaut, Sylvain. Supplément au *Lexicon linguae aethiopicae* de August Dillman (1865) et édition du *Lexique* de Juste d'Urbin (1850–55). Paris, Imprimerie Nationale, 1952. v, 521 pages.

Guidi, Ignazio. Vocabulario amarico-italiano. Rome, Casa Editrice Italiana, 1901. xv pages, 918 columns. (Supplement, Rome, 1940. vii pages, 268 columns).

Walker, Craven Howell. English-Amharic dictionary. London, Sheldon Press, 1928. xii, 236 pages.

BANDA (Ubangi-Shari-Chad region)

Tisserant, Charles. Dictionnaire banda-français. Paris, Institut d'Ethnologie, 1931. 616 pages. (Université de Paris. Travaux et Mémoires de l'Institut d' Ethnologie, XIV).

BEMBA (North-East Rhodesia—Kasama Province)

White Fathers. Bemba dictionary. Chilubula, White Fathers, 1947. 1505 pages.

BISA (language of the Boussanse, a Mandingo tribe in Mossi territory)

Prost, André. La langue bisa: grammaire et dictionnaire. Ouagadougo, Upper Volta, Centre IFAN, 1950. 199 pages. (Etudes Voltaïques, Mémoire I).

BUSHMAN

Bleek, Dorothea Frances. Comparative vocabularies of Bushman languages. Cambridge University Press, 1929. iv, 94 pages. (University of Cape Town. Publications of the School of African Life and Languages).

CHAGGA (Tanganyika–Kilimanjaro region)

Müller, Emil. Wörterbuch der Djaga-Sprache (Madjame-Mundart) gesprochen am Kilimandjaro in Ostafrika. Hamburg, Eckardt & Messtorff, 1947. lv, 466 pages. (Zeitschrift für Eingeborenen-Sprachen. Beihefte, 25. Heft).

COKWE (North-east Angola and Belgian Congo)

Macjannet, Malcolm Brooks. Chokwe-English, English-Chokwe dictionary and grammar lessons. 2nd edition. Biula, C.P., 1949. (first published 1927. Errata and addenda. Biula, 1950. 18 pages).

COMORO (Comoro archipelago)

Fischer, François. Grammaire-dictionnaire comorien. Strasbourg, Société d'Edition Basse Alsace, 1949. 292 pages.

CUNAMA

Castelnuovo del Zappa, Giuseppe Fermo da.   Vocabolario della lingua cunama.   Rome, Curia Generalizia dei Fr. Min. Cappuccini, 1950. xi, 604 pages.

DAGOMBA (Gold Coast)

Blair, H. A.   Dagomba (Dagbane) dictionary.   Accra, Government Printer, 1910.   111 pages.

DAHOMEY

Alapini, Julien.   Le petit dahoméen: grammaire-vocabulaire: lexique en langue du Dahomey.   Avignon, Presses Universelles, 1950.   284 pages.

DINKA (Southern Sudan—Upper Nile and northern Bahr-el-Ghazal Provinces)

Nebel, A.   Dinka-dictionary: [English-Dinka, Dinka-English-Italian] with abridged [Dinka] grammar.   Verona, Missioni Africane, 1936. xli, 311 pages.

DYIMINI (Senegal)

Bazin, Hippolyte.   Dictionnaire bambara-français, précédé d'un abrégé de grammaire bambara.   Paris, Imprimerie Nationale, 1906.   xxiv, 693 pages.

Sauvant, M.   Dictionnaire français-bambara et bambara-français. Algiers, 1926.

Travélé, Moussa.   Petit dictionnaire français-bambara et bambara-français.   2nd edition.   Paris, Geuthner, 1923.   xii, 281 pages.   (first published 1913).

DYOLA (Senegal)

Wintz, Edouard.   Dictionnaire français-dyola et dyola-français, précédé d'un essai de grammaire.   Elinkine, Casamance, Mission Catholique, 1909.   264 pages.

EDO (Southern Nigeria—Benin Division of Benin Province)

Butcher, Hugh Louis Montague.   An elementary dictionary of the Benin language.   Benin City, Church Missionary Society, 1932. 116 pages.   (Benin-English, English-Benin).

Melzian, Hans Joachim.   A concise dictionary of the Bini language of Southern Nigeria.   London, Kegan Paul, 1937.   xviii, 232 pages.

EFIK (the literary language throughout most of Southern Nigeria)

Adams, R. F. G.   English-Efik and Efik-English dictionary.   2nd and 3rd editions.   Liverpool, Philip, 1943, 1953.   279 pages.   (first published 1939).

Goldie, Hugh. Dictionary of the Efik language. I. Efik and English.
II. English and Efik. Glasgow, Dunn & Wright, 1874–86. 2 parts.

EWE (Togoland, Dahomey, and some eastern districts of the Gold
Coast)

Westermann, Diedrich. Evefiala, or Ewe-English dictionary. Berlin,
Reimer, 1928. 347 pages.

Westermann, Diedrich. Gbesela yeye, or English-Ewe dictionary.
Berlin, Reimer, 1910. 347 pages. (reprinted 1930).

Westermann, Diedrich. Wörterbuch der Ewe-Sprache. I. Ewe-deutsch.
II. Deutsch-ewe. Berlin, Reimer, 1905–06. 2 volumes. (revised
edition, 1954).

EWONDE (South Cameroons—spoken by the Fang group of tribes)

Heepe, M. Jaundes-Wörterbuch: unter Mitwirkung von H. Nekes.
Hamburg, Friederichsen, 1926. (Hamburg University. Abhandlung
aus dem Gebiet der Auslandskunde, XXII). xvi, 258 pages.

FULANI (French Guinea and Senegal)

Cremer, Jean. Dictionnaire français-peul (dialectes de la Haute-Volta).
Paris, Geuthner, 1923. xxix, 109 pages. (Société Française d'Ethno-
graphie. Matériaux d'ethnographie et de linguistique soudanaises.
Tome I.).

Dauzats, André. Lexique français-peul et peul-français. 2nd edition.
Albi, Imprimerie Albigeoise, 1952. 444 pages.

Gaden, H. Le poular, dialecte peul du Fouta sénégalais. Tome second:
Lexique poular-français. Paris, Leroux, 1914. xi, 263 pages.
(Collection de la *Revue du Monde Musulman*).

Reichardt, Charles Augustus Ludwig. Vocabulary of the Fulde language.
London, Church Missionary Society, 1878. 357 pages.

Taylor, Frank William. A Fulani-English dictionary. Oxford, Clarendon
Press, 1932. vi, 242 pages.

GA (Gold Coast)

Schopf, J. *and* Richter, L. An English-Accra or Gâ dictionary. 2nd
edition. Basle, 1912. xi, 256 pages.

GALLA (Southern Ethiopia and northern Kenya)

Cecchi, Antonia. Da Zeila alle frontiere del Caffa. Rome, 1885–87.
(third volume contains extensive Galla dictionary—reprinted with
additions 1892).

Foot, E. C. A Galla-English, English-Galla dictionary. Cambridge
University Press, 1913. viii, 118 pages.

GANDA (Buganda)

Kitching, Arthur Leonard *and* Blackledge, George Robert. A Luganda-English and English-Luganda dictionary. Revised edition. London, Society for the Promotion of Christian Knowledge, 1952. xv, 234 pages. (first published 1925).

GBANDI (Belgian Congo)

Lekens, Benjamin. Dictionnaire ngbandi (Ubangi, Congo belge). Français-ngbandi, ngbandi-français. Antwerp, de Sikkel, 1952. xii, 348 pages. (Annales du Musée du Congo Belge, Sciences de l'Homme (Linguistique). Tome I).

GBEA (French Congo)

Calloc'h, J. Vocabulaire français-gbéa, précédé d'éléments de grammaire. Paris, Geuthner, 1911. 170 pages.

HAUSA (Nigeria, French colony of Niger, northern Cameroons, and a lingua franca from the Atlantic to the Mediterranean).

Abraham, Roy Clive *and* Malam Mai Kano. Dictionary of the Hausa language. London, Crown Agents for the Colonies, on behalf of the Government of Nigeria, 1949. xxvii, 992 pages.

Bargery, George Percy. A Hausa-English dictionary and English-Hausa vocabulary, compiled for the Government of Nigeria. London, Oxford University Press, Milford, 1934. liv, 1226 pages. (reprinted 1951).

Robinson, Charles Henry. Dictionary of the Hausa language. 4th edition. Cambridge University Press, 1925. 2 volumes.

HERERO (South-West Africa)

Brincker, P. H. Wörterbuch und kurzgefasste Grammatik des Otji-Hérero. Leipzig, Weigel, 1886. viii, 382 pages.

IDOMA (Northern Nigeria)

Abraham, Roy Clive. The Idoma language, Idoma wordlists, Idoma chrestomathy, Idoma proverbs. Idoma, published by the author, on behalf of the Idoma Native Administration, 1951. 272 pages.

IDZING (Belgian Congo—Province of Congo-Kasai)

Mertens, Joseph. Dictionnaire idzing-français, suivi d'un aide-mémoire français-idzing. Brussels, Institut Royal Colonial Belge, 1939. 240 pages. (Mémoires, Tome IV, 3éme partie). (constitutes the third part of a work entitled *Les Badzing de la Kamtsha*).

IGBO (Southern Nigeria)

Thomas, Northcote Whitridge. English-Ibo and Ibo-English dictionary. London, Harrison, 1913. 391 pages.

Thomas, Northcote Whitridge. Addenda to Ibo-English dictionary. 1914. v, 184 pages. (*i.e.* volumes II and V of the *Anthropological report on the Ibo-speaking peoples of Nigeria.* 1913-14).

KAMBA (Kenya)

African Inland Mission. A Kikamba-English dictionary. Nairobi, 1939. 231 pages.

Brutzer, Ernst. Handbuch der Kambasprache. Berlin, 1906. (Friedrich-Wilhelms-Universität, Berlin. Seminar für orientalische Sprachen. Mitteilungen. Jahrgang 9, Abteilung 3, pages 1-100).

KANURI (Northern Nigeria—Bornu Province)

Lukas, Johannes. A study of the Kanuri language, grammar and vocabulary. London, published for the International Institute of African Languages and Cultures, by Oxford University Press, 1937. xvii, 253 pages.

KAONDE (Northern Rhodesia)

Woods, R. E. Broughall. A short introductory dictionary of the Kaonde language, with English-Kaonde appendix. London, Religious Tract Society, 1924.

KIKUYU (Central Kenya)

Beecher, Leonard James *and* Beecher, Gladys Sybil Bazett. A Kikuyu-English dictionary, with a general introduction to the phonetics, orthography and spelling of Kikuyu. Kahuhia, Church Missionary Society, 1935. xv, 231 pages.

Gecaga, B. M. *and* Kirkcaldy-Willis, W. H. English-Kikuyu, Kikuyu-English vocabulary. Nairobi, Eagle Press, 1952. 70 pages.

KOMBE

Fernández, Leoncio P. Diccionario español-kômbò. Madrid, Instituto de Estudios Africanos, 1951. 541 pages.

KONGO (Lower Congo)

Bentley, William Holman. Dictionary and grammar of the Kongo language, as spoken at San Salvador, the ancient capital of the old Kongo empire, West Afrika, and Appendix. London, Baptist Missionary Society, and Trübner, 1887-95. 2 volumes.

Laman, Karl Edvard. Dictionnaire kikongo-français avec une étude phonétique décrivant les dialectes les plus importants de la langue dite kikongo. Brussels, Institut Royal Colonial Belge, Section des sciences morales et politiques, 1936. xciv, 1183 pages. (Mémoires . . . II. 1936).

KPELLE (Liberia)

Wellmers, William Everett.   Spoken Kpelle.   Monrovia, Lutheran Mission in Liberia, 1948.

Westermann, Diedrich.   Die Kpelle-Sprache in Liberia: grammatische Einführungen, Texte und Wörterbuch.   Berlin, Reimer, 1924.   vii, 278 pages.

LAMBA (North-West Rhodesia—Ndola district;   southern Belgian Congo—Katanga district)

Doke, Clement Martyn.   English-Lamba vocabulary.   Johannesburg, University of the Witwatersrand Press, 1933.   134 pages.

Madan, Arthur Cornwallis.   Lala-Lamba-Wisa and English, English and Lala-Lamba-Wisa dictionary.   Oxford University Press, 1913.   328 pages.

LANGO (Northern Uganda—Lango district)

Driberg, Jack Herbert.   The Lango: a Nilotic tribe of Uganda.   London, Fisher Unwin, 1923.   468 pages.   (contains vocabularies).

LEGA (Belgian Congo)

Burk, Ellen I. A small handbook of the Kilega language as spoken by the Warega tribe of the Congo Belge, with grammar and vocabulary also in English and Kingwana.   Pittsburg, Pa., The Pittsburg Bible Institute Press, 1940.   118 pages.

LENJE (North-West Rhodesia)

Madan, Arthur Cornwallis.   Lenje handbook: a short introduction to the Lenje dialect spoken in North-Western Rhodesia.   Oxford, Clarendon Press, 1908.   154 pages.

LIMBA (Sierra Leone)

Clarke, Mary Lane.   A Limba-English (English-Limba) dictionary.   Freetown, Government Printer, 1929.   150 pages.

LOZI

Jalla, A.   Dictionary of the Lozi language: Lozi-English.   London, U.S.C.L., 1937.   393 pages.

LUBA

Clercq, A. de.   Dictionnaire luba.   Première partie: luba-français.   Léopoldville, Procurie des Missions Belges, 1937.   316 pages.

LUENA (East-central Angola and Northern Rhodesia)

Horton, A. E.   A dictionary of Luvale.   El Monte, Calif., Rahn, 1953.   iv, 434 pages.

LUNDA (Northern Rhodesia)

White, C. M. N. A Lunda-English vocabulary. Balovale, the author, 1943.

LUO (Western Kenya)

Dholuo grammar. By a Member of St. Joseph's Society, Mill Hill. Kisumu, Kisumu Stores, 1936. 262 pages. (contains vocabularies).

LUR (North-West Congo, and the neighbouring part of Uganda)

Vanneste, M. Woordenboek van de Alur-Taal, Mahagi (Belgisch Congo). Boechout, Seminarie der Witte Paters, 1940. 427 pages. (Alur-Dutch only).

MALAGASY (Madascar)

Dama-Ntsoha: dictionnaire étymologique de la langue malgache. Tananarive, Antaninandro, 1952–   volume 1–

Malzac, V. Dictionnaire français-malgache. new edition. Paris, Société d'Editions Géographiques, Maritimes et Coloniales, 1949. 860 pages. (first published in Tananarive, 1888–93).

MALINKE (Gambia and French West Africa)

Abiven, P. O.   Dictionnaire français-malinké et malinké-français, précédé d'un abrégé de grammaire malinkée. Conakry, 1906.

Delafosse, Maurice. La langue mandingue et ses dialectes (Malinké, Bambara, Dîoula). I. Introduction, grammaire, lexique français-mandingue. Paris, Geuthner, 1929. 674 pages. (Bibliothèque des langues orientales vivantes).

Hopkinson, Emilius. Mandingo vocabulary. 1911, with addenda, 1924. Bathurst, Gambia, Government Printing Office, 1928. 84 pages.

MASAI (Southern Kenya and Northern Tanganyika)

Hinde, *Mrs.* Hildegarde. The Masai language: grammatical notes together with a vocabulary. Cambridge University Press, 1901. ix, 76 pages. (reprinted 1950).

Hollis, *Sir* Alfred Claud. The Masai: their language and folklore. Oxford University Press, 1905. xxviii, 360 pages.

MBUNDU (Angola—central and Luanda areas)

Johnson, Amandus. Mbundu English-Portuguese dictionary, with grammar and syntax. (first series). Philadelphia, Pa., International Printing Co., 1930. 110 pages.

MENDE (Sierra Leone—central and eastern areas)

Schön, James Frederick. Vocabulary of the Mende language. London, Society for the Promotion of Christian Knowledge, 1884. 255 pages.

Sumner, A. T. A handbook of the Mende language. Freetown, Government Printing Office, 1917. 191 pages.

MONGO (Equatorial regions of the Congo Basin)

Hulstaert, G. Dictionnaire français-lomongo (lonkundo). Tervuren, Ann. Mus. Roy. Congo Belge; Antwerp, de Sikkel, for Commission de Linguistique Africaine, 1952. xxi, 466 pages.

Ruskin, E. A. *and* Ruskin, L. Lomongo dictionary. London, Christian Literature Society, 1928. viii, 651 pages.

MOSSI (Upper Volta)

Alexandre, G. Dictionnaire möré-français et lexique français-möré. Maison Carrée, Alger, Imprimerie des Pères Blancs, 1934–35. 2 volumes.

NDANDE

Baudet, Guibert. Eléments de grammaire kinande suivis d'un vocabulaire kinande-français et français-kinande. Brussels, Etablissements Généraux d'Imprimerie, 1949. 186 pages.

NANDI (West-Central Kenya)

Hollis, *Sir* Alfred Claud. The Nandi: their language and folklore. Oxford University Press, 1909. xl, 328 pages.

NGALA (a lingua franca, spoken mostly by Bantu tribes along the vast stretch of the central part of the main Congo River)

Guthrie, Malcolm. Grammaire et dictionnaire de lingala: avec un manuel de conversation français-lingala. 2nd edition. Léopoldville, Librairie Evangélique du Congo, 1951. 190 pages. (first published 1935).

Vocabulaire lingala-français: français-lingala. Nouvelle-Anvers, Mission de Scheut, 1937. 344 pages.

NUBIAN (Sudan)

Murray, George William. An English-Nubian comparative dictionary. London, Milford, 1923. xli, 194 pages. (Harvard African Studies, volume IV).

NUER (Southern Sudan—Upper Nile and Bahr el Ghazal Provinces)

Huffman, Ray. Nuer-English dictionary. Berlin, Reimer, 1929. 63 pages.

Huffman, Ray. English-Nuer dictionary. London, Oxford University Press, 1931. viii, 80 pages.

Kiggen, J. Nuer-English dictionary. Steyl bij Tegelen, Drukkerij van het Missiehuis, 1948. 346 pages. (reprinted Mill Hill, 1954).

Stigand, Chauncey Hugh. A Nuer-English vocabulary. Cambridge University Press, 1923. 33 pages.

NUPE (Central Nigeria)

Banfield, A. W. Dictionary of the Nupe language. 1. Nupe-English. 2. English-Nupe. Shonga, Nigeria, Niger Press, 1914–16. 2 volumes.

NYAMWEZI

Dahl, Edmund. Nyamwezi-Wörterbuch. Hamburg, Friederichsen, 1915. xv, 696 pages. (Abhandlungen des Hamburgischen Kolonial-instituts, Band 25, Reihe B, Band 15).

NYANEKA (Angola)

Bonne Foux, B. M. Dicionario olunyaneka-portuguès. Huila, Angola, Missão da Huila, 1940. viii, 206 pages.

NYANJA (Nyasaland)

Scott, David Clement. Dictionary of the Nyanja language, being the encyclopaedic dictionary of the Mang'anja language, edited and enlarged by Alexander Hetherwick. London, Religious Tract Society, 1929. viii, 612 pages. (new edition, 1951).

NIKA

Krapf, Ludwig *and* Rebmann, Johannes. A Nika-English dictionary. Edited by T. H. Sparshott. London, Society for the Promotion of Christian Knowledge, 1887. vii, 391 pages.

NYORO (Northern Uganda)

Davis, M. B. A Lunyoro-Lunyankole-English and English-Lunyoro-Lunyankole dictionary. Kampala, Uganda Book Shop; London, Society for the Promotion of Christian Knowledge, 1938. xi, 332 pages. (reprinted 1953: Kampala, Uganda Book Shop; London, Macmillan).

OTETELA

Hagendorens, J. Dictionnaire français otetela. Tshumbe Sainte Marie, Imprimerie de la Mission Catholique, 1943. 369 pages.

RIF (or Berbèr. Rif Mountains of North Morocco)

Ibáñez, Esteban. Diccionario español-rifeño. Madrid, Ministerio de Asuntos Exteriores, Junta de Relaciones Culturales, 1944. xxxii, 440 pages.
Ibáñez, Esteban. Diccionario rifeño-español (etimologico). Madrid, Instituto de Estudios Africanos, 1949. 336 pages.

RONGA (Portuguese East Africa and South Africa)

Quintão, José L. Dicionarios xironga-português e português-xironga. Lisbon, Agéncia Geral das Colónias, 1951. 177 pages.

RUNDI

Dictionnaire français-kirundi, kirundi-français.   Roesselare, Belgium, De Meester, 1909.

Burgt, J. M. M. van der.   Dictionnaire français-kirundi.   Bois le Duc, the Netherlands, Société Illustration Catholique, 1903.   cxix, 640 pages.

SANGA (Belgian Congo—Katanga Province)

Roland, Hadelin.   Vocabulaire français-kisanga.   Abbaye de Saint André lez Bruges, 1938.   150 pages.

SANGO (Ubangi-Shari)

Calloc'h, J.   Vocabulaire français-sango et sango-français: langue commerciale de l'Oubangi-Chari, précédé d'un agrégé grammatical. Paris, Geuthner, 1911.   viii, 86 pages.

SERER (Senegal)

Greffier, H.   Dictionnaire français-sérère, précédé d'un abrégé de la grammaire sérère.   St. Joseph de Ngasobil, Imprimerie de la Mission, 1901.   x, 330 pages.

SHAMBALA (Tanganyika)

Lang, Heinrich F.   Schambala-Wörterbuch.   Hamburg, 1921.   502 pages.   (Abhandlungen des Hamburgischen Kolonialinstituts, Reihe B, Band 23).

SHILLUK (Southern Sudan—Upper Nile Province, especially round Malakal)

Kohnen, B.   Grammatica della lingua scilluk con l'aggiunta di un piccolo dizionario italiano-scilluk.   Cairo, Missione dell'Africa Centrale, 1931.   201 pages.

SHONA (Southern Rhodesia, Mashonaland and Moçambique)

Barnes, Bertram H.   A vocabulary of the dialects of Mashonaland in the new orthography.   London, Sheldon Press, 1932.   214 pages.

Biehler, Edward.   A Shona dictionary, with an outline Shona grammar. revised edition.   Salisbury, Southern Rhodesia, Jesuit Fathers, 1950.   xi, 337 pages.

SIGUI (French Sudan—Mopti District)

Leiris, Michel.   La langue secrète des Dogons de Sanga, Soudan français.   Ouvrage publié avec le concours de la recherche scientifique coloniale.   Paris, Institut d'Ethnologie, 1948.   xxxii, 530 pages. (Université de Paris.   Travaux et Mémoires de l'Institut d'Ethnologie. tome LX).

SOTHO (Basutoland and Orange Free State)

Casalis, A. English-Sotho vocabulary. 11th edition. Morija, Basutoland, Morija Sesuto Book Depot, 1950. 166 pages.

Kriel, T. J. The new Sesotho-English dictionary. Johannesburg, Afrikaanse-Pers-Boekhandel, 1950. 452 pages.

Mabille, Adolphe *and* Dieterlen, H. Southern Sotho-English dictionary; reclassified, revised and enlarged by R. A. Paroz. 7th edition. Morija, Basutoland, Morija Sesuto Book Depot, 1950. xvi, 445 pages. (first published in 1878, under the title: *Sesuto-English vocabulary.* The fifth and sixth editions were called *Sesuto-English dictionary*).

SUDAN

Tucker, Archibald Norman. The eastern Sudanic languages. volume 1. London, published for the International Institute of African Languages and Cultures, by Oxford University Press, 1940. xv, 434 pages. (this volume covers the Eastern Sudanic languages in general, and the Moru-Madi group).

SUK (Kenya)

Beech, Mervyn Worcester Howard. The Suk: their language and folklore. Oxford, Clarendon Press, 1911. xxiv, 151 pages.

SWAHILI (Kenya—and lingua franca throughout many parts of East and Central Africa)

Inter-Territorial Language Committee of the East African Dependencies. A standard English-Swahili [and Swahili-English] dictionary. [Prepared] under the direction of the late Frederick Johnson. London, Oxford University Press, 1939. 2 volumes.

Krapf, Ludwig. Swahili dictionary: being Dr. Krapf's original Swahili-English dictionary [published 1882] revised and re-arranged by the Rev. Canon Binns. London, S.P.C.K., 1925. vii, 301 pages.

Sacleux, Charles. Dictionnaire swahili-français [et français-swahili]. Paris, Institut d'Ethnologie, 1939-49. 2 volumes. (Travaux et Mémoires de l'Institut d'Ethnologie, de l'Université de Paris, XXXVI–XXXVIII, LIV). (the first volume, Swahili-French, is 2nd edition, 1949).

Velten, C. Suaheli-Wörterbuch. Leipzig, Harrassowitz, 1933. 2 volumes.

TEDA

Le Coeur, Charles. Dictionnaire ethnographique téda, précédé d'un lexique français-téda. Dakar, Centre IFAN, 1950. 213 pages. (Mémoires de l'Institut Français d'Afrique Noire, IX).

TEMNE (Sierra Leone)

Schlenker, Christian Friedrich. An English-Temne dictionary. London, Church Missionary Society, 1880. viii, 403 pages.

Thomas, Northcote Whitridge. Timne-English dictionary. London, Harrison, 1916. (Anthropological Report on Sierra Leone, part II). 139 pages.

TESO (Uganda—Eastern Province)

Kitching, Arthur Leonard. The Ateso language. London, 1915. 144 pages.

TIV (Northern Nigeria—alternative name of Munshi or Munci)

Abraham, Roy Clive. A dictionary of the Tiv language. London, Crown Agents for the Colonies, on behalf of the Government of Nigeria, 1940. ix, 331 pages.

Malherbe, W. A. Tiv-English dictionary: with grammar, notes and index. Lagos, Government Printer; London, Crown Agents for the Colonies, 1931. xxxix, 207 pages.

TOGA

Colomb, A. Dictionnaire toga-français et français-toga-anglais . . . Paris, Chadenat, 1890. xxii, 422 pages.

TONGA (Northern Rhodesia—Victoria Falls region)

Griffin, A. W. Chitonga vocabulary of the Zambesi valley. London, Oxford University Press, 1915. 160 pages.

Torrend, J. An English-vernacular dictionary of the Bantu-Botatwe dialects of Northern Rhodesia. London, Kegan Paul, 1932. viii, 649 pages.

TSWA (Moçambique—Inhambane District)

Persson, J. A. An English-Tswa dictionary. Johannesburg, Inhambane Mission Press, 1928. 249 pages.

TSWANA

Brown, John. Secwana dictionary: English-Secwana and Secwana-English. London, London Missionary Society, 1895. 466 pages.

TUAREG (French Sudan)

Foucauld, Charles de. Dictionnaire touareg-français: dialecte de l'Ahaggar. Paris, Imprimerie Nationale de France, 1951–52. volumes 1–4.

TURUKA (French Congo)

Calloc'h, J. Vocabulaire français-gbéa, précédé d'éléments de grammaire. Paris, Geuthner, 1911. 170 pages.

TWI (Gold Coast—Asante, Akwapem, Akem and Brong regions)

Christaller, Johann Gottlieb. Dictionary of the Asante and Fante language called Tshi (Twi). 2nd edition. Basle, Basel Evangelical Missionary Society, 1933. xxxii, 607 pages. (first published 1881).

VENDA

Marole, L. T. *and* Gama, L. J. de. English-Tshivenda vocabulary. Morija, Basutoland, Morija Printing Works, 1936. 93 pages.

Warmelo, N. J. van. Tshivenda-English dictionary. Pretoria, Union of South Africa, Department of Native Affairs, 1937. 345 pages. (Ethnological Publications, VI).

WOLOF (Senegal and Gambia)

Guy-Grand, V. J. Dictionnaire français-volof et volof-français. Dakar 1923. viii, 627 pages.

XHOSA (Cape Province—eastern and north-eastern districts. The literary language of Kaffraria and the Transkei)

Bold, J. D. Dictionary and phrase-book of Fanagalo, Kitchen Kafir: the lingua franca of Southern Africa, the Rhodesias, Portuguese East Africa, Nyasaland, Belgian Congo, etc. Cape Town, Central News Agency, 1951. 76 pages.

Kropf, Albert. A Kaffir-English dictionary. 2nd edition. Lovedale, Lovedale Mission Press, 1915. 525 pages. (first published 1899).

McLaren, James. A concise English-Kafir dictionary. London, Longmans, Green, 1923. viii, 319 pages.

McLaren, James. A concise Xhosa-English dictionary, Revised in the new orthography by W. G. Bennie. London, Longmans, Green, 1936. xix, 196 pages.

YANZI

Swartenbroeckx, P. Dictionnaire kiyansi ou kiyei. Brussels, Commission Belge d'Ethnologie, 1948. 2 volumes.

YOMBE (Belgian Congo)

Bittremieux, Leo P. Mayombische Idiotikon. Deel 1 & 2. Ghent, Erasmus Press, 1923. 821 pages. (Congo-Bibliothek, X & XI).

YORUBA (Southern Nigeria and Dahomey)

A dictionary of the Yoruba language. 2nd edition. Lagos, Church Missionary Society, 1937. ii, 461 pages. (first published 1913. reprinted, Oxford University Press, 1950).

Baudin, Noël. Dictionnaire français-yoruba [et yoruba-français]. Lyons, Séminaire des Missions Africaines, 1885. 2 parts.

11   D.F.L.

ZANDE (Southern Sudan—Western Mongalla and Bahr el Ghazal Provinces. Belgian Congo—northern districts—and French Equatorial Africa)

Gore, E. C. Zande and English dictionary. London, Sheldon Press, 1932. vii, 309 pages.

Lagae, C. R. *and* Van den Plas, V. H. Dictionnaire français-zande et zande-français. Brussels, Van Campenhout, 1922–25. 2 volumes.

ZARMA (Nigerian frontier region, east of River Niger)

Ardant du Picq, *Colonel*. La langue songhay, dialecte dyerma: grammaire et lexique français-dyerma et dyerma-français. Paris, Larose, 1933. 170 pages.

Marie, E. Vocabulaire français-djerma et djerma-français. Paris, Leroux, 1914. iv, 99 pages.

ZULU (Zululand and the greater part of Natal)

Bryant, Alfred T. A Zulu-English dictionary. With notes of pronunciation . . . a synopsis of Zulu grammar and a concise history of the Zulu people from the most ancient times. Pinetown, Natal, Mariannhill Mission Press, 1905. 889 pages.

Bryant, Alfred T. An abridged English Zulu word book. 4th edition. Mariannhill, Mariannhill Mission Press, 1940. 471 pages.

Colenso, John William. Zulu-English dictionary. 4th edition. Pietermaritzburg, Vause, Slatter, 1905. xiv, 728 pages. (first published 1861).

Doke, Clement Martyn *and* Vilakazi, Benedict Wallet. Zulu-English dictionary. 2nd edition. Johannesburg, University of the Witwatersrand Press, 1954. xxvi, 918 pages. (first published 1948).

Samuelson, Robert Charles Azariah. The King Cetewayo Zulu dictionary. Durban, 1923. xliii, 995 pages.

DICTIONARIES OF THE LANGUAGES
OF ASIA

The languages of Asia have a far richer lexicographical history than that of any other continent. Throughout their existence a lively curiosity has kept alive the study of derivations and meanings in a way which has benefited modern scholarship and made the task of the research worker easier. This interest comes from many sources: in the first place, the literary men and the scholars in the individual countries have been keen to record details of the grammar and orthography of their native languages and, in such a case as that of Amarasimha, these valuable guides to contemporary opinion have survived almost sixteen hundred years of wars and famines and religious strife. In fact, the survival of ancient manuscripts of all types—in spite of their fragility—has provided a store of examples of the development of each individual language which even now has only briefly been explored.

In other languages of Asia the work which Amarasimha did for Sanskrit was performed by the early travellers from the West. There is, for instance, the remarkable case of the Jesuit, Alexandre de Rhodes, who spent most of his life in South-East Asia. Persecuted, banished and treated at times with great cruelty, Alexandre de Rhodes yet succeeded in spreading the Gospel in China and Indo-China and, from the unpublished materials of Gaspar de Amaral and Antonio Barbosa, in compiling his *Dictionarium annamiticum, lusitanum et latinum* as early as 1651.

Alexandre de Rhodes was a missionary and his was but one of the first of innumerable efforts of the missionaries of the many Christian churches to give the world an ordered account of the languages of the countries in which they were serving. The contribution of Christian missionaries in Africa and Asia to the serious study of philology has never been properly assessed or appreciated. Didactic though their efforts were of necessity, the remarkable honesty and objective attitude with which they invariably approached their task has made their dictionaries of the utmost value to the professional lexicographers. Amateurs in the subject, they showed that ability to adapt and to train themselves in an unfamiliar field which has characterised their work in other fields such as medicine, bridge-building, and forestry, where they have contributed so much to the health and prosperity of the districts which they tended. A typical case is that of Thomas Stephens, S.J., the first Englishman in India, who reached Goa in 1579 and stayed there some forty years. He was the first to make a scientific study of Konkani and Marathi and to write manuals of piety and practical grammars in those languages.

Of the later missionaries, a typical and memorable example is that of Adoniram Judson, an American who was born in Massachusetts in 1788. Judson went to Burma and quickly gained a fluent knowledge of the language. By 1849 he was publishing the first part of his *Burmese and English dictionary* at Moulmein on his own hand-press which had been sent out to him by a group of American well-wishers. By 1852 he had completed his task, and this in spite of the ill-treatment he had received in a Burmese prison during the British invasion of 1826. A glance at the following pages will reveal many similar instances of early missionary work of great importance, and the majority of the twentieth-century dictionaries are based on these pioneer efforts.

As in the Near East field, not every lexicographer had a close acquaintance with the country whose language he was recording. Bernhard Dorn, the early authority on the language of Afghanistan, was Professor of Asiatic Geography in the Oriental Institute at St. Petersburg (and later Librarian of the Imperial Library in the same city) but he does not appear to have visited the east at any time.

In recent times the missionaries, the scholars of both East and West, and the representatives of industry and commerce, have joined forces to produce more comprehensive and authoritative dictionaries of the main languages. With the increasing independence of these newly industrialised countries has come a desire to put the history and the language of each nation on a more satisfactory footing. In fact, in Asia at the present time, a movement closely akin to the activities of the early Academies of Europe appears to be taking place, and generally under the happiest circumstances. The new national dictionary of Sinhalese is a notable example. In other cases, especially in India and in Indo-China, there has been a remarkable revival in indigenous philology, with the result that many great dictionaries have been produced during the last fifty years with little or no help from western scholars. Work, for instance, has commenced on a new dictionary of Sanskrit on historical principles as is shown in the programme of work in *A dictionary of Sanskrit on historical principles* (Poona, Deccan College, 1949. 8, xxxv pages).

Another and very pleasing characteristic has been the tendency to institute new and revolutionary methods of approach in the case of the more difficult languages.   In Japan, Oreste Vaccari and his wife have produced two fine dictionaries based on completely new and more helpful systems of classification, and in China there have been many different systems propounded by the various universities and missions working in the field.   Some of these efforts may have been misguided or even misleading, but they have all contributed to the lively interest and intelligent exploration of a field in which there cannot be too much research at the present time.

Below are given the principal dictionaries of the main languages of Asia arranged alphabetically in each of two sections, the first being devoted to the languages of Afghanistan, India, Pakistan and South-East Asia, and the second to those of the nations of the Far East.

Afghanistan, India, Pakistan and South-East Asia

AFGHAN

Dorn, Bernhard. A chrestomathy of the Pushtū or Afghan language; to which is subjoined a glossary in Afghan and English. St. Petersburg, Imperial Academy of Sciences, 1847. 617 pages.

Gilbertson, George Waters. The Pakkhto idiom: a dictionary. Hertford, the author, 1932. 2 volumes.

Lorimer, John G. Grammar and vocabulary of Waziri Pashto. Calcutta, Government Printer, 1902. 345 pages.

Morgenstierne, Georg. An etymological vocabulary of Pashto. Oslo, Dybwad, 1927. 120 pages. (Skrifter, hist.-fil, Kl. 1927, no. 3, Oslo Academy).

Vaughan, Sir John Luther. A grammar and vocabulary of the Pushtú language (as spoken in the Trans-Indus territories under British rule, etc., etc.). 2nd edition. Calcutta, Thacker, Spink, 1901. vii, 289 pages.

ANNAMITE

Association pour la Formation Intellectuelle et Morale des Annamites (AFIMA). Dictionnaire annamite. Hanoï, Imprimerie Trung-Bắc Tân-văn, 1929–   volume 1–

Barbier, Victor. Dictionnaire annamite-français [et français-annamite]. Hongkong, Hanoï, Imprimerie d'Extrème-Orient, 1919–22. 2 volumes.

Bonet, Jean. Dictionnaire annamite-français (langue officielle et langue vulgaire). Paris, Imprimerie Nationale, 1899-1900. 2 volumes. (Publications de l'Ecole des Langues Orientales Vivantes, sér. 5, tom. 1 & 2).

Cordier, Georges. Dictionnaire français-annamite à l'usage des élèves des écoles et des annamitisants. Hanoï, Imprimerie Tonkinoise, 1930. 1433 pages.

Dào-duy-Anh. Dictionnaire français-annamite (avec transcription en caractères chinois des termes sino-annamites). Hanoï, Lêvăn-Tân, 1936– volume 1–

Emeneau, Murray Barnson *and* Steinen, Diether von den. Annamese-English dictionary, with an English-Annamese index based on work done by John Sherry. Berkeley, Calif., Army Specialised Training Programme, University of California, 1945. vi, 279 leaves.

Génibrel, J. F. M. Dictionnaire annamite-français. 2nd edition. Saigon, 1898.

Hue, Gustave. Dictionnaire annamite-chinois-français. Hanoï, Imprimerie Trung-hoà, 1937. 1210 pages.

Masseron, G. Nouveau dictionnaire français-annamite. Saïgon, Imprimerie de la Mission, 1922. 1083 pages.

Rhodes, Alexandre de. Dictionarium annamiticum lusitanum et latinum. Rome, 1651. 569 pages. (the earliest known Annamite dictionary).

ARDHAMAGADHI

Kapadia, Hiralal Rasikdas. The student's English-Pāiya dictionary (with three appendices). Surat, Karsandas Narandas, 1941. ix, 190 pages.

Ratnachandraji. An illustrated Ardha-Magadhi dictionary, literary, philosophic and scientific, with Sanskrit, Gujrati, Hindi and English equivalents, references to the texts and copious quotations. Dhamandi, published for the S.S. Jain Conference by Ajmer; London, Probsthain, 1923–32. 4 volumes.

ASSAMESE

Anglo-Assamese dictionary. 2nd edition. Nalbari, Baruah, 1952. 752 pages.

Assam Sahitya Sabha, *Jorhat*. Chandra-kanta Abidhani: a comprehensive dictionary of the Assamese language. Jorhat, Assam Sahitya Sabha, 1933. xxx, 1045 pages.

Baruyā, Hemachandra. Hem-Kosa. 2nd edition. Jorhat, Bara-Kataki, 1941. 1030 pages. (Assamese-English only. First published 1900. An etymological dictionary).

Bronson, Miles. A dictionary in Assamese and English. Sibsagor, American Baptist Mission Press, 1867. vii, 609 pages. (compiled with the aid of Jaduram Deka Barua. The first Assamese dictionary: words are written phonetically, and no etymologies are given).

BALUCHI

Dames, Miles Longworth. A sketch of the northern Balochi language, containing a grammar, vocabulary and specimens of the language. Calcutta, Asiatic Society, 1881. 171 pages. (Journal of Asiatic Society, Bengal, volume 49, part 1. Extra number, 1880).

Gilbertson, George Waters *and* Haddíání, Ghan Khán. English-Balochi colloquial dictionary. Hertford, the author, 1925. 2 volumes.

Mayer, T. J. L. English-Balochi dictionary. Lahore, Government Press, 1910. 227 pages.

BENGALI

Dev, Ashu Tosh. Students' favourite dictionary, Anglo-Bengali [and Bengali-English]. Calcutta, the author, 1934–48. 2 volumes. (frequent reprints).

Subalachandra Mitra. The student's Anglo-Bengali [and Bengali-English] dictionary. Calcutta, Mitra; the New Bengali Press, 1923–32. 2 volumes. (frequent reprints).

BIHARI

Hoernle, A. F. Rudolf *and* Grierson, Sir George Abraham. A comparative dictionary of the Bīhārī language. (Index to the Rámáyan of Tulsí Das). Calcutta, 1885-89. Parts I and II. (no more published).

BURMESE

Hough, George Henry. An Anglo-Burmese dictionary. Moulmein, American Mission Press, 1845. 3 parts. (a second edition of Part I: Monosyllables was published in 1861. A projected fourth part was never published).

Htûn Ngyein. The student's English-Burmese dictionary. Revised and enlarged edition. London, Luzac, 1933. 991 pages.

Judson, Adoniram. Burmese-English dictionary. Revised and enlarged by Robert C. Stevenson; edited by F. H. Eveleth. London, Kegan Paul, 1921. 1123 pages.

Judson, Adoniram. English and Burmese dictionary. 8th edition. Rangoon, American Baptist Mission Press, 1922. 928 pages.

Stewart, John A. *and others*. A Burmese-English dictionary, compiled under the direction of J. A. Stewart, from material supplied by a large number of contributors; revised and edited by C. W. Dunn and Hla Pe. London, published under the auspices of the University of Rangoon, by Luzac, 1940– volume 1–

BURUSHASKI

Lorimer, David Lockhart Robertson. The Burushaski language. Volume 3: Vocabularies and indexes (Burushaski-English, Werchikwar-

English, Indexes of English words). Oslo, Aschehoug: Cambridge, Mass., Harvard University Press, 1938. xvi, 545 pages. (Instituttet for Sammenlignende Kulturforskning, Serie B, 29.3).

CAMBODIAN

Dictionnaire cambodgien. Phnôm-Penh, Editions de la Bibliothèque Royale de Cambodge, 1938– volume 1– (entirely in Cambodian).

Guesdon, J. Dictionnaire cambodgien-français. Paris, Plon-Nourrit, 1930. 1997 pages.

GUJARATI

Belsāre, Malhār Bhikājī. An etymological Gujarati-English dictionary. 3rd edition. Ahmedábád, R. M. Shah, 1927. xii, 1207 pages. (first published in 1895).

Mehta, Bhanusukhram Nirgunram *and* Mehta, Bharatram Bhanusukhram. The modern Gujarati-English dictionary. Raopura, Kothari; London, Kegan Paul, 1925. 2 volumes.

Oza, Shantilal S. Taraporevala's up-to-date Gujarati-English dictionary. Bombay, Taraporevala, 1938. 1296 pages.

Vyas, Vithalrai Goverdhanprasad *and* Patel, Shankerbhai Galabhai. The standard English-Gujarati dictionary. 6th edition. Bombay, Tripathi; London, Kegan Paul, 1923. 2 volumes. (first published in 1894).

GURKHALI

Cornelius, A. W. Gurkhali to English [and English to Gurkhali] dictionary. Dehra Dun, Jugal Kishire, 1944. 2 volumes.

HINDI (see also HINDUSTANI, URDU and PUNJABI—the four languages have close affinities, and are together spoken by some 150 million people)

Bhargava's standard illustrated dictionary of the Hindi language: Anglo-Hindi, Hindi-English. Edited by R. C. Pathak. Benares, Shree Ganga Pustakalaya, 1946–47. 2 volumes. (Concise Hindi-English edition published 1950. 1090 pages).

Lal, Mukundī *and* Sahay, Raj Vallabh. Hindī sábd Sangrah. Benares, 1930. 600 pages. (includes quotations).

Lal, Ram Narain. Student's practical dictionary: Hindi-English. Allahábád, Lal, 1949. 1350 pages.

HINDUSTANI (see also URDU)

Craven, Thomas. The new royal dictionary: English into Hindustani and Hindustani into English. 1932 edition, revised by J. R. Chitambar. Lucknow, Methodist Publishing House, 1932. 700 pages.

Fallon, S. W. A new English-Hindustani dictionary, with illustrations from English literature and colloquial English, translated into Hindustani. Lahore, Gulab Singh, 1941. ii, 703 pages.

Fallon, S. W. A new Hindustani-English dictionary, with illustrations from Hindustani literature and folklore. Benares, Medical Hall Press; London, Trübner, 1879. xxxiii, 1219 pages.

INDONESIAN

Boer, D. W. N. de. De indonesische aanvulling van het maleise woorden-boek; in het bijzonder de Z. G. " Kata 'Istilah ", vaktechnische termen en uitdrukkingen. Leiden, Brill, 1949. xiv, 68 pages. (the dictionary referred to is H. C. Klinkert's *Nieuw maleisch-nederlandsch woordenboek*, 1947—see page 150).

Gericke, J. F. C. *and* Roorda, T. Javaansch-nederlandsch handwoorden-boek. Vermeerderd en verbeterd door A. C. Vreede, met medewerking van J. G. H. Gunning. Leiden, Brill, 1901. 2 volumes.

Pino, E. *and* Wittermans, T. English-Indonesian, Indonesian-English dictionary. London, Luzac, 1953. 2 volumes.

Pernis, H. D. van. Woordenboek bahasa Indonesia-Nederlands. Groningen & Jakarta, Wolters, 1950. xii, 317 pages.

Poerwadarminta, W. J. S. *and* Teeuw, A. Indonesisch-nederlands woordenboek. 2nd edition. Groningen & Jakarta, Wolters, 1952. xiv, 383 pages. (first published 1950).

Van Goor's Indonesisch zakwoordenboek: indonesisch-nederlands en nederlands-indonesisch, bewerkt door A. L. N. Kramer. The Hague, Van Goor, 1950. viii, 573 pages. (a concise edition was published in 1952. 359 pages).

KANNADA

Bucher, J. *and* Watsa, C. A Kannada-English school dictionary. 2nd edition. Mangalore, 1923. 539 pages. (first published 1899).

Kittel, Ferdinand. A Kannada-English dictionary. Mangalore, Basel Mission Book & Tract Depository, 1894. li, 1752 pages.

Ziegler, F. English-Kanarese school dictionary. revised edition. London, Kegan Paul, 1929. 614 pages. (first published in 1919).

KASHMIRI

Grierson, *Sir* George Abraham. A dictionary of the Kāshmīrī language. Compiled partly from materials left by the late . . . Iśvara Kaula, by Sir George A. Grierson . . . assisted by . . . Mukandarāma Śāstrī. Calcutta, Asiatic Society, 1916–32. xxiii, 1252 pages. (Bibliotheca Indica, new series).

MALAY

Clifford, *Sir* Hugh Charles *and* Swettenham, *Sir* Frank Athelstane.
A dictionary of the Malay language: Malay-English. Parts I to V
(A to G). Taiping, the authors, 1894–1902. vi, 509 pages. (no
more published).

Klinkert, H. C.   Nieuw nederlandsch-maleisch (en maleisch-nederlandsch) woordenboek.   Leiden, Brill, 1926–47.   2 volumes. (3rd
and 5th editions respectively).

Swettenham, *Sir* Frank Athelstane.   Vocabulary of the English and
Malay languages, with notes.   7th-8th editions.   Shanghai, Hongkong, Kelly & Walsh, 1908–09.   2 volumes.

Wilkinson, Richard James.   A Malay-English dictionary (romanised).
Mytilene, Salavopoulos & Kinderlis;   Singapore, Kelly & Walsh,
1932.   2 volumes in 1.   (abridged edition published in 1952. 270
pages).

Winstedt, *Sir* Richard Olof.   An English-Malay dictionary (roman
characters).   3rd edition.   Singapore, Kelly & Walsh;   London,
Kegan Paul, 1949.   iii, 524 pages.

Winstedt, *Sir* Richard Olof.   A practical modern English-Malay dictionary.   Singapore, Kelly & Walsh;   London, Kegan Paul, 1952.
388 pages.   (an abridgement of the *English-Malay dictionary* with
some additions).

MALAYALAM

Gundert, Hermann.   A Malayalam and English dictionary.   Mangalore,
Basel Mission Book and Tract Depository, 1872.   xviii, 1116 pages.
(Malayalam-English only).

Zacharias, Tobias.   Anglo-Malayalam dictionary.   Revised and enlarged
by Oliver F. E. Zacharias.   2nd edition.   Mangalore, Basel Mission
Book and Tract Depository, 1933.   1362 pages.

MARATHI

Ranade, Nilkanth Babaji.   The twentieth century English-Marathi
dictionary: pronouncing, etymological, literary, scientific and
technical.   Bombay, Nirnaya-Saga Press, 1916.   2 volumes.

MUNDARI

Bhaduri, Maṇīndra-Bhūshaṇa.   A Mundari-English dictionary.   Calcutta
University Press;   London, Longmans, Green, 1931.   xv, 229 pages.

NEPALI

Kilgour, Robert.   English-Nepali dictionary, revised and arranged
by H. C. Duncan.   Darjeeling, Government Branch Press, 1923.
391 pages.

Pushkara Ṣamṣer *and others*. Angrejī-Nepali kosa. Compiled by Pushkara Ṣamṣer, Devavīra Pāṇḍe, Khangamāna Malla, and Pūrṇamāna Sreshṭha. 1936-38. 2 volumes.

Turner, Ralph Lilley. A comparative and etymological dictionary of the Nepali language; with indexes of all words quoted from other Indo-Aryan languages; compiled by Dorothy Rivers Turner. London, Kegan Paul, 1931. xxiv, 935 pages.

ORIYA

Pūrṇṇachandra oria bhāṣākoṣa: [Oria-Bengali-Hindi-English]. Cuttack, Utkala Sahitya Press, 1931-40. 7 volumes.

PALI

Andersen, Dines *and* Smith, Helmer. A critical Pāli dictionary. Begun by V. Trenckner; revised, continued and enlarged by D. Andersen and H. Smith. Copenhagen, Kongelige Dansk Videnskabernes Selskab, 1924– volume 1–

Buddhadatta Mahāthera, A. P. Concise Pāli-English dictionary. Colombo, Colombo Apothecaries' Company, 1949. xii, 281 pages.

Childers, Robert Caesar. A dictionary of the Pali language. London, Trübner, 1875. xxxvi, 624 pages. (reprinted in 1909).

Pali Text Society. Pali-English dictionary: edited by T. W. Rhys Davids and William Stede. Chipstead, the Society, 1925. 743 pages. (reprinted 1949).

Widurupola Piyatissa Mahā Nāyaka Thera, *Pandit*. The English-Pāli dictionary. Colombo, Colombo Apothecaries' Company, 1949. xvii, 747 pages.

PUNJABI

Hares, Walter Pullin. An English-Punjabi dictionary. Lahore, Civil & Military Gazette; London, Kegan Paul, 1929. iii, 478 pages.

Jawahir Singh. English to Punjabi dictionary. Amritsar, Wazir-i-Hind Press, 1905. vii, 241 pages.

Māyā Siṃha. The Panjábí dictionary. Lahore, Singh, 1895. vi, 1221 pages. (Panjabi-English only).

SANSKRIT

Amarasiṃha. Cosha; or, dictionary of the Sanskrit language, by Amera Sinha; with an English interpretation, and annotations, by H. T. Colebrooke. Serampore, Carey, 1808. vii, 641 pages.

Amarasiṃha. Amarasara; or, an abridgment of Amarakosha. Being a Sanskrit-English and English-Sanskrit pocket dictionary, by Mahader Shivram Gole. 3rd edition, revised and rearranged by K. G. Oka. Poona, 1915. x, 524 pages.

Āpte, Vāmana Sivarāma. The student's English-Sanskrit [and Sanskrit-English] dictionary. Bombay, Sagoon; Gopal Narayen, 1893–1922. 2 volumes.

Böhtlingk, Otto von. Sanskrit-Wörterbuch herausgegeben von der Kaiserlichen Akademie der Wissenschaften, bearbeitet von Otto Böhtlingk und Rudolph Roth. St. Petersburg, 1855–75. 7 volumes.

Böhtlingk, Otto von. Sanskrit-Wörterbuch in kürzerer Fassung. St. Petersburg, K. Akademie der Wissenschaften, 1878–89. 7 volumes. (reprinted 1923–25).

Cappeller, Carl. A Sanskrit-English dictionary, based upon the St. Petersburg (i.e. Böhtlingk's) lexicons. Strasbourg, Trübner; London, Luzac, 1891. viii, 672 pages.

Macdonell, Arthur Anthony. A practical Sanskrit dictionary; with transliteration, accentuation, and etymological analysis throughout. Oxford University Press, 1924. xii, 382 pages. (first published in 1893).

Mahīpa. The Anekārtha-Tilaka of Mahīpa: critically edited by Madhukar Mangesh Patkar. Poona, Deccan College Postgraduate & Research Institute, 1947. 219 pages. (Sources of Indo-Aryan Lexicography, I). (This is the first of a series of early Sanskrit lexicons which is being published as part of the preparatory work for the issue of a new historical Sanskrit dictionary on a comprehensive scale).

Mayrhofer, Manfred. Kurzgefasstes etymologisches Wörterbuch des Altindischen. A concise etymological dictionary of Sanskrit. Heidelberg, Winter, 1954–   volume 1– . (to be completed in 8 to 10 fascicles. Basic language German, but English introduction, key to abbreviations and equivalents of Sanskrit words given).

Monier-Williams, Sir Monier. A dictionary, English and Sanskrit. London, William H. Allen, 1851. xiv, 860 pages. (English-Sanskrit only).

Monier-Williams, Sir Monier. A Sanskrit-English dictionary, etymologically and philologically arranged with special reference to cognate Indo-European languages. New edition, greatly enlarged and improved, with the collaboration of E. Leumann, C. Cappeller, and other scholars. Oxford, Clarendon Press, 1899. xxxvi, 1333 pages. (first published in 1872).

Shchupak, N. and others. Dictionnaire sanskrit-français, par N. Stchoupak, L. Nitti et L. Renou. Paris, Maisonneuve, 1931–32. 897 pages. (Publications de l'Institut de Civilisation Indienne). (transcribed into roman; restricted to classical Sanskrit).

Vira, Raghu *and others*. Āmgala-saṃskṛta-hindī-mahājoṣa: an exhaustive English-Sanskrit-Hindi dictionary. Nágpur, International Academy of Indian Culture, 1952–   volume 1–   (to be completed in 10 volumes).

SANTALI

Bodding, Paul Olaf. A Santal dictionary. Oslo, Dybwad, 1929–36. 5 volumes. (Norske Videnskaps-Akademi i Oslo).

Campbell, A. A Santali-English and English-Santali dictionary. 2nd edition, edited by R. M. Macphail. Pokhuria, Santal Mission Press, 1933. 906 pages.

SINDHI

Bulchand, Dulamal. English-Sindhi dictionary. Hyderabad, Kaiseria Press, 1904. 333 pages.

Navani, Khan Chand H. Pocket English-Sindhi dictionary. 1928. 322 pages.

Premier concise English-Sindhi dictionary. Hyderabad, Advani, 1917. 339 pages.

SINHALESE

Carter, Charles. A Sinhalese-English [and English-Sinhalese] dictionary. Colombo, Ceylon Observer, 1924–36. 2 volumes. (first published in 1889).

Geiger, Wilhelm. An etymological glossary of the Sinhalese language. Colombo, 1941–   volume 1–

Jayatilaka, *Sir* D. B. A dictionary of the Sinhalese language. Colombo, Royal Asiatic Society, Ceylon Branch, 1935–   volume 1–

Ratnasuriya, M. Dharmasiri *and* Wijeratne, P. B. F. The shorter Sinhalese-English dictionary. Colombo, University of Ceylon Press Board, 1949-   volume 1-   (based on extracts from Jayatilaka's dictionary. To be completed in 5 volumes).

TAMIL

Ṣaṅkaranārāyaṇa, P. An English-Tamil etymological dictionary, with full Tamil meanings, copious English synonyms, brief and accurate definitions and clear derivations. 2nd edition. Madras, Kameswara, 1911. 1477 pages.

Tamil lexicon. Published under the authority of the University of Madras. Madras, Madras Law Journal Press; London, Luzac, 1926–37. 6 volumes.

—— Supplement. 1938–39.

TELUGU

Brown, Charles Philip. An English and Telugu dictionary . . . revised and enlarged by M. Venkata Ratnam. 2nd edition. Madras, Society for the Promotion of Christian Knowledge, 1895. xxv, 1454 pages.

Brown, Charles Philip. A Telegu-English dictionary. New edition . . . by M. Venkata Ratnam, W. H. Campbell and K. Veeresalingam Pantulu Garu. 2nd edition. Madras, Society for the Promotion of Christian Knowledge, 1903. viii, 1416 pages.

Galletti di Cadilhac, Arthur M. A. C. Galletti's Telugu dictionary: a dictionary of current Telugu. London, Oxford University Press, 1935. xvii, 434 pages.

Saṅkaranārāyaṇa, P. An English-Telugu medium dictionary, with English synonyms and definitions (abridged from the author's larger dictionary). Revised and enlarged edition. Ellore, Venkatrama, 1936. 997 pages.

Saṅkaranārāyaṇa, P. A Telugu-English [and English-Telugu] dictionary. Madras, Sastrulu, 1927-28. 2 volumes.

THAI

Amnuay Silpa School *and* Dansuputra, C. Scholars' Siamese-English dictionary: a useful manual for students of both languages, containing more than 13,500 entries by the Amnuay Silpa School staff in collaboration with C. Dansuputra. 3rd edition. Bangkok, Amnuay Silpa School, 1936. 788 pages. (first published in 1932).

Cartwright, Basil Osborn. A Siamese-English dictionary. Bangkok, American Presbyterian Mission Press, 1907. 751 pages.

Haas, Mary Rosamond. Special dictionary of the Thai language. Berkeley, Calif., Army Specialised Training Program, University of California, 1945. 2 volumes. (a revision and expansion of a phonetic dictionary of the Thai language is now being undertaken by the author).

Halliday, Robert. A Mon-English dictionary. Bangkok, Siam Society, 1922. xxx, 512 pages.

McFarland, George Bradley. Thai-English dictionary. Bangkok, Times Press, 1941. xxiii, 1058 pages. (reprinted, Stanford University Press; London, Milford, 1944).

McFarland, Samuel Gamble. An English-Siamese dictionary, containing 14,000 words and idiomatic expressions; originally prepared by S. G. McFarland, 1865: revised and enlarged by George B. McFarland . . . 10th edition. London, Kegan Paul, 1937. 661 pages. (first published 1865).

Pallegoix, Jean Baptiste. Dictionnaire siamois français-anglais, revu par J. Vey. Bangkok, Imprimerie de la Mission Catholique, 1896. 1234 pages. (first published in 1854).

So Sreshthaputra. The new model English-Thai dictionary. Bangkok, 1940. 4 volumes.

TIBETAN

Bell, *Sir* Charles Alfred. English-Tibetan colloquial dictionary. 2nd edition. Calcutta, Bengal Secretariat Book Depot, 1920. 562 pages.

Gould, Sir Basil John *and* Richardson, Hugh Edward. Tibetan word book; with a foreword by Sir Aurel Stein. London, Milford, 1943. xvi, 447 pages.

Jäschke, Heinrich August. A Tibetan-English dictionary, with special reference to the prevailing dialects, to which is added an English-Tibetan vocabulary. Prepared and published at the charge of the Secretary of State for India in Council. London, Kegan Paul, 1934. xxxii, 671 pages. (reprint of 1st ed., 1882).

Sarachchandra Dāsa. A Tibetan-English dictionary with Sanskrit synonyms. Revised and edited under the orders of the Government of Bengal, by Graham Sandberg and A. William Heyde. Calcutta, Bengal Secretariat Book Depot, 1902. xxiv, 1353 pages.

Zla-Ba Bsam 'Grub, *Kazi*. An English-Tibetan dictionary, containing a vocabulary of approximately twenty thousand words with their Tibetan equivalents. Calcutta, the University, 1919. xiv, 989 pages.

URDU

Abdul Huq. The standard English-Urdu dictionary. Aurangabad, Anjuman-e-Urdu Press, 1937. x, 1538 pages.

Ferozson's English-Urdu dictionary. English words with their equivalents in Urdu. Compiled by a Board of Editors. Karachi, Ferozson, 1950. 835 pages.

Majīd, 'Abdul. Jāmi' ul-Lugāt: a new Urdu dictionary. Lahore, Jāmi' ul-Lugāt Press, 1935. 4 volumes. (the largest of recent Urdu dictionaries—to some extent treatment is encyclopaedic, short biographies and some religious and geographical information being included).

Platts, John Thompson. A dictionary of Urdū, classical Hindī and English. 4th impression. London, Crosby Lockwood, 1911. viii, 1259 pages. (first published in 1884).

VIETNAMESE

Dao-Duy-Anh. Pháp-Viet Tov-Diêń, Chú Thêm chûv Hán: dictionnaire français-vietnamien, avec transcription en caractères chinois des termes sino-vietnamiens. Paris, Minh-Tân, 1951.

The Far East
CHINESE

N.B. It will be noted that several of the dictionaries listed below are published by the Harvard-Yenching Institute whose work in this field is well known throughout the world. A great Chinese-English dictionary has long been in preparation at the Institute, the intention being to supersede the existing bilingual dictionaries which are generally admitted to be unsatisfactory. It is planned to include all available Chinese lexicographical materials and to cover every period of the language from antiquity to modern times. The first fruits of this vast project have already appeared in the shape of a pilot effort: *Chinese-English dictionary project: fascicle 39.0.1: preliminary print.* (Harvard University Press, 1953. iv, 95 pages).

Chang, P'êng-yün. Han-Ying ta-tz'u-tien. revised edition. Shanghai, Republican Press, 1930. 807 pages. (Chinese-English).
—— Supplementary volume. 1937. 415 pages.

Chao, Yüan-Jên *and* Yang, Lien Sheng. The concise dictionary of spoken Chinese. Cambridge, Mass., Harvard University Press for the Harvard-Yenching Institute, 1947. xxxix, 291 pages. (Mandarin, with indications of obsolete and dialect forms where important).

Ch'en Shou-jung. A concise English-Chinese dictionary, with romanised standard pronunciation. Palo Alto, Stanford University Press, 1946. 390 pages.

Chinese encyclopedic dictionary. Shanghai, Commercial Press, 1915. 2 volumes. (Supplement, 1931).

Fenn, Courtenay Hughes. The five thousand dictionary: a Chinese-English pocket dictionary and index to the character cards of the College of Chinese Studies, California College in China . . . 5th edition. Peking, 1940. 697 pages. (reprinted in revised American edition, by Harvard University Press, 1942. 694 pages).

Giles, Herbert Allen. A Chinese-English dictionary. 2nd edition. Shanghai, Kelly & Walsh; London, Quaritch, 1912. 2 volumes.

Goodrich, Chauncey. A pocket dictionary (Chinese-English) and Pekingese syllabary. Shanghai, Kwang Hsueh Publishing House, 1933; New York, Columbia University Press, 1944. vi, 308 pages. (first published 1891. reprint of 1918 issue).

Hemeling, Karl E. English-Chinese dictionary of the standard Chinese spoken language . . . Shanghai, Inspectorate of Customs, 1916. 1726 pages.

Hillier, *Sir* Walter Caine. An English-Chinese dictionary of Peking colloquial. New edition, enlarged by Sir Trelawny Backhouse and Sidney Barton. London, Kegan Paul, 1924. 1030 pages.

Huang Shi-fu *and* Chiang T'ieh. Tsung-ho Ying-Han ta-tz'u-tien. 2nd edition. Shanghai, Commercial Press, 1948. xvi, 1674 pages. (English-Chinese).

Mathews, Robert Henry. Mathews' Chinese-English dictionary. revised American edition. Cambridge, Mass., Harvard University Press for the Harvard-Yenching Institute, 1943. xxiv, 1226 pages. (first published in 1931).

—— Index. 1947. 186 pages.

Nash, Vernon. Trindex: an index to three dictionaries: Giles' Chinese-English dictionary, K'ang Hsi tzu tien, P'ei wen yun fu . . . Peiping, Yenching University, Index Press, 1936. lxx, 584 pages.

Shu Hsin-ch'eng *and others*. Tz'u-hai. Shanghai, Chung-hua-shu-chü, 1939. (frequently reprinted).

Simon, W. A beginner's Chinese-English dictionary of the national language (Gwoyeu).* London, Lund Humphries, 1947. cxxxiv, 1064 pages.

Soothill, William Edward. The student's four thousand . . . and general pocket dictionary. 19th edition. London, Kegan Paul, 1949.

Ting-I Fu. Dictionary of compound expressions. Peiping & Shanghai, Fu-chin shu-shê, 1943. 10 volumes and index volume.

Wang Hsüeh-che. Hsien-tai Han-Ying tz'u tien; edited by Wang Yün-wu. Chungking, Commercial Press, 1946. 735 pages.

Wang Yün-wu ta-tz'u-tien. Shanghai, Commercial Press, 1930. 1641 pages.

Webster, Noah. Webster's collegiate dictionary with Chinese translation. Editors: P. W. Kuo and S. L. Chang. Shanghai, Commercial Press, 1933. xliii, 1768 pages.

Williams, Samuel Wells. A syllabic dictionary of the Chinese language arranged according to the Wu-Fang Yüan Yin . . . alphabetically rearranged according to the romanisation of Sir Thomas F. Wade, by a Committee of the North China Mission of the American Board. Tung Chou, North China Union College, 1909. lxxxiv, 1056 pages.

Yen, Hui-ch'ing. An English and Chinese standard dictionary . . . 4th edition. Shanghai, Commercial Press, 1916. 1377 pages.

JAPANESE

Daniels, Otome. Dictionary of Japanese (Sōsho) writing forms. London, Lund Humphries, 1944. xix, 357 pages.

---

* The system of romanisation for Chinese words called Gwoyeu Romatzyh (literally, National Language Latin script) was first promulgated by the Chinese Ministry of Education in 1928.

Fuzambo's comprehensive English-Japanese dictionary. Cambridge, Mass., Harvard University Press, 1942. 1865 pages.

Hepburn, James Curtis. A Japanese-English and English-Japanese dictionary. 4th edition. Tokio, Maruya; London, Trübner, 1888. xxxiii, 962 pages.

Ishikawa, Rinshiro. Sanseido's new concise dictionary. Minneapolis, Harrison & Smith, 1944. 2 volumes.

Jones, J. Ira *and* Peeke, Harmon van Slyck. 6000 Chinese characters with Japanese pronunciation and Japanese and English renderings. 4th edition. Tokio, Kyobun kwan, 1936. xix, 223 pages.

Karlgren, Bernhard. Analytic dictionary of Chinese and Sino-Japanese. Paris, Geuthner, 1923. 436 pages.

Kenkyusha's new English-Japanese dictionary on bilingual principles. Y. Okakura, general editor. Berkeley, Cal., University of California Press, 1942. 2514 pages. (first published in 1936).

Kenkyusha's new Japanese-English dictionary . . . Takenobu Yoshitaro, general editor. Tokio, The Kenkyusha; London, Lund Humphries, 1942. 2285 pages.

Lu, Jo-ming. Sōsho dictionary . . . South Pasadena, Cal., Perkins, 1944. 152 pages.

Miyazaki, Seiji. The Japanese dictionary explained in English. Tokio, The Kenkyusha, 1950. 888 pages.

Otsuki, Buengen. Daigenkai. Tokio, Fuzambo, 1932– volume 1–

Pierson, Jan Lodewÿk. 10,000 Chinese-Japanese characters. Leiden, Brill, 1926. xxvi, 748 pages.

Rose-Innes, Arthur. Beginners' dictionary of Chinese-Japanese characters . . . American edition. Cambridge, Mass., Harvard University Press, 1942. 532 pages. (reprint of 1927. also reprinted 1950, etc.).

Saito, Hidesaburo. Saito's Japanese-English dictionary. Tokio, Nichieisha, 1931. 1160 pages.

Satow, Sir Ernest Mason *and* Ishibashi, Masakata. An English-Japanese dictionary of the spoken language. 4th edition, by E. M. Hobart-Hampden and Harold G. Parlett. Tokio, The Sanseidō, 1919. ix, 1550 pages. reprinted Tokio, 1936; South Pasadena, Cal., Perkins, 1942).

Suski, Peter Marie. The dictionary of " kanji " or Japanese characters, with pronunciations, intonations and definitions in English. Los Angeles, Science Society; London, Kegan Paul, 1928. 237 pages.

Takahashi, M. Romanised* English-Japanese and Japanese-English dictionary. London, Bailey Brothers & Swinfen, 1952. 2 volumes.

---

*The system of the Romanisation of Japanese was officially approved 21st September, 1937.

Takehara, Tsuneta. A standard English-Japanese dictionary. 17th edition. Tokio & Osaka, Hōbunkan, 1925. viii, 1677 pages.

Ueda, Mannen. Daijiten: a Japanese dictionary of Chinese characters and compounds. American edition. Cambridge, Mass., Harvard University Press, 1942. 2918 pages.

Vaccari, Oreste *and* Vaccari, *Mrs*. Enko Elisa. A.B.C. Japanese-English dictionary: an entirely new method of classification of the Chinese-Japanese characters. Tokio, Vaccari; New York, Brentano, 1949. 2 volumes.

Vaccari, Oreste *and* Vaccari, *Mrs*. Enko Elisa. The up-to-date English-Japanese conversation dictionary (Romanised). 6th edition. Tokio, Vaccari, 1950. xxxix, 438 pages. (first published in 1939).

KOREAN

Gale, James Scarth. Unabridged Korean-English dictionary. 3rd edition, edited by Alexander A. Pieters. Seoul, Christian Literature Society, 1931. 1781 pages.

Lew, Hyungki J. New life Korean-English, English-Korean dictionary. Washington, D.C., Educational Services, 1952. 2170 pages. (reprint of 1st edition, printed in 2 volumes, Seoul, 1947-50).

Underwood, Horace Grant *and* Underwood, Horace Norton. An English-Korean dictionary. Revised by Edwin Wade Koons and Oh Seung Kun. Seoul, YMCA Printing Department, 1925. 746 pages.

MANCHU

Hauer, Erich. Handwörterbuch der Mandschusprache. Wiesbaden, Harrassowitz, 1953-54. (issued in 3 parts).

MONGOLIAN

Bleichsteiner, R. *and others*. Wörterbuch der heutigen mongolischen Sprache mit kurzem Abriss der Grammatik und ausgewählten Sprachproben. Vienna & Peking, Siebenberg-Verlag, 1941. 135 pages. (includes technical terms).

Boberg, Folke. Mongolian-English, English-Mongolian dictionary. Stockholm, Förlaget Filadelfia AB; New York, Stechert-Hafner, 1955. 3 volumes. (published with the support of the Langman Cultural Fund of Uppsala. 3rd volume is English-Mongolian).

Kowalewski, Józef Szczepan. Dictionnaire mongol-russe-français . . . Kazan, Imprimerie de l'Université, 1844–49. 3 volumes.

Shmidt, Iakov Ivanovich. Mongolisch-deutsch-russisches Wörterbuch, nebst einem deutschen und einem russischen Wortregister. St. Petersburg, K. Akademie der Wissenschaften, 1835. viii, 613 pages.

U.S. Department of the Army. Mongolian vocabulary (modern Khalkha language). (Mongolian-English, English-Mongolian). Compiled by D. A. Trozel. Washington, D.C., 1953. v, 725 pages. (Technical Manual TM 30-537).

N.B. Work on the preparation of a new Mongolian-English dictionary has commenced at the Institute of East Asiatic Studies, University of California, under the direction of Dr. Ferdinand Lessing.

APPENDICES

I. Technical Dictionaries

II. General Bibliography

TECHNICAL DICTIONARIES

From time to time even the large general dictionaries prove inadequate and recourse must be had to more specialised lexicons which deal with a single subject or with a group of related topics. The provision is however very unequal: some languages are well provided with technical vocabularies, while others have few or none. Moreover, some of the best general dictionaries sometimes contain more technical words on a given subject than the smaller vocabularies devoted to that topic: it has been said, for instance, that Mansion has proved the best technical dictionary in the French language for many a specialised subject, and a glance at the sub-titles of many of the larger general dictionaries listed in the main body of this work will reveal how much attention has been paid to modern science and technology. Nevertheless, technical dictionaries are needed, and there is a vast number of specialised vocabularies available, and new titles are now being published at very frequent intervals. Here have been listed a selection of those available, and they have been listed (with rather less detail than that given to the general dictionaries) in the following order: I. General Technical Dictionaries —(a) Polyglot, and (b) Single Languages arranged alphabetically by language. II. Specialised Dictionaries, arranged alphabetically by subject.

Readers are also reminded that the classified sections of many foreign business directories can act as auxiliaries, through their practice of giving the subject-headings in several languages. Moreover it is increasingly the custom of editors of directories of specific products and groups of products to include vocabularies of foreign-language equivalents of technical trade terms.

For further titles the excellent lists published by the Science Library should be consulted, and for those in science and technology Dr. J. E. Holmstrom's *Bibliography of interlingual scientific and technical dictionaries* (Paris, Unesco; London, H.M.S.O., 1954. xlvii, 178 pages), and its previous editions, should be used at all times. The latter, with its skilful arrangement and detailed information concerning 1629 dictionaries in 75 languages, arranged under 237 subject headings, is an essential reference tool.

GENERAL DICTIONARIES

Polyglot

Airas, V. *and others*. Technical vocabulary: German, English, Finnish, Swedish, Russian. 2nd edition. Helsinki, Otava, 1950.

Baudry, H. "D.A.": dictionnaire d'abbréviations: françaises et étrangères, techniques et usuelles, anciennes et nouvelles. Paris, 1951.

Bildorboken: svenska, engeliska, franska, tyska. Stockholm, Forum, 1947.

Bosch, A. ten. Viertalig technisch woordenboek: nederlands-engels-frans-duits. 4th edition. Deventer, N.V. Uitgevers-Maatschappij, 1948.

Boyd, A. Guide to fourteen Asiatic languages. London, Pilot Press, 1947.

Britannica world language dictionary. New York, Funk & Wagnalls, 1954. (English, French, German, Italian, Spanish, Swedish, Yiddish equivalents of about five thousand most commonly used English words).

Buecken, Francisco J. Vocabulário técnico . . . Portuguese-English-French-German. 2nd edition. New York, Stechert-Hafner, 1952. (first published São Paulo, Melhoramentos, 1947).

Dony, Y. P. de. Léxico del lenguaje figurado. Buenos Aires, Desclée, de Brouwer, 1951. (comparative lexicon in Spanish, French, German, English, of nearly thirty thousand idiomatic phrases, distributed in more than four thousand groups).

Duden pictorial encyclopedia, in five languages: English, French, German, Italian, Spanish. New York, Murray, 1943. (about thirty thousand words, illustrated by pictures).

Glahn, H. E. *and* Weincke, O. Teknisk ordbog: I. Dansk-tysk-engelsk-fransk. II. Tysk-dansk. Engelsk-dansk. Fransk-dansk. 3rd edition. Copenhagen, Hirschsprung, 1950.

Greiser, J. Lexikon der Abkürzungen . . . mit Anhang: Abkürzungen aus dem Finanz- und Steuerrecht. Osnabrück, Fromm, 1953. (international in scope).

Hoyer, E. von *and* Kreuter, F. Technologisches Wörterbuch. 6th edition. Ed. by Alfred Schlomann. New York, Unger, 1944. 3 volumes. (English, French, German). (reprint of the Berlin, Springer, 1922 edition).

Hvad hedder det? Politikens billedordbog-dansk-engelsk-fransk-tysk. Copenhagen, Politikens Forlag, 1948.

Langford, R. A. *and* Aeberhard, R. W. Langford's technical and commercial dictionary. 2nd edition. Zurich, The English Institute; London, Foyle; New York, Chemical Publications Co., 1952. (English, French, German. first published 1949).

Newmark, M. Dictionary of science and technology in English-French-German-Spanish. London, Pitman, 1945.

Oppegaard, S. Teknisk ordliste: tysk, norsk, engelsk. Med alfabetisk register. 2nd edition. Trondheim, Bruns, 1945.

Rabaté, H. Glossaire trilingue (français, anglais, allemand) special aux industries: des cires, huiles, gommes, résines, pigments, vernis, encres, peintures, produits d'entretien et préparations assimilées. Paris, " Peintures, Pigments, Vernis ", 1948.

Thali, H. Technical dictionary of the terms used in electrical engineering, radio, television, telecommunications, including the most used terms of accoustics, illumination, mathematics, materials, mechanics, optics, heating, etc. Lucerne, Thali, 1946-53. 3 volumes.

Afrikaans

Malherbe, D. F. du T. Vakwoordeboek: scientific and technical dictionary. Pretoria, de Bussy, 1932. 2 volumes. (English-Afrikaans: Afrikaans (Dutch)-English).

Danish

Hansen, H. *and* Hinrichsen, H. Danish-English technical dictionary. 2nd edition. Copenhagen, Harcks, 1950.

Warrern, A. Dansk-engelsk [engelsk-dansk] teknisk ordbog. Copenhagen, Clausens, 1948–49. 2 volumes.

French

Cusset, F. Vocabulaire technique anglais-français et français-anglais. 3rd edition. Paris, Berger-Levrault, 1948.

De Vries, L. French-English science dictionary. 2nd edition. New York & London, McGraw-Hill, 1951.

Kettridge, J. O. French-English and English-French dictionary of technical terms and phrases used in civil, mechanical, electrical and mining engineering, and allied sciences and industries. 3rd edition. London, Routledge, 1948. 2 volumes.

Macquinghen, R. Dictionnaire de termes commerciaux et techniques. Paris, Dunod, 1954. (French-English, English-French).

Malgorn, G. Lexique technique anglais-français. 3rd edition. Paris, Gauthier-Villars, 1950.

German

Brockhaus-Bildwörterbuch: englisch-deutsch. Wiesbaden, Brockhaus, 1953. (edited by Will Héraucourt. First of a new series of bilingual dictionaries. Includes differences between English and American idiom and pronunciation).

De Vries, L. German-English science dictionary for students in chemistry, physics, biology, agriculture and related sciences. 2nd edition. New York & London, McGraw-Hill, 1946.

—— German-English technical and engineering dictionary. New York & London, McGraw-Hill, 1950.

Ernst, R. German-English, English-German technical dictionary: a representation of the vocabulary of industrial technics, including related fields of science and civil engineering. Wiesbaden, Brandstetter; Hamburg, Tauchnitz, 1948-53. 2 volumes.

Leibiger, O. W. *and* Leibiger, I. S. German-English and English-German dictionary for scientists, comprising chemistry, physics, mathematics, engineering, aeronautics, dynamics, biology, physiology, medicine and other sciences. Ann Arbor, Edwards Bros., 1950.

Leidecker, K. F. German-English technical dictionary of aeronautics, rocketing, space navigation, atomic physics, high mathematics, jet-engines, turbines, hydraulics, petroleum . . . Based on data compiled by the U.S. Air Force. New York, Vanni, 1951. 2 volumes.

Lenk, Gotthard *and* Börner, H. Technical dictionary for the basic industries: mining, non-metallic mineral industry, dressing, metallurgy, metal working industry, building materials industry, auxiliary sciences. English-German; German-English. Göttingen, Vandenhoeck & Ruprecht, 1949–54. 2 volumes.

Webel, A. A German-English technical and scientific dictionary. 3rd edition. London, Routledge, 1952.

Hindi

Raghu Vira. The consolidated great English-Indian dictionary of technical terms. Nagpur, International Academy of Indian Culture, 1950. (Supplement. 3rd edition. published 1952).

—— Hindi-English dictionary of technical terms. Nagpur, International Academy of Indian Culture, 1951. (these two volumes constitute volumes 19 and 25 respectively of the Sarasvati Vilhara Series).

Hungarian

Cserépy, S. English and Hungarian glossary of technical terms. Revised and enlarged by Tibor Gyengö. 2nd edition. Budapest, Fövárosi Könyukiadó, 1947.

English-Hungarian technical dictionary, compiled by the editorial staff of English technical dictionaries of Akadémiai Kiadó . . . Budapest, Akadémiai Kiadó, 1952. (cover title: *Angol-Magyar müszaki szóta'r*).

Italian

Marolli, G. Technical dictionary, English-Italian, Italian-English. 5th edition. Florence, Monnier, 1954. (first published in 1946).

Japanese

Fujita, Nintaro. Kenkyusha English-Japanese dictionary: commercial and technical terms. South Pasadena, Calif., Perkins, 1944.

Norwegian

Ansteinsson, J. Engelsk-norsk teknisk ordbok. 2nd edition. Trondheim, Bruns, 1950.

Portuguese

Furstenau, E. E. Dicionário de têrmos técnicos: inglês-português. 2nd edition. Rio de Janeiro, Gertum Carneiro, 1948.

Sell, L. L. English-Portuguese comprehensive technical dictionary. New York & London, McGraw-Hill, 1953.

Russian

Bel'kind, L. D. Anglo-russkii politekhnicheskii slovar'. Moscow, Gostekhizdat, 1946.

Bray, A. Russian-English scientific-technical dictionary. New York, International University Press, 1945.

Callaham, L. I. Russian-English technical and chemical dictionary. New York, Wiley, 1947.

Chernukhin, A. E. English-Russian technical dictionary. New York, International University Press, 1944. (reprint of 2nd edition. Moscow, 1938).

Kondratov, L. N. Russko-angliĭskiĭ politekhnicheskiĭ slovar'. Moscow, Gostekhizdat, 1948.

Spanish

Guinle, R. L.   A modern Spanish-English and English-Spanish technical and engineering dictionary.   London, Routledge, 1946.

Perol Guerrero, A.   New technical and commercial dictionary.   London, Cassell, 1942.

" Popular Mechanics Magazine."   Vocabulario técnico inglés-español. Traducción de términos técnicos que generalmente no se encuentran en diccionarios inglés-español, por Samuel Melo.   Chicago, Windsor Press, 1948.

Robayo, L. A.   Spanish-English, English-Spanish technical, legal and commercial dictionary.   Montreal, Dictionary Publishing Company, 1952.

Sell, L. L.   English-Spanish comprehensive technical dictionary of aircraft, automobile, electricity, radio, television . . . petroleum, steel products . . . New York & London, McGraw-Hill, 1944.

Swedish

Blomgren, A. S. *and* Nilsson, B.   Engelsk-svensk och svensk-engelsk ordbok.   Till tjänst för rederier, befraktare, fartygsbefäl, m. fl. Tillika nautisk och sjöfartsteknisk uppslagsbok.   Lund, Gleerup, 1939.

Engstrom, Einar.   Svensk-engelsk teknisk ordbok.   3rd edition.   Stockholm, Svensk Trävaru-Tidnings, 1947.

—— Engelsk-svensk teknisk ordbok.   6th edition.   Stockholm, Svensk Trävaru-Tidnings, 1953.

Welsh

Cardiff.   University of Wales.   Board of Celtic studies.   Termau technegol [Saesneg-Cymraeg].   Cardiff, University of Wales, 1950.

SPECIALISED DICTIONARIES

Abbreviations (see also pages 65 to 66).

Baudry, H.   " D.A.": dictionnaire d'abbréviations: françaises et étrangères, techniques et usuelles, anciennes et nouvelles. Paris, 1951.

Greiser, J. Lexikon der Abkürzungen . . . mit Anhang: Abkürzungen aus dem Finanz- und Steurerrecht. Osnabrück, Fromm, 1953.

Academic Matters

International glossary of academic terms. Paris, International Federation of University Women, 1939. (French and English).

Accounting

Dobbek, O. Finance and accounting: Fachwörterbuch für Buchhaltungs und Finanzwesen. Frankfurt-am-Main, 1948. 2 volumes in 1.

Administration

Jéraute, J. Vocabulaire français-anglais et anglais-français de termes et locutions juridiques, administratifs, commerciaux, financiers et sujets connexes. Paris, Librairie Générale de Droit et de Jurisprudence, 1953.

Malka, E. Nouveau dictionnaire pratique d'arabe administratif: arabe-français, avec un index français-arabe correspondant. Tangiers, Ed. Internationales, 1951. (Publication de la Direction de l'Instruction Publique). (Legal and administrative terms used in Arabic documents in Morocco).

Quemner, T. A. Dictionnaire juridique: t.I. français-anglais. (Droit, finances, commerce, douanes, assurances, administration). Paris, Ed. de Navarre, 1953.

Advertising

International Chamber of Commerce. Dictionary of advertising and distribution in eight languages. Basle, Verlag für Recht & Gesellschaft, 1954. (English, French, German, Spanish, Italian, Dutch, Portuguese, Swedish).

International Chamber of Commerce. Terms commonly used in distribution and advertising. Basle, Verlag für Recht & Gesellschaft, 1940–47. 4 volumes. (English, French, German, Italian, Spanish, Dutch, Portuguese, Swedish).

Agriculture

Bading, H.   Dictionary of agriculture: German-English, English-German. Hamburg, Park Verlag, 1947.

Bezemer, T. J. *and others.* Dictionary of terms relating to agriculture, horticulture, forestry, cattle breeding, dairy industry, and apiculture in English, French, German and Dutch. London, Allen & Unwin, 1934.

De Vries, L.   French-English science dictionary for students in agricultural, biological and physical sciences. New York, McGraw-Hill, 1940.

Archaeology

Agrawala, Vasudeva S.   Some archeological and art terms (useful for preparing labels, guide-books and catalogues in Indian languages). Bombay, 1945. (also published in Indian Museums Association. *Journal of Indian museums*, volume I, no. 2, page 93 onwards).

Réau, L.   Dictionnaire polyglotte des termes d'art et d'archéologie. Paris, Presses Universitaires de France, 1953.   viii, 251 pages. (Comité International d'Histoire de l'Art).

Architecture

Azorín, F.   Universala terminologio de la arkitekturo (arkeologio, arto, konstruo kaj metio). Kun 2.000 desegnoj. Madrid, Chulilla y Angel, 1932. (Esperanto, Sanskrit, Greek, Latin, Gothic, Arabic, Hebrew, Spanish, Portuguese, Italian, French, English, German, Russian, Polish, Swedish).

Bodson, F.   Dictionnaire des termes récents, symboles et abbréviations: architecture, art de construire, génie civil. Brussels, Editec, 1948.

Art

Agrawala, V. S.   Some archeological and art terms (useful for preparing labels, guide-books, and catalogues in Indian languages). Bombay, 1945. (also published in Indian Museums Association. *Journal of Indian museums*, volume I, no. 2, page 93 onwards).

Pei, M. A. *and* Gaynor, F.   Liberal arts dictionary in English, French, German, Spanish. New York, Philosophical Library, 1952.

Réau, L. Dictionnaire polyglotte des termes d'art et d'archéologie. Paris, Presses Universitaires de France, 1953. (Comité International d'Histoire de l'Art).

Atomic Energy

Leidecker, K. F. German-English technical dictionary of aeronautics, rocketing, space navigation, atomic physics, higher mathematics . . . Based on data compiled by the U.S. Air Force. New York, Vanni, 1950-51. 2 volumes.

United Nations. Secretariat. Department of Conference and General Services. Atomic energy: glossary of technical terms. Lake Success, 1948. (English, French, Russian, Chinese, Spanish).

Automobiles

Centre d'Etudes Techniques de l'Automobile et du Cycle. Lexique illustré de l'automobile: français, anglais, italien, allemand. Paris, Bibliothéque de l'Argus de l'Automobile, 1948.

Dierfeld, B. R. Autodictionaer, Dreisprachen-Wörterbuch des Kraftfahrwesens. 2nd edition. Zurich, Gallus, 1938-40. 4 volumes. (English, French, German, Spanish, Portuguese).

Henslowe, L. Henslowe's motor dictionary. English-French, French-English. London, Cassell, 1938.

Maul, M. Engelsk-dansk automobilordbog. Copenhagen, Branner, 1944.

Renssen, S. van. Viertalig technisch woordenboek voor de automobiel en motorrijwielbranche. 2nd edition. Deventer, Kluwer, 1939.

Sell, L. L. English-French comprehensive technical dictionary of the automobile and allied industries: a practical and theoretical nomenclature of internal combustion engines and their operating principles. New York, McGraw-Hill, 1932.

Union Technique de l'Automobile, du Motorcycle et du Cycle. Lexique illustré de l'automobile: français, anglais, italien, allemand, espagnol, Paris, Ed. S.N.E.E.P., 1950.

Aviation

Aeronautical dictionary in French and English. Compiled by technicians of the Free French Air Force. London, Harrap, 1943.

Fontanet, G. L. Aviation: a technical dictionary. London, Harrap, 1945. (English-French, French-English).

International Civil Aviation Organisation. Lexicon of terms used in connection with international civil aviation: English, French, Spanish. Montreal, ICAO, 1952.

Janarmo, K. W. English-Finnish aviation dictionary. Helsinki, Julkaisija Ilmailuvirkailijat ry, 1949.

Rotol, Ltd. Aeronautical glossary: English-Spanish.

Serrallés, J. K.   English-Spanish and Spanish-English dictionary of aviation terms. New York, McGraw-Hill, 1944.

Ballet

Beaumont, C. W. A French-English dictionary of technical terms used in classical ballet. revised edition. London, Beaumont, 1935. (first published in 1931).

Banking

De Kaminski, M. *and others.* " Pentax " banking encyclopaedia (terminology and phraseology) in English, French, Italian, Spanish and German. London, Hirschfeld, 1928.

Herendi, L. A complete dictionary of banking terms in three languages (English, German, French) . . . London, Pitman, 1928.

Bees and Bee-Keeping

Bezemer, T. J. *and others.* Dictionary of terms relating to agriculture, horticulture, forestry, cattle breeding, dairy industry, and apiculture in English, French, German and Dutch. London, Allen & Unwin, 1934.

Crane, E. E. Dictionary of bee-keeping terms, with allied scientific terms, giving translations from and into English-French-German-Dutch. With Latin index. London, Bee Research Association, 1951.

Bibliography

Buonocore, D. Vocabulario bibliográfico: términos relativos al libro, al documento, a la biblioteca y a la imprenta, para uso de escritores, bibliógrafos . . . Santa Fe, Argentina, Librería y Editorial Castellví, 1952. (Serie Bibliotecológia, I).

Biology

De Vries, L. French-English science dictionary for students in agricultural, biological and physical sciences. New York, McGraw-Hill, 1940.

Lépine, P. Dictionnaire français-anglais, anglais-français, des termes médicaux et biologiques. Paris, Flammarion, 1952.

Plans y Sanz de Bremond, F. *and* Turner, C. J. Diccionario inglés-español y español-inglés de términos médicos biológicos. Madrid, Lib. Ed. Cientifico Médica, 1947.

Sharaf, M. English-Arabic dictionary of medicine, biology and allied sciences. Cairo, Government Press, 1928.

Book Trades

Buonocore, D. Vocabulario bibliográfico: términos relativos al libro, al documento, a la biblioteca y a la imprenta, para uso de escritores, bibliógrafos . . . Santa Fe, Argentina, Librería y Editorial Castellví, 1952. (Serie Bibliotecológia, I.).

Orne, J. The language of the foreign book trade: abbreviations, terms and phrases. Chicago, American Library Association, 1949.

Botany

Backer, C A. Dutch-English taxonomic-botanical vocabulary. Leiden, Flora Malesiana & Rijksherbarium, 1949.

Bedevian, A. K. Illustrated polyglottic dictionary of plant names in Latin, Arabic, Armenian, English, French, German, Italian and Turkish languages, including economic, medicinal, poisonous and ornamental plants and common weeds. Cairo, Argus & Papazian Presses, 1936.

Coninck, A. M. C. J. Dictionnaire latin-grec-français-anglais-allemand-hollandais des principaux terms employés en botanique et en horticulture, ainsi qu'une liste de genres de plantes, dérivés de mots, dont l'explication se trouve dans ce dictionnaire. 2nd edition, reprinted. New York, Stechert, 1926. (this edition first published 1907).

Greenway, P. J. A Swahili dictionary of plant names. Dar-es-Salaam, East African Agricultural Research Station, Amani, Tanganyika Territory, 1937.

Steinmetz, E. F. Codex vegetalis: botanical drugs and spices: trade-dictionary in five languages (Latin, Dutch, German, English and French) with the botanical origin and with the families. Amsterdam, Steinmetz, 1947.

—— Vocabularium botanicum: plant-terminology: nomenclature in six languages (Latin, Greek, Dutch, German, English and French) of the principal scientific words used in botany. Amsterdam, Steinmetz, 1947.

Buddhism

Hackmann, Heinrich. Erklärendes Wörterbuch zum chinesischen Buddhismus (chinesisch-sanskrit-deutsch). Nach seinem handschriftlichen Nachlass überarbeitet von Johannes Nobel. Herausgegeben von der religionskundlichen Sammlung der Universität Marburg/Lahn. Leiden, Brill, 1953– volume 1- (to be completed in about 12 Lfg.).

13

Nyanatiloka. Buddhist dictionary: manual of Buddhist terms and doctrines. Colombo, Ceylon, Frewin, 1950. (Island Hermitage Publications, no. 1). (Pali and English).

Building

Azorín, F. Universala terminologio de la arkitekturo (arkeologio, arto, konstruo kaj metio). Kun 2.000 desegnoj. Madrid, Chulilla y Angel, 1932. (Esperanto, Sanskrit, Greek, Latin, Gothic, Arabic, Hebrew, Spanish, Portuguese, Italian, French, English, German, Russian, Polish, Swedish).

Bodson, F. Dictionnaire des termes récents, symboles et abbréviations: architecture, art de construire, génie civil. Brussels, Editec, 1948.

Liebe, P. W. Fachwörterbuch für das Bauwesen: deutsch-englisch, englisch-deutsch. Stuttgart, Franckh, 1949.

Chemistry and Chemical Engineering

Fouchier, J. *and* Billet, F. Chemical dictionary: English, French German. Baden-Baden, Wervereis, 1953. 3 volumes in 1.

Goldberg, M. English-Spanish chemical and medical dictionary: comprising terms employed in medicine, surgery, dentistry, veterinary, biochemistry, biology, pharmacy, allied sciences and related scientific equipment. New York, McGraw-Hill, 1947.

—— Spanish-English chemical and medical dictionary . . . New York, McGraw-Hill, 1952.

Herzfeld, K. M. English-Russian dictionary on pure and applied chemistry. 2nd edition. Moscow, State Publishing Office of Technical and Theoretical Literature, 1953.

Molina Font, J. Diccionario químico, comercial, industrial y farmacéutico. Español-inglés, inglés-español. Mexico, Ed. de Libros Científicos, 1949.

Patterson, A. M. A French-English dictionary for chemists. 2nd edition. New York, Wiley; London, Chapman & Hall, 1954.

—— A German-English dictionary for chemists. 3rd edition. New York, Wiley; London, Chapman & Hall, 1950. (first published in 1917).

Cinematography

Alvey, G. H. Dizionario dei termini cinematografici (Dictionary of terms for the cinema): italiano-inglese, English-Italian. Rome, Mediterranea, 1952.

Santen, J. J. M. van. Amalux fototolk: viertalig, verklarend woordenboek voor fotografie en cinematografie. Bloemendaal, Focus, 1948. (Dutch, English, French, German).

Commerce

Bons, A. *and* Kleinbentink, S. F. Engels handelswoordenboek (engels-nederlands). Deventer, Kluwer, 1939.

Business terms, phrases and abbreviations; with equivalents in French, German, Spanish and Italian. 12th edition. Pitman, 1953.

Eichborn, R. von. Spezialwörterbuch für Handel und Wirtschaft. 2nd edition. Stuttgart, Deutsche Verlags-Anstalt, 1949. 2 volumes. (English-German, German-English).

Gaynor, F. International business dictionary in five languages: English, German, French, Spanish, Italian. New York, Philosophical Library, 1946.

Giraud, A. F.-S. Novísimo diccionario comercial: " El secretario " . . . para la correspondencia comercial. Española-inglesa, inglesa-española . . . Madrid, Juventud, 1948.

International Chamber of Commerce. Dictionary of advertising and distribution in eight languages: English, French, German, Spanish, Italian, Dutch, Portuguese and Swedish. Basle, Verlag für Recht & Gesellschaft, 1954.

—— Terms commonly used in distribution and advertising. Basle, Verlag für Recht & Gesellschaft, 1940–47. 4 volumes. (English, French, German, Italian, Spanish, Portuguese, Swedish).

—— Trade terms: annotated synoptic tables. Paris, I.C.C., 1953. (Document no. 16). (English, French, American).

Kettridge, J. O. French-English and English-French dictionary of commercial and financial terms, phrases and practice. London, Routledge, 1931.

Ludvigsen, V. Engelsk-dansk og dansk-engelsk handelsordbog. Copenhagen, 1919.

Marangoni, F. A. Dizionario commerciale fraseologico: italiano-inglese ed inglese-italiano . . . Milan, Hoepli, 1951.

Quemner, T. A. Dictionnaire juridique: t.I.: français-anglais. (Droit, finances, commerce, douanes, assurances, administration). Paris, Ed. de Navarre, 1953.

Robb, L. A. Dictionary of business terms: Spanish-English and English-Spanish. New York, Wiley, 1950.

Spinelli, N. Dizionario commerciale: italiano-inglese e inglese-italiano. Ed. 1953 con un'appendice . . . Turin, Lattes, 1953.

Tejadar y Sainz, J. de D. Spanish and English legal and commercial dictionary. 2nd edition. Santa Maria, Cuba, Var-I-TEK, 1945. (a revision and enlargement of the author's *Law translator's reference glossary*).

Vasquez, G. M. L.   Commercial correspondence dictionary: English-
Spanish and Spanish-English. New York, Latin American Inst.
Press, 1953.

Cookery *see* **Gastronomy and Cookery**

Customs and Excise

Quemner, T. A.   Dictionnaire juridique: t.I.: français-anglais. (Droit,
finances, commerce, douanes, assurances, administration).   Paris,
Ed. de Navarre, 1953.

Dams

Dictionnaire technique des barrages (technical dictionary of dams).
Paris, Commission Internationale des Grands Barrages de la Con-
férence Mondiale de l'Energie, 1950. (French, English, German).

Dentistry

Goldberg, M.   English-Spanish chemical and medical dictionary:
comprising terms employed in medicine, surgery, dentistry, veter-
inary, biochemistry, biology, pharmacy, allied sciences and related
scientific equipment. New York, McGraw-Hill, 1947.
—— Spanish-English chemical and medical dictionary . . . New York,
McGraw-Hill, 1951.
Marie, J. S. F.   Dental vocabulary, including many medical terms:
English-Spanish, Spanish-English. Lancaster, Pa., Jacques Cattell
Press, 1943.

Dyes

Interessengemeinschaft Farbenindustrie Aktiengesellschaft. Fachwörterbuch für die Farbstoffe und Textilhilsmittel verbrauchenden
Industrien: German-English. New York, Dictionaries Inc., 1947.

Economics

Eichborn, R. von.   Spezialwörterbuch für Handel und Wirschaft.
2nd edition. Stuttgart, Deutsche Verlags-Anstalt, 1949. 2 volumes.
(German-English, English-German).
Gunston, C. A. *and* Corner, C. M.   Glossary of German financial and
economic terms. London, English Universities Press, 1953.
" The Oriental Economist." Japanese-English dictionary of economic
terms. Tokyo, Tokyo Keizai Shimpo Sha, 1949. 671 pages.

Electrical Engineering

Freeman, H. G. Elektrotechnisches Englisch. Essen, Giradet, 1948.

Heiler, L. B. *and* Dozorov, N. J. English-Russian electro-technical dictionary. Moscow, State Publishing House for Technical & Theoretical Literature, 1951.

Swoboda, G. *and* Filipowsky, R. Wörterbuch der Elektrotechnik: englisch-deutsch. Vienna, Manzsche, 1948.

Thali, H. Technical dictionary of the terms used in electrical engineering, radio, television, telecommunications, including the most used terms of accoustics, illumination, mathematics, materials, mechanics, optics, heating, etc. Lucerne, Thali, 1946– . (English, German, French. to be completed in three volumes).

Electronics

Regen, B. R. *and* Regen, R. R. German-English dictionary for electronics engineers and physicists, with a patent-practice vocabulary. Ann Arbor, Mich., Edwards, 1946.

Engineering

Amburger, P. G. English-Russian dictionary on civil engineering. 2nd edition. Moscow, State Publishing House for Technical & Theoretical Literature, 1951.

Bosch, A. ten. English-Dutch engineering dictionary. 3rd edition. Deventer, Kluwer, 1950.

Goerner, E. *and* Thomas, H. Technical dictionary for civil engineers. Berlin, Schmidt, 1947. 2 volumes.

Kučera, J. V. *and* Stuchlik, A. English-Czech engineering dictionary. Prague, Neubert, 1948.

Robb, L. A. Engineers' dictionary: Spanish-English and English-Spanish. 2nd edition. New York, Wiley, 1949. (first issued 1944).

Finance

Dobbek, O. Finance and accounting: Fachwörterbuch für Buchhaltungs und Finanzwesen. Frankfurt-am-Main, 1948. 2 volumes in 1.

Greiser, J. Lexikon der Abkürzungen . . . Mit Anhang: Abkürzungen aus dem Finanz- und Steuerrecht. Osnabrück, Fromm, 1953. (international in scope).

Gunston, C. A. *and* Corner, C. M. Glossary of German financial and economic terms. London, English Universities Press, 1953.

Kettridge, J. O. French-English and English-French dictionary of commercial and financial terms, phrases and practice. London, Routledge, 1931.

Langguth, K. T.   Financial dictionary.   London, Routledge, 1933.
2 volumes. (English, German).

Quemner, T. A.   Dictionnaire juridique: I. français-anglais. (Droit,
finances, commerce, douanes, assurances, administration). Paris,
Ed. de Navarre, 1953.

Fishing and Fisheries

Oddenino, C. J.   Nomenclature des poissons, crustacés et mollusques
de la Méditerranée, et quelques nations sur leur pêche: vocabulaire
des noms locaux et provençaux. Paris, Rousset.

Slater, R. A. Shipping and fisheries dictionary: Dutch-English, English-
Dutch. New York, Oceanic Exchange Company, 1946.

Forestry

Aro, P. *and others*. Finnish, Swedish, German, English forest dictionary.
Helsinki, Otava, 1944.

Bezemer, T. J. *and others*. Dictionary of terms relating to agriculture,
horticulture, forestry, cattle breeding, dairy industry and apiculture
in English, French, German and Dutch. London, Allen & Unwin,
1934.

Bruttini, A.   Dictionnaire de sylviculture en cinq langues: français
(texte), allemand, anglais, espagnol, italien . . . Paris, Lechevalier,
1930. (Encyclopédie Economique de Sylviculture, IV).

Organisation for European Economic Co-operation.   Bois tropicaux
africains (African tropical timber): nomenclature-description. Paris,
OEEC, 1951. (with botanical, English, Belgian, French, Dutch
and Portuguese equivalents).

Games *see* Sports and Games

Gastronomy and Cookery

Duchamp, H. *and* Jenning, A. The menu-translator: French, English,
German. 7th edition. Zurich, Fussli, 1940.

Eijkern, W. H. N. van.   Culinair handwoordenboek in vier talen.
Doetinchem, Misset; New York, Stechert-Hafner, 1947. (German,
English, French, Dutch).

Gytkiaer, E. *and* Smith, J. Dictionnaire gastronomique français-English-
deutsch-dansk. Copenhagen, Haase, 1951.

Schumacher, A.   Dictionnaire des menus: français-English-deutsch-
dansk og dansk-fransk. Copenhagen, 1908.

Geography (see also Map-Reading)

Fischer, E. *and* Elliott, F. E. A German and English glossary of geographical terms. New York, American Geographical Society, 1950. (Library Series, no. 5).

Geology

Cooper, S. A. Concise international dictionary of mechanics and geology: English, French, German and Spanish. London, Cassell, 1949.

Novitzky, A. Diccionario minero-metalurgico-geologico-mineralogico-petrografico y de petroleo: ingles-español, frances, aleman, ruso. Buenos Aires, the author, 1951.

Heating

Dusnickis, I. *and* Chaumelle, P. Dictionnaire technique anglais-français: chauffage industriel. Paris, Dunod, 1954. (includes American terms).

Heraldry

Académie Internationale d'Héraldique. Vocabulaire-atlas héraldique en six langues: français-English-deutsch-español-italiano-neder-landsch, par le Baron Stalins . . . Paris, Société du Grand Armorial de France, 1952.

Horology

Oelschlaegel, H. Trade dictionary of precious metals, gemstones, jewellery and horological products. The Hague, Moulton, 1939. (French, English, German, Italian, Spanish, Portuguese, Czech and Dutch).

Horticulture

Bezemer, T. J. *and others*. Dictionary of terms relating to agriculture, horticulture, forestry, cattle breeding, dairy industry, and apiculture in English, French, German, and Dutch. London, Allen & Unwin, 1934.

Coninck, A. M. C. J. Dictionnaire latin-grec-français-anglais-allemand-hollandais des principaux termes employés en botanique et en horticulture, ainsi qu'une liste de genres de plantes, dérivés de mots, dont l'explication se trouve dans ce dictionnaire. 2nd edition, reprinted. New York, Stechert, 1926. (this edition originally published 1907).

Housing

Spiwak, H. J. International glossary of technical terms used in housing and town planning. 2nd edition. Amsterdam, International Federation for Housing and Town Planning, 1951. (English, French, German, Italian and Spanish).

Insurance

Glass, G. Dictionnaire technique d'assurances: français-anglais-allemand-flamand-hollandais. Brussels, Office des Assureurs.

Quemner, T. A. Dictionnaire juridique: I. français-anglais. (Droit, finances, commerce, douanes, assurances, administration). Paris, Ed. de Navarre, 1953.

Thomsen, A. English-French-German-Danish insurance dictionary. Copenhagen, 1924.

Iron and Steel

Verein Deutscher Eisenhüttenleute. Aus der Fachsprache des Eisenhüttenmannes: deutsch-englisch, englisch-deutsch. 2nd edition. Düsseldorf, Verlag Stahleisen, 1948.

Islam

Wensinck, A. J. *and* Kramer, H. J. Handwörterbuch des Islam. Im Auftrag der Kon. Akademie van Wetenschappen. Amsterdam, Leiden, Brill, 1941.

Jewellery

Oelschlaegel, H. Trade dictionary of precious metals, gemstones, jewellery, and horological products. The Hague, Moulton, 1939.

Judaism

Jastrow, M. Dictionary of the Targumim, the Talmud Babli and Yerushalmi, and the Midrashic literature. With an index of Scriptural quotations. London, Luzac; New York, Putnam, 1903. 2 volumes. (reprinted, London, Vallentine, 1926).

Law

Basedow, K. H. Dictionary of legal terms. Hamburg, Heldt, 1947–48. 2 volumes. (German and English).

Beseler, D. von. Englisch-deutsches und deutsch-englisches Taschenwörterbuch der Rechts- und Geschäftssprache. 2nd edition. Berlin, de Gruyter, 1947.

Dalrymple, A. W. French-English dictionary of legal words and phrases. 2nd edition. London, Stevens, 1948.

Ito, Jujiro. A Japanese-English dictionary of legal terms. Tokyo, Daigaku Shobo, 1950.

Kniepkamp, H. P. Rechtswörterbuch: englisch-deutsch, deutsch-englisch. Berlin-Dahlem, Colloquium Verlag; New York, Oceana Publications, 1954. (English-German part first published in 1941: present issue revised).

Malka, E. Nouveau dictionnaire pratique d'arabe administratif: arabe-français avec un index français-arabe correspondant. Tangiers, Ed. Internationales, 1951. (Publication de la Direction de l'Instruction Publique).

Quemner, T. A. Dictionnaire juridique, I: français-anglais. (Droit, finances, commerce, douanes, assurances, administration). Paris, Ed. de Navarre, 1953.

Tejadar y Sainz, Juan de Dios. Spanish and English legal and commercial dictionary. 2nd edition. Santa Maria, Cuba, Var I TEK, 1945. (revision and enlargement of the author's *Law translator's reference glossary*).

Weissenstein, R. F. Anglo-amerikanisches Rechtswörterbuch. Zurich, Schulthess, 1950– (to be completed in 2 volumes).

Leather

Freudenberg, W. International directory of the leather and allied trades. 2nd edition. Berlin, Springer, 1951. (German, English, French, Spanish, Russian. Compiled for the International Council of Tanners, London).

Libraries

Buonocore, D. Vocabulario bibliográfico: términos relativos al libro, al documento, a la biblioteca y a la imprenta, para uso de escritores, bibliógrafos . . . Santa Fe, Argentina, Librería y Editorial Castellví, 1952. (Serie Bibliotecológia, I).

Gross, O. Library terms: Fachausdrücke des Bibliothekswesens und seiner Nachbargebiete: englisch-deutsch und deutsch-englisch. Hamburg, Stichnote, 1952.

Mamiya, Fujio. A complete dictionary of library terms: technical terms used in libraries, bibliographies and by printing and binding trades in English, German, French, Chinese and Japanese languages. revised edition. Tokyo, Japan Library Bureau, 1952. (first published 1925).

Thompson, A. Vocabularium bibliothecarii: English, French, German. Begun by Henri Lemaître, revised and enlarged by Anthony Thompson. Paris, UNESCO; London, H.M.S.O., 1953.

Map-Reading

War Office. General Staff. Geographical Section. Short glossaries for use on foreign maps. London, War Office, 1943–46.

Marine Fauna

Oddenino, C. J. Nomenclature des poissons, crustacés et mollusques de la Méditerranée, et quelques notions sur leur pêche: vocabulaire des noms locaux et provençaux. Paris, Rousset,

Maritime Affairs

Askim, P. Engelsk-norsk [norsk-engelsk] maritim-teknisk ordbok. 5th edition. Oslo, Grøndahl, 1952–53. 2 volumes.

Carroll, E. J. The yachtsmen's glossary of nautical terms and expressions: English-French-Spanish-Dutch-Portuguese. 2nd edition. London, Simpkin Marshall, 1945.

Kønig, G. A. F. and Ottesen, C. Marine-teknisk ordsamling. Engelsk-dansk, dansk-engelsk. Copenhagen, 1901.

Lefrançois, Gabriel. Le vocabulaire du navire (anglais-français): recueil des termes techniques employés en construction navale, dans la réparation des navires et la construction mécanique de marine. 2nd edition. Paris, Société d'Editions Géographiques, 1953.

Littleton, A. C. Vocabulary of sea words in English, French, German, Spanish and Italian. Portsmouth, Griffin, 1879.

Navarro Dagnino, J. Vocabulario marítimo: inglés-español, español-inglés. 2nd edition. Barcelona, Gili, 1947.

Slater, R. A. Shipping and fisheries dictionary, Dutch-English, English-Dutch. New York, Oceanic Exchange Company, 1946.

Technical marine encyclopaedia. Naples, Edizioni Tines, 1951. (English, French, Italian).

Wolfhagen, H. Marineordbog. I. Maritime udtryk paa dansk, engelsk, fransk, tysk. II. Sproglige vink paa engelsk, fransk, tysk. Copenhagen, 1903–04.

Marketing

International Chamber of Commerce. Dictionary of marketing terms prepared by Richard Webster. Basle, Verlag für Recht und Gesellschaft, 1952. (Document no. 12).

Mathematics

American Mathematical Society. Russian-English vocabulary, with a grammatical sketch: to be used in reading mathematical papers. New York, 1950.

Herland, L. Dictionary of mathematical sciences. New York, Ungar, 1951-54. 2 volumes. (English and German).

Leidecker, K. F. German-English technical dictionary of aeronautics, rocketry, space navigation, atomic physics, higher mathematics . . . Based on data compiled by the U.S. Air Force. New York, Vanni, 1950–51. 2 volumes.

Mechanics

Cooper, S. A. Concise international dictionary of mechanics and geology: English, French, German and Spanish. London, Cassell, 1949.

Medicine

Clairville, A. L. Dictionnaire polyglotte des termes médicaux. Paris, SIPUCO, 1950– (volume I. français-anglais-allemand-latin. 1950. II. Portuguese. 1953. III. Spanish. 1952. Arabic and Italian volumes in preparation).

De Vries, L. German-English medical dictionary. New York & London, McGraw-Hill, 1952.

Goertz, M. *and* Unseld, D. W. Medizinisches Wörterbuch der deutschen und englischen Sprache. 2nd edition. Stuttgart, Wissenschaftliche Verlagsgesellschaft, 1949. 2 parts in 1.

Goldberg, M. English-Spanish [Spanish-English] chemical and medical dictionary. New York & London, McGraw-Hill, 1947–52. 2 volumes.

Lépine, P. *and* Krassnoff, G. D. Dictionnaire français-anglais, anglais-français des termes médicaux et biologiques. Paris, Ed. Médicales Flammarion, 1952.

Marconi, R. *and* Zino, E. Dizionario inglese-italiano per le scienze mediche. Turin, Minerva, 1949.

Marie, J. S. F. Dental vocabulary, including many medical terms: English-Spanish, Spanish-English. Lancaster, Pa., Jacques Cattell Press, 1943.

Plans y Sanz de Bremond, F. *and* Turner, C. J. Diccionario inglés-español y español-inglés de términos médicos biológicos. Madrid, Lib. Ed. Cientifico Médica, 1947.

Schoenewald, F. S. German-English medical dictionary. London, H. K. Lewis, 1949.

Sharaf, M.   English-Arabic dictionary of medicine, biology and allied sciences.   Cairo, Government Press, 1928.

Takasima, R.   Pocket Japanese-English-German medical dictionary. Tokyo, Bunkodō, 1951.

Tomaszewski, W.   Slownik lekarski angielsko-polski i polsko-angielski. 2nd edition.   London, Livingstone, 1953.

Tuḥfat Al-Aḥbab.   Glossaire de la matière médicale marocaine.   Texte avec traduction, notes critiques et index par H. J. P. Renaud et Georges S. Colin.   Paris, Geuthner, 1934.   (Publications de l'Institut des Hautes Etudes Marocains, XXIV).

Veillon, E.   Medical dictionary.   Bern, Huber, 1950.   (English, French, German)

Metallurgy

Novitzky, A.   Diccionario minero-metalurgico-geologico-mineralogico-petrografico y de petroleo: ingles-español, frances, aleman, ruso. Buenos Aires, the author, 1951.

Singer, T. E. R.   German-English dictionary of metallurgy, with related material on ores, mining and minerals.   New York, McGraw-Hill, 1945.

Meteorology

Meteorological Office.   The meteorological glossary.   3rd edition. London, H.M.S.O., 1939.   253 pages.   (reprinted 1950, incorporating Amendment Lists, numbers 1 to 4.   Includes Danish, Dutch, French and German equivalents (pages 226 to 253) of some terms in the main glossary).

Military Affairs

Canada.   Department of National Staff.   General Staff.   Military dictionary, English-French, French-English; prepared under the direction of the Chief of General Staff, Canada.   Ottawa, Government Printers, 1945.

Carstenn, L. von.   English-German, German-English military dictionary. London, Harrap, 1941.   2 volumes in 1.

Davidson-Houston, J. V. *and* Dewar-Durie, R. V.   Chinese and English modern military dictionary.   Peiping, 1935.

Dictionnaire des termes militaires et de l'argot poilu.   Paris, Larousse, 1916.

Kettridge, J. O.   French and English military dictionary, including air service.   London, Routledge, 1940.

Noblet, A. French-English, English-French dictionary of technical military terms. London, Crosby Lockwood, 1940.

War Office. General Staff. Vocabulary of German military terms and abbreviations (revised to 1942). London, H.M.S.O., 1943.

Mining and Minerals

Seebach, H. J. von. Dictionary for mining engineering and economics. 2nd edition. Essen, Glückauf, 1947. 2 volumes in 1. (German and English).

Singer, T. E. R. German-English dictionary of metallurgy, with related material on ores, mining and minerals. New York, McGraw-Hill, 1945.

Navy

Bataille, L. *and* Brunet, M. From keel to truck: dictionary of naval terms, English, French, German, Spanish and Italian. 5th edition. London, Philip, 1937.

Lefrançois, G. Le vocabulaire du navire (anglais-français): recueil des termes techniques employés en construction navale, dans la réparation des navires et la construction mécanique de marine. 2nd edition. Paris, Société d'Editions Géographiques, 1953.

U.S. Naval Academy. Department of Foreign Languages. New naval phraseology in English, French, Spanish, Italian, German, Portuguese. Annapolis, U.S. Naval Institute, 1944.

Office Economy

Bruckbauer, V. *and* Kirste, L. Office terms in three languages. Vienna, Dokumentationszentrum für Technik & Wirtschaft, 1954. (German, English, French).

Oil

Allied Control Commission for Germany (French Element). Oil Section. Dictionnaire des termes techniques de l'industries du pétrole (en français, anglais, russe et allemand). 2nd edition. Berlin, the Commission, 1946.

Molyn, J. H. Dictionary, Dutch-English, English-Dutch: petroleum; prospecting, drilling, production, refining, laboratories, transportation, applications. Hilversum, OCECO, 1946.

Novitzky, A. Diccionario minero-metalurgico-geologico-mineralogico-petrografico y de petroleo: ingles-español, frances, aleman, ruso. Buenos Aires, the author, 1951.

" Petroleo Interamericano." Glossary of the petroleum industry: containing more than 12,000 technical terms and idiomatic expressions ... by Oscar B. Irizarry. Tulsa, Oklahoma, 1947.

Ornithology

Jørgensen, H. I. *and* Blackburne, C. I. Glossarium europae avium. Copenhagen, Munksgaard, 1941. (Latin, Czech, Danish, German, English, Spanish, French, Italian, Icelandic, Hungarian, Dutch, Norwegian, Polish, Portuguese, Russian, Finnish, Swedish, Turkish).

Paints and Varnishes

Merz, O. Deutsch-englisches und englisch-deutsches Fachwörterbuch, für Fachausdrück aus dem Lack- und Farbengebiet. Stuttgart, Verlagsgesellschaft, 1947.

Rabaté, H. Glossaire trilingue (français, anglais, allemand), special aux industries: des cires, huiles, gommes, résines, pigments, vernis, encres, peintures, produits d'entretien et préparations assimilées. Paris, " Peintures, Pigments, Vernis ", 1948.

Paper

Argy, M. *and* Supper, H. L. Vocabulaire papetier: français-anglais et anglais-français. Paris, " La Papeterie ", 1948.

Labarre, E. J. Dictionary and encyclopaedia of paper and papermaking, with equivalents of the technical terms in French, German, Dutch, Italian, Spanish and Swedish. 2nd edition. Oxford University Press, 1952. (first published 1937).

Patents and Trade Marks

Polak, M. Patent and trade mark dictionary: Dutch-English, English-Dutch. New York, Oceanic Exchange Company, 1949.

Pharmacology

Goldberg, M. English-Spanish [Spanish-English] chemical and medical dictionary: comprising terms employed in medicine, surgery, dentistry, veterinary, biochemistry, biology, pharmacy, allied sciences and related scientific equipment. New York, McGraw-Hill, 1947–51. 2 volumes.

Molina Font, J. Diccionario químico, comercial, industrial y farmacéutico: español-inglés, inglés-español. Mexico, Ed. de Libros Científicos, 1949.

Steinmetz, E. F. Codex vegetalis: botanical drugs and spices: trade dictionary in five languages (Latin, Dutch, German, English and French) with the botanical origin and with the families. Amsterdam, Steinmetz, 1947.

Suid-Afrikaanse Akademie vir Wetenskap en Kuns. Interim glossary of pharmaceutical terms, English-Afrikaans, Afrikaans-English. Johannesburg, A.P.S. Journal for Pharmaceutical Society of South Africa, 1950.

Philately

Singer, E. The philatelic dictionary: English-French-German. London, Robson Lowe, 1946.

Philology

Doke, C. M. Bantu linguistic terminology. London, Longmans, Green, 1937. (with French and German equivalents for most of the terms).

Grandsaignes d'Hauterive, R. Dictionnaire des racines des langues européennes (grec, latin, ancien français, français, espagnol, italien, anglais, allemand). Paris, Larousse, 1949.

Marouzeau, J. Lexique de la terminologie linguistique: français, allemand, anglais, italien. 3rd edition. Paris, Geuthner, 1951.

Philosophy

Rau, C. V. Shankar. A glossary of philosophical terms. Madras, 1941. (Sanskrit-English). (Sri Venkatesvara Oriental Series, no. 3).

Photography

Photowords in four languages. London, Focal Press, 1950.

Santen, J. J. M. van. Amalux fototolk: viertalig, verklarend woordenboek voor fotografie en cinematografie. Bloemendaal, Focus, 1948. (Dutch, English, French, German).

Plastics

Wittfoht, A. M. Plastics technological dictionary: English-German, German-English nomenclature used in processing, fabricating and using plastics, in testing and mold construction. Munich, Hanser, 1948.

Postal Services

Wirkberg, J. Recueil polyglotte des expressions postales en français, en anglais, en allemand, en suédois, en finnois, et en russe, avec quelques expressions correspondantes en italien et en espagnol. Helsinki, Central Press, 1924.

Precious Metals

Oelschlaegel, H. Trade dictionary of precious metals, gemstones, jewellery and horological products. The Hague, Moulton, 1939. (French, English, German, Italian, Spanish, Portuguese, Czech and Dutch).

Printing

Buonocore, D. Vocabulario bibliográfico: términos relativos al libro, al documento, a la biblioteca y a la imprenta, para uso de escritores, bibliógrafos . . . Santa Fe, Argentina, Librería y Editorial Castellví, 1952. (Serie Bibliotecológia, I).

Hostettler, R. The printer's terms. St. Gallen, Switzerland, Zollikofer; London, Alvin Redman, 1949. (English, German, French, Italian, Dutch). (Schweizer Graphische Mitteilungen Books, I).

Mamiya, Fujio. A complete dictionary of library terms; technical terms used in libraries, bibliographies and by printing and binding trades in English, German, French, Chinese and Japanese languages. revised edition. Tokyo, Japan Library Bureau, 1952. (first published 1925).

Moselund, L. Typografiske og deres betydning. Udarbejdet paa dansk-tysk-engelsk, engelsk-dansk, tysk-dansk, svensk-dansk. Copenhagen, 1944.

Psychoanalysis

Strachey, A. New German-English psychoanalytical vocabulary. London, Baillière, 1943.

Psychology

Piéron, H. Vocabulaire de la psychologie. Paris, Presses Universitaires de France, 1951.

Public Works

Chabrerie, A. P. *and* Rozinoer, R. Lexique technique, français et anglais-français, concernant le matériel de travaux publics: tables de correspondance, des unités métriques. Paris, Institut Technique du Batiment et des Travaux Publics, 1949.

Radio and Television

Adam, M. Dictionnaire de radiotechnique en 3 langues . . . allemand-français, anglais-français. Paris, Librairie de la Radio, 1949.

Clason, W. E. Elsevier's dictionary of television, radar and antennas. Elsvieer, 1955. (English, French, Spanish, Italian, Dutch, German).

Sander, P. Diccionario ilustrado de radio y television: con todos los terminos tecnicos modernos explicados en español y su traduccion al italiano, francés, inglés y alemán. Madrid, Ibérica, 1945.

Rubber

Imperial Chemical Industries Ltd. Dyestuffs Division. A vocabulary of technical terms used in the rubber industry: French-English, German-English, Spanish-English. Manchester, I.C.I., 1953.

Sanitation

Scott, R. R. A glossary of some scientific terms used in sanitary practice by Swahili-speaking Africans. Dar-es-Salaam, Government Printer, 1929.

Shipping *see* Maritime Affairs. Navy

Social Services

Paula Ferreira, Francisco de. Glossário do serviço social: português-espanhol-françes-inglês. Rio de Janeiro, Associação Brasileira de Assistentes Sociais, 1952.

Sports and Games

Axtmann, Horst. Special dictionary for sports and games: English-German, German-English. Heidelberg, Groos, 1949.

Frohberg, W. O. Langenscheidt's language guide for the sportsman: German-English. Berlin-Schöneberg, Langenscheidt, 1936.

Sportszótár . . . (Sports dictionary). Budapest, Akadémiai Kiado, 1952. (Hungarian, Russian, French, German, English).

Sulonen, K. *and* Leikkola, U. Dictionary of sports: English-German-Swedish-Finnish. Helsinki, Söderström, 1952.

Taxonomy

Backer, C. A. Dutch-English taxonomic-botanical vocabulary. Leiden, Flora Malesiana & Rijksherbarium, 1949.

Telecommunications

Germany. Territory under Allied Occupation, 1945– . (Vereinigtes Wirtschaft). Glossary of telecommunication. Brunswick, Westermann, 1948–49. 2 volumes. (German and English).

Television *see* Radio and Television

Textiles

Interessengemeinschaft Farbenindustrie Aktiengesellschaft. Fachwörterbuch für die Farbstoffe und Textilhilsmittel verbrauchenden Industrien: German-English. New York, Dictionaries Inc., 1947.

Puppinck, P. Les termes anglais employés dans l'industrie lainière et Vocabulaire technique textile en quatre langues: français-anglais-allemand-espagnol. Roubaix, Verschave, 1948.

Tas, J. Viertalig textiel-woordenboek voor de handel. Doetinchem, Misset, 1951. (Dutch, German, English, French).

Timber *see* **Wood and Timber**

Town Planning

Bardet, G. Petit glossaire de l'urbaniste en six langues. Paris, Vincent, 1948. (French, English, German, Italian, Spanish, Portuguese).

Spiwak, H. J. International glossary of technical terms used in housing and town planning. 2nd edition. Amsterdam, International Federation for Housing and Town Planning, 1951. (English, French, German, Italian and Spanish).

Trade Marks *see* **Patents and Trade Marks**

Veterinary Science

Goldberg, M. English-Spanish [Spanish-English] chemical and medical dictionary: comprising terms employed in medicine, surgery, dentistry, veterinary, biochemistry, biology, pharmacy, allied sciences and related scientific equipment. New York, McGraw-Hill, 1947-51. 2 volumes.

Welding

Thompson, R. N. *and* Haim, G. Welding dictionary: French, German, Spanish, English. London, Cassier, 1950.

Wood and Timber

Mrugowski, H. English and German dictionary for the wood and timber trade . . . Hanover, Schaper, 1948. (English and German).

Organisation for European Economic Co-operation. Bois tropicaux africains (African tropical timber): nomenclature-description. Paris, OEEC, 1951. (with botanical, English, Belgian, French, Dutch and Portuguese equivalents).

Wool

Puppinck, P. Les termes anglais employés dans l'industrie lainière et Vocabulaire technique textile en quatre langues: français, anglais, allemand, espagnol. Roubaix, Verschave, 1948.

Workshop Practice

Bastyr, W. *and* Paszkowski, E. Anglo-Polish translation of workshop terms. Edited by the Association of Polish Engineers in Great Britain. London, the Association, 1941.

Yachting *see* **Maritime Affairs**

Zoology

Malouf, Amin. Arabic zoological dictionary. Cairo, Al-Muktataf Press, 1932.

GENERAL BIBLIOGRAPHY

Geneva. *University. Ecole d'Interprètes. Library.* Dictionnaires techniques. Geneva, Imprimerie la Sirène, 1953–   volume 1–

Linguistic Bibliography. Published by the Permanent International Committee of Linguists. Utrecht, Spectrum, 1949 to date. (issued annually; first two volumes covered the years 1939–1947).

Liverpool. *Public Libraries.* Select list of general dictionaries in the Picton Reference Library, William Brown Street. Liverpool, 1950. 52 pages.

Meillet, Antoine *and* Cohen, Marcel. *editors.* Les langues du monde. new edition. Paris, Centre Nationale de la Recherche Scientifique, 1952. xlii, 1296 pages. (Société de Linguistique de Paris).

Science Library. Technical glossaries and dictionaries. London, 1952. 82 pages. (Series no. 707).

Stechert-Hafner book news. New York, Stechert-Hafner, 1946 to date. (invaluable for its news of new dictionaries and its information concerning the issue of new parts of the larger dictionaries now appearing).

United Nations. *Geneva. Library.* Monthly list of books catalogued in the Library of the United Nations. (Section VIII—Reference works, Library science—in each issue).

United Nations Educational, Scientific and Cultural Organisation, *Paris.* Bibliography of interlingual scientific and technical dictionaries. 3rd edition. Paris, 1953. xlvii, 178 pages. (compiled by Dr. J. E. Holmstrom. previous editions should be retained, since they contain some items not reprinted in the present work. Dr. Eugen Wüster of Wieselburg, Austria, is preparing—as a complement to this work— a bibliography of glossaries containing both national standard and other definitions of terms in single languages, to be published by Unesco).

United States. *Library of Congress. Division of Bibliography.* Foreign language-English dictionaries: a selected list. Compiled by Grace Hadley Fuller, under the direction of Florence S. Hellman. Washington, D.C., 1942. ii, 132 pages.

—— Supplement. Washington, D.C., 1944. ii, 42 pages.

* Winchell, Constance M. Guide to reference books. 7th edition. Chicago, American Library Association, 1951. (pages 216 to 252).

—— Supplement, 1950–52. By Constance M. Winchell and Olive A. Johnson. Chicago, American Library Association, 1954. (pages 41 to 48. continued in the July issue each year of *College and research libraries*).

The year's work in modern language studies: by a number of scholars. Edited for the Modern Humanities Research Association. Cambridge University Press, 1930 to date.

* A reliable and up-to-date guide to the best dictionaries, especially valuable for its long lists of French and Spanish dialect dictionaries. The introductory note to the section on Dictionaries in the main work, stating the principles governing the selection of dictionaries, &c., is worthy of detailed study. For tracing items not listed in this or any other of the works mentioned above, the reader is reminded of the resources of the catalogues issued by the British Museum, the Library of Congress, and the Bibliothèque Nationale, the first two institutions publishing subject as well as author catalogues.

INDEX

Authors, compilers, editors, principal contributors, official bodies, titles, alternative titles, languages and dialects (in small capitals), areas and regions, allusions, etc., are listed in one alphabetical sequence. To economize in space, the words "dictionary" and "vocabulary"—and their foreign equivalents— have been abbreviated to "d." and "v." respectively, except where they occur as the first word in a title entry.

Aasen, I., 73.
Aavik, J., 104.
Abayev, V. I., 66.
Abbott-Smith, G., 90.
Abbreviations, 65-6, 164, 169.
ABC Japanese–English dictionary, 159.
Abdul Huq, 155.
Abdurakhmanov, R., 66.
Abiven, P. O., 135.
Abkariyus, Yuhanna, 116.
Abraham, R. C., xii, 132, 140.
Abrahams, P., 94-5.
Abridged d. of the Ladine (or Romansh) language, 40.
Abridged English–Zulu word book, 142.
Abxazsko–russkii slovar', 67.
Academia Brasileira de Letras, 56.
Academia das Ciencias de Lisboa, 55, 56.
Academia Española, 45-7.
Academia Romana, 109.
Academic matters, 169.
Académie Française, xii, 1-2.
Académie Internationale d'Héraldique, 179.
Accademia della Crusca, xii, 35-6, 43.
Accounting, 169.
ACCRA, 131.
Achaemenidan inscriptions, 122.
Achmanov, O. S., 68.
ACHOLI, 128.
Acordo Ortografico Luso-Brasileiro, 55, 56.
Adam, M., 188.
Adams, G. S. C., 10.
Adams, R. F. G., 130.
Additions aux d. arabes, 116.
Adelung, J. C., 17, 25.
Adjarean, H., 118.
Adler, A., 85.
Administration, 169.
Advertising, 169.
Aeberhard, R. W., 165.
Aeronautical d. in French and English, 171.
Aeronautical glossary, 171.
AFGHAN, 144, 145.
AFIMA, 145.
African Inland Mission, 133.
AFRICAN LANGUAGES, 152-42.
African tropical timber, 178.
AFRIKAANS, 33-4.
Afrikaanse woordeboek, 34.

Afzelius, J. A., 79.
Agrawala, V. S., 170.
Agriculture, 170.
Aguilo y Foster, M., 51.
Ahaggar, 140.
Ahbab, T. al-, 184.
Aillaud, J. P., 60.
Ainsworth, R., 93.
Airas, V., 164.
Akadémiai Kiado, 167.
Akademiia Nauk, 63.
AKKADIAN, 119.
Akhmanova, O. S., 67.
Al-Ahbab, T., 184.
Alanne, S., 105.
Alapini, J., 130.
Alba, R. de, 47.
ALBANIAN, 99, 101.
Albeck, U., 82.
Albertoni, A., 38.
Alcala Venceslada, A., 51.
Alcover Sureda, A. M., 51.
Aldrete, B. J., 45.
Alemany y Bolufer, J., 48.
Aleppo, 117.
Alessio, G., 39-40.
Alexander II, of Russia ,99.
Alexandre, G., 136.
"Aleksandrov, A.", 67-8.
Allgemeine Synonymik, 23.
Allgemeines englisch-deutsches ... Wörterbuch, 28.
Allied Control Commission for Germany, 185.
Allodoli, E., 38.
Almeida e Araujo Corrêa de Lacerda, J. M. de, 60.
Alnaes, J., 74.
Alsace-Lorraine, 27.
Alterneuhochdeutsches Wörterbuch, 25.
Altfranzösisches Wörterbuch, 33.
Altfriesisches Wörterbuch, 26.
Althochdeutscher Sprachschatz, 26.
Althochdeutsches Wörterbuch, 25-6.
Altiranisches Wörterbuch, 122.
Altitalisches Wörterbuch, 96.
Altnordisches Glossar, 70.
Alt-Wienerisch, 27.
Alunno, F., 35.
ALUR, 135.
Alvey, G. H., 174.
Amador, E. M. Martinez, 54.
Amalux fototolk, 174, 187.
Amarakosha, 151.

Amaral, G. de, 143.
Amaral, V. Botelho de, 59.
Amarasara, 151.
Amarasimha, 143, 151.
Amburger, P. G., 177.
American Council of Learned Societies, 30.
American Mathematical Society, 183.
Amgala-samskrta-hindi-mahajosa, 153.
AMHARIC, 128.
Amnuay Silpa School, 154.
Anadilden derlemeler, 124.
Analytical d. of Chinese & Sino-Japanese, 158.
Ance, 10.
Ancient Persian lexicon, 122.
Andalusia, 51.
Andersen, D., 151.
Anderson, J. G., 14.
Andrejcin, L. D., 101.
Andriotes, N. P., 90.
Anekartha-Tilaka, 152.
Angliski-latviska vardnica, 107.
Anglo-amerikanisches Rechts-wörterbuch, 181.
Anglo-Assamese d., 146.
Anglo-Burmese d., 147.
Anglo-Malayalam d., 150.
Anglo-Polish translation of work-shop terms, 190.
Anglo-russkii politekhnischeskii slovar', 167.
Anglo-russkii slovar', 67.
Angol-magyar és magyar-angol iskolai és kéziszotar, 106.
Angol-magyar kéziszotar, 106.
Angreji-Nepali, 151.
Annamese–English d., 146.
ANNAMITE, 145-46.
Année philologique, 98.
Annovazzi, A., 40.
Ansteinsson, J., 167.
Antennas, 188.
Appleton's new English-Spanish ... d., 53-4.
Apte, V. S., 152.
Arabe vivant, 116.
ARABIC, 115-17.
Arabic zoological d., 190.
Arabisches Wörterbuch, 116.
Aragon, 51.
ARAMAIC, 117-18, 121.
Araujo Corrêa de Lacerda, J. M. de Almeida e, 60.
Archæology, 170.

193

DATE DUE
